PRETEND PLAY
AS IMPROVISATION

Conversation in the Preschool Classroom

PRETEND PLAY
AS IMPROVISATION

Conversation in the Preschool Classroom

R. Keith Sawyer
Washington University

LEA LAWRENCE ERLBAUM ASSOCIATES, PUBLISHERS
1997 Mahwah, New Jersey

Lawrence Erlbaum Associates, Inc., Publishers
10 Industrial Avenue
Mahwah, New Jersey 07430

Cover design by Kathryn Houghtaling

Library of Congress Cataloging-in-Publication Data

Sawyer, R. Keith (Robert Keith)
Pretend play as improvisation : conversation in the
preschool classroom / R. Keith Sawyer.
    p.   cm.
Includes bibliographical references and index.
ISBN 0-8058-2119-8
1. Symbolic play. 2. Play—Psychological aspects. 3.
Role playing. 4. Drama—Psychological aspects. 5. Fan-
tasy games—Psychological aspects. I. Title.
BF717.S333 1996
155.4'18—dc20
96-27823
CIP

Books published by Lawrence Erlbaum Associates are printed
on acid-free paper, and their bindings are chosen for strength
and durability.

Printed in the United States of America
10   9   8   7   6   5   4   3   2   1

But how can we speak of mere play, when we know that it is precisely play and play alone, which of all man's states and conditions is the one which makes him whole and unfolds both sides of his nature at once?

—Friedrich Schiller, 1967
On the Aesthetic Education of Man (p. 105)

Contents

    Improvisations

       A Typical Day   *143*
       The Polyphony of Play   *149*
       The Improvisationality of Play   *154*
       Summary   *164*

8   **Improvisation and Development**   **165**

       Scripts and Improvisations   *168*
       Metapragmatics and Social Development   *170*
       A Model of Improvisational Socialization   *172*
       Implications for Developmental Research   *177*
       Implications for the Study of Situated Action   *179*
       Suggestions for Future Work   *182*

    References   **185**

    Author Index   **199**

    Subject Index   **203**

Foreword

More than 20 years ago, in my first ethnographic study of preschool children's play and peer culture, I was struck by a type of play that I called *spontaneous fantasy*. Through their talk and manipulation of objects (toy human and animal figures, cars, blocks and building materials, etc.) around a small sand table, the children created elaborate fantasy events. It took me some time, however, to appreciate the full complexity of this play and to determine its significance in the children's peer culture. Of all the children's activities I had observed, spontaneous fantasy was the most difficult for me to follow and understand. In this type of play, the children seldom made explicit reference to a specific pretend frame or plot; they often produced rapid bursts of speech accompanied by coordinated manipulations of the play objects and then fell completely silent for several minutes, and they relied heavily on implicit paralinguistic cues like voice, stress, and pitch to establish shared understanding and to extend the play in new directions. I was often baffled about how to join such play, and I seldom got beyond the simple strategy of repeating a sound, phrase, or object movement that had been produced by one of the children. After I observed numerous episodes of spontaneous fantasy and videotaped several others, I was able to make some limited headway in capturing the complexity of this type of play. I isolated three underlying themes (lost–found, danger–rescue, and death–re-

birth) that provided some plot structure for many of the events, and I documented several communicative strategies (repetition, use of paralinguistic cues,
coordinated movement of objects, and semantic tying or extension) that the
children used to produce and organize spontaneous fantasy.

In the years after this initial research I returned to analyze children's fantasy
play from time to time, and I kept abreast of other research done on this topic.
In my work and the related literature there was some further specification of
the communicative complexity of this type of play and the documentation of
its existence over time and across a range of play settings and subcultural and
cultural groups. Yet, I always felt that there was something missing in my analysis
and that of other researchers in this area. We seemed unable to capture fully
the "spontaneous" aspects of what I called spontaneous fantasy.

Then, a few years ago, Keith Sawyer, then a graduate student at the
University of Chicago, called and asked if he could come to visit me at Indiana
University. He wanted to discuss his dissertation research on children's pretend
play. During the time of our first meeting, Keith was struggling with the analysis
of a very rich set of data. He had derived a highly elaborate coding scheme that
had become unwieldy when he applied it to his data. I urged Keith to simplify
his codes and to supplement the quantitative analysis with a more inductive,
discourse analysis. I believed that such an approach would help him to develop
further some highly innovative ideas that he had about improvisation and
metapragmatics. I was very impressed with the potential of Keith's ideas in this
area, especially his empirical documentation of the powerful but highly abstract
work of Michael Silverstein on metapragmatics. Keith moved forward, carefully
refining his analysis, and the result was an innovative, insightful, and important
dissertation. This dissertation has now become a wonderful monograph, which
shines through with careful scholarship and ground-breaking analysis of children's play.

The monograph has a number of key strengths. First, Sawyer does an
impressive job in reviewing, evaluating, and integrating the now diverse number
of research studies on children's pretend play as well as more general work in
conversation and discourse analysis. For example, he carefully ties his notion of
the improvisational exchange in pretend play to work on related research on
children's play entry, friendships, and peer cultures. Of crucial importance in
this regard is Sawyer's insistence on a collective unit (interactional events) for
data collection and analysis rather than an individual unit of analysis such as
individual children or individual verbalizations or actions out of context. This
decision leads to many important insights as, for example, Sawyer's identification of the children's "play motifs" which are seen as collectively shared in the
local peer culture and similar to the "riffs" or "figures" shared and used by jazz
musicians. The children's "motifs," like jazz musicians' "riffs," are employed not
just to reach shared understanding, but also to offer opportunities for repetition,
variation, and embellishment at various points in the emerging play frame.

Thus, argues Sawyer, the "intersubjectively agreed upon, denotationally en-acted frame is only the tip of the iceberg. Underneath the surface, there is a complex jumble of material that has been mentioned, but has not entered the frame because it has not been accepted by more than one child. These proposals are not yet intersubjective. But they are like seeds that the child plants, in the hopes that they may later grow" (p. 150).

These ideas regarding improvisations as collective productions are related to a second strength of the book, Sawyer's important empirical application and extension of work on metapragmatics and the poetic function of conversation. In line with Silverstein (1993), Sawyer notes that interaction proceeds at two levels simultaneously, the levels of denotational and interactional texts. The interactional text is the regulatory or metapragmatic level of interaction. One key aspect of metapragmatics, notes Sawyer, is what Silverstein (1993) called *indexical entailment*, meaning that utterances often index potential directions that interaction may take (p. 40). Thus, such metapragmatic entailment effects can be seen as poetic, "because they derive from the line-by-line structure of the interaction" (p. 45). Sawyer finds that in pretend play children rely on what Gumperz (1982) referred to as *contextualization cues* to serve a range of metapragmatic functions that result in collectively produced multiple turns at talk that reinforce one another, creating complex poetic structures. Sawyer's empirical demonstration of these powerful concepts regarding human commu-nication in children's pretend play is highly impressive and original.

A third strength of the volume is Sawyer's innovative discussion of the developmental implications of his work (p. 8). Here, I am again impressed by the originality of Sawyer's analysis, but I also have a few reservations. Sawyer links his analysis of improvisational play and development to related work on children's play and the theoretical work of Bakhtin, particularly Bakhtin's notion of *heteroglossia*. Sawyer notes that Bakhtin used the notion of hetero-glossia to capture the diversity of artistically organized voices in the novel (p. 173). Sawyer sees this artistic blending of voices as the most advanced level of children's spontaneous pretend play. He argues that children advance through a series of phases in communicative competence. At around 2 years of age, children produce social speech but in a single voice (what Bakhtin termed *monoglossic*), and they develop a rudimentary dialogic interaction with caretak-ers at around age 3. Then, over the period of 3 to 6 years of age, through interaction and the repeated production of pretend play episodes with peers, children develop full heteroglossia. At this point, notes Sawyer, children produce less improvisational fantasy play, because it has served its developmen-tal purpose. Around 6 years of age, he argues, children have "mastered the interactional skills practiced in fantasy play, and are able to use them during everyday conversation. These skills also allow children to participate in more complex social relationships, developing relatively permanent friendships and entering primary school" (p. 177). Sawyer's functionalist argument that improvisational play contributes to the development of adult communicative competence is insightful and promising. Children's participation in improvisational fantasy play in the preschool years may indeed contribute to their acquisition and the taken-for-granted use of metapragmatic skills in everyday conversation as older children and adults. However, Sawyer's study, which focuses only on the preschool years, cannot really capture this developmental trajectory. More importantly, however, I would argue that we should not be so quick to equate fully the skills of improvisational pretend play to metapragmatic skills in everyday conversation. Sawyer may indeed be correct that the former contribute to the development of the latter. But the specific types and the range of skills necessary to participate competently and effectively in improvisational pretend play (and for that matter in adult improvisational comedy or jazz) may whither away without use and practice. Here we may have a case where the improvisational skills of preschool children actually surpass those of most older children and adults, but most children lose this improvisational edge as they become part of and participate in the social worlds of older children and adults where opportunities to routinely use and sharpen these skills are severely limited. This intriguing possibility is clearly something Sawyer may wish to pursue in future research. It also demonstrates again the importance of taking children's peer interactions and their production of peer cultures seriously and as worthy of study in their own right.

—William A. Corsaro
Indiana University, Bloomington

REFERENCES

Bakhtin, M. M. (1981). Discourse in the novel. In M. M. Bakhtin (Ed.), *The dialogic imagination* (pp. 259–422). Austin, TX: University of Texas Press.

Gumperz, J. J. (1982). *Discourse strategies.* New York: Cambridge University Press.

Silverstein, M. (1993). Metapragmatic discourse and metapragmatic function. In J. A. Lucy (Ed.), *Reflexive language* (pp. 33–58). New York: Cambridge University Press.

Preface

I have been an improvising and performing musician for over 20 years, as a jazz pianist, a bluegrass guitarist, and as a keyboardist in an improvisational rock band. I began my graduate study in psychology at the age of 30, after my performing days were largely over. Entering the University of Chicago, I didn't expect these experiences to be relevant to psychological study. The ideas presented in this book began to emerge during my first years there, due to the influence of my advisors. Tom Trabasso introduced me to developmental psychology. Mike Csikszentmihalyi introduced me to the field of creativity research. Rick Shweder introduced me to cultural psychology, and the notion that people's behavior is intimately related to the situations they find themselves in. Michael Silverstein introduced me to the study of situated language use, and to his own comprehensive theory of the creativity of everyday language use. My own intuitions about group improvisation seemed to fall at the intersection of current and neglected issues in each of these fields. As I learned from Bill Corsaro, research on play discourse had recently begun to consider how children collectively manage the flow of their play dialogue. Sociocultural psychology had begun to examine the more improvised aspects of group collaborations. However, creativity research had not yet examined improvisational creativity, and the study of conversation in social and cultural context had rarely focused on its most creative manifestations.

While I was conducting this study, I joined the University of Chicago improvisational comedy group, "Off-off Campus," as their pianist. I was fascinated by the improvised dialogue that these actors created on stage. I visited most of the professional improvisational theater groups that were active in Chicago during 1993 and 1994. This exposure to staged improvised dialogue, together with my earlier experiences with musical improvisation, led to the central theme of this book: Children's play conversation is an improvised group activity. I use this theme to integrate the several bodies of literature that are relevant to play conversation, including developmental psychology, creativity theory, sociocultural psychology, and discourse analysis.

During the initial phases of the project, I was supported by a University Fellowship for graduate study from the University of Chicago, Committee on Human Development. As I wrote the final draft of the manuscript, I was supported by a Postdoctoral Fellowship in the Department of Psychology at the University of California, Santa Cruz, where I received wonderful mentoring and support from Barbara Rogoff. I am extremely grateful to several colleagues who invested the time required to read an entire draft of the book: Maureen Callanan, Bill Corsaro, Bruce Dorval, Greta Fein, and Tom Rizzo. Their feedback was constructive and invaluable, and allowed me to clarify and strengthen several parts of the manuscript. The analyses of chapters 5 and 6 would not have been possible without two research assistants, Anne Wright and Andrea Sadow, who helped me develop the coding schemes and code the large corpus of data. I also want to thank my editor at Lawrence Erlbaum, Judi Amsel, who supported me throughout the process by providing excellent feedback and comments.

I would like to thank the administration, teachers, and students of the preschool, who must remain anonymous.

—R. Keith Sawyer

Introduction:
Play as Improvisational Performance

The movement which is play has no goal which brings it to an end; rather it renews itself in constant repetition. ... It is the game that is played—it is irrelevant whether or not there is a subject who plays. The play is the performance of the movement as such.
—Hans-Georg Gadamer (1975, p. 93)

I study how linguistic interaction is collectively managed and created, and how this process varies in different social situations and in different cultures. Linguistic interactions range from informal situations, in which people have informal conversations, to formal situations, where talk may be more structured and formulaic. We all have an intuitive sense that the most important uses of language are found in formal events like marriages, funerals, or job interviews. These formal uses of language tend to be quite constrained, often to the point of being scripted. For example, most U.S. weddings are entirely scripted. Although these types of social interactions display a high degree of structure, formality, and ritualization, it is rare for our everyday conversations with others to follow a preexisting script. Because conversations usually occur in common, everyday contexts, and because almost everyone can participate, it is easy for us to fail to realize how amazing and creative an accomplishment conversation is. Everyday conversations, including gossip, boasting, flirting, teasing, and informative discussions, are highly creative interactions. Because these inter-actions are not scripted, I refer to them as improvised.

I became interested in children's play because it is often *improvisational*. One of the most improvisational activities of 3- to 5-year-old children is *social pretend play*, also called fantasy play, sociodramatic play, or role play. Children's imagi-nation has free reign during pretend play. They manipulate dinosaur figurines to create a drama of panic after an earthquake. They play out a story in which a duck and a dinosaur are best friends. They build spaceships with elaborate systems of weaponry and controls, and go on adventures to exotic planets. Conversations in these play episodes are more improvisational than the average adult conversation. Adults usually know, immediately after meeting someone, what type of interaction is about to occur, and what the parameters constraining the interaction will be. Because pretend play dialogue occurs in a dramatized, fantasy world, it is less constrained by social and physical reality.

By referring to pretend play as a form of improvisational *performance*, I am drawing an analogy with adult performance genres. The two types of adult improvisation that drive my analogy are small-group jazz performance and ensemble improvisational theater. I focus particularly on comparisons between children's play and improvisational theater. These parallels are not surprising, because improvisational theater evolved directly from a series of games devel-oped for children's peer play. These games were developed by Spolin in the 1930s and 1940s (Coleman, 1990; Spolin, 1963). Her son, Paul Sills, was the founder of the first improvisational comedy group, The Compass Players, at the University of Chicago in 1955. The Compass Players later evolved into the well-known improv group, The Second City, the model for the popular TV show "Saturday Night Live."

Since its origins in the 1950s, improvisational theater has grown dramatically in Chicago and in other urban centers. With this growth has come a remarkable variety of styles and approaches to improvisation. These styles can be grouped loosely into two main approaches. The most well-known groups perform short *games*, 5 minutes or less, which start from one or two audience suggestions. There are dozens of different games widely used by improvisational ensembles; each game is distinguished by a unique set of constraints on how the perform-ance will proceed. A common game is *freeze tag*. After asking for an audience suggestion, perhaps a location or a starting line of dialogue, two performers begin to improvise a scene. The actors accompany their dialogue with exagger-ated gestures and broad physical movements. The audience is instructed to shout "freeze" whenever they think the actors are in interesting physical positions. Immediately, the actors must freeze themselves in position; a third actor then walks up to these two and taps one of them on the shoulder. The tapped actor leaves the stage, and the new actor must take his place, in the same position, and then begin a completely different scene with the next line of dialogue, playing on the ambiguities inherent in the physical relationship of the frozen actors.

A second style of performance is referred to as *long-form improv.* The ensemble asks for an audience suggestion, and then begins to improvise a one-act play that typically lasts for 30 minutes without interruption. Although these performances often are so dramatically true that many audience members assume a script is being followed, this is never the case with authentic improv groups. The actors work very hard to avoid repeating even brief segments of a performance from a prior night. Long-form improv is less focused on comedy than are game performances, instead focusing on character and plot development.

All improvisational performance genres share several characteristics: (a) there is no script, thus, they are created in the moment; (b) nonetheless, there are loose outlines of structure that guide the performance (more so in jazz, with its lead sheets, than in improv theater); (c) they are collective—no one person decides what will happen. Because the performance is collective, each performer's acts are influenced by the others'. Although each individual's participation seems not to be scripted, a highly structured performance emerges. Studying improvisation thus requires being able to model the ways in which genre and group processes constrain individual acts, and the mechanisms whereby participants may creatively influence the emerging performance. Because group improvisational genres are collective and unscripted, improvisational creativity is a collective social process.

How does an improvisational analogy contribute to developmental research? One discovers from the pretend play literature that this improvisational behavior is most prevalent during the same years that many other social skills are developing. Between the ages of 3 and 5, children learn a wide range of cognitive and social skills. Children begin to develop representations of their own mental states and of others' mental states, as shown by research in the *theory of mind* (Astington, Harris, & Olson, 1988) and in *social cognition* (Shantz, 1983). In parallel with a recent trend toward *narratological studies* in a wide range of social science disciplines, developmental psychologists have identified these years as the period when the child learns to represent and construct narratives (Galda, 1984; Scarlett & Wolf, 1979). Freudian psychologists and other personality theorists have identified these years as critical in the development of the personality. These studies show a remarkable consensus on the importance of this age range for social development. If we can demonstrate that children's improvisational abilities develop during these years, and that their fantasy improvisations become more complex and creative, it might suggest that these social skills are linked to the child's developing ability to improvise with other creative performers.

Moving From Structure to Process

The canonical works of Piaget and Vygotsky don't have much to say about improvisational play. Piaget referred to sociodramatic play as *collective symbolism*, but devoted only two pages to it in his important work *Play, Dreams, and Imitation in Childhood* (Piaget, 1946/1962). Rather than study the improvisational aspects of social play, Piaget focused on games with rules. Vygotsky, often considered a sociocultural counterweight to Piaget, also considered social play to be characterized by obedience to rules. I discuss the work of both of these important researchers in chapter 1. By focusing on rule-governed play, both Piaget and Vygotsky neglected the improvisational play that occurs between ages 3 and 5.

Developmental conceptualizations of pretend play have tended to follow in the Piagetian tradition, proposing stages of play development. Although Piaget's most detailed elaboration of the stage model was developed for children less than 2 years old, other researchers have applied the stage metaphor to social play, following on Parten's work in the early 1930s (Parten, 1932). Stages are usually defined in terms of the structure of the interaction: the number of children and the nature of their role relationships. Piagetian models vary somewhat, but they always propose a development from solitary play to social play. Here's an example of what most developmental researchers would consider the highest level of development, which Parten referred to as *cooperative role-play:*

Example 1. Karl, Kathy, Corinna, Yung-soo, and Jan are pretending that they are going on a camping trip. They are loading up the car and bus (both are laundry baskets big enough for the children to sit inside) and getting ready to leave.

(1)	Jan	Who gonna drive the car
(2)		who gonna drives the bus
(3)		I'm already driving the car
(4)	Corinna	Let's get in the car, Yung-soo
(5)		Let's get in the car, Yung-soo
(6)	Kathy	Well, there's two people in this one.
(7)		That's not a really big car.
(8)		This is (Points to "bus")
(9)	Corinna	And then someone will sit right there.
(10)	Karl	Yung-soo
(11)	Kathy	Now sit down!
(12)	Jan	Wait! I forgot my backpack.
(13)	Karl	Oh shucks I forgot I have to drive!

Parten called this "role play" because the children are enacting dramatic roles, in this case family members; she called it "reciprocal" because the children enact different roles that have identifiable relationships.

When children enact similar roles, without identifiable relationships, most researchers suggest that the play is less advanced. In Parten's model, the following example is less complex than cooperative play, because there are no clear relationships between distinct dramatic roles. In Parten's scheme, the following exchange would be called *associative play*:

Example 2. Artie, Eddy, and Muhammed are in the block area. Each of them builds his own rocket using wooden blocks. They are about 5 feet from each other, and each boy's gaze is focused on his own construction as he speaks. They don't look at each other, except for occasional glances.

(1)	Eddy	I am making a rocket like…
(2)	Artie	That's not even a rocket, that's a small rocket
(3)		Mine is bigger than yours
(4)	Eddy	Mine is even bigger, mine smaller than yours
(5)	Artie	You can't even sit on it
(6)	Eddy	I am this…
(7)		make a rocket…
(8)		looks like a rocket, but it's not a real rocket
(9)	Artie	That not a real rocket at all
(10)		(laughs)
(11)	Muhammed	Mine shoots poison in their eyes
(12)	Eddy	Mine shoots poison all the poison in their eyes
(13)	Muhammed	Mine shoots billions and billions of poison in their eyes
(14)		…kind of poison
(15)	Artie	Doesn't this look like a dumb rocket?
(16)	Eddy	(laughs as his rocket falls down)
(17)	Artie	I eat lots of food
(18)	Muhammed	I don't need lots of food
(19)	Artie	Yes we do, I have been in space for 9 years

This has similarities with what Piaget called *collective monologue* because the children are speaking on the same topic. Unlike the traditional conception of collective monologue, the children are clearly listening and responding to each other. Both of the previously discussed transcripts fall into the improvisational category neglected by Piaget and Vygotsky: The play is social, but is not rule-governed.

Structuralist developmental models of play can be compared to the structuralist tradition in developmental linguistics, which posits that language acquisition proceeds from lower structural levels to higher ones. In the canonical model, the child first learns phonemes, then a lexicon, then syntactic rules, and finally, the *pragmatics* of how to use language appropriately to convey goals and meanings in specific situations. Both psychology and linguistics have focused on what the child learns during the early solitary stages of development, before entering the social world. For Parten and Piaget, the final stage is social play; for Chomskian linguists, the final stage of linguistic development is pragmatic ability.

Structural models of both linguistic development and play development have come under attack in the past two decades, on both theoretical and empirical grounds. The Chomskian model began to be undermined in the 1970s by the research of Bruner (1975, 1981, 1983), Bates (1975, 1976), and others, who demonstrated that children acquire pragmatic skills preverbally, and that these skills are prerequisites for learning language. This research, focusing on the preverbal child's interaction with the parents, demonstrated how interactional skills are developed through gesture, gaze, and action. This research suggested an alternative to Chomsky's biological determinism: Language competence might result not only from genetically determined development, but in some part from social interaction, as well.

Staged models of play which propose a developmental sequence from solitary to social play have also been criticized in some recent studies. These studies suggest that even infants engage in some social play, and that solitary play remains as prominent as social play up to age of 6. Thus, development through the preschool years cannot be adequately characterized as a shift from solitary to social play (see the review in Hartup, 1983). There is social interaction throughout these years, and researchers must examine how it becomes more sophisticated and complex.

In this book, I explore how the improvisational conversations of play become more sophisticated and complex during the preschool years. The improvisational analogy suggests how social development may follow a path of increasing interactional complexity. To get at this increasing complexity, I examine improvised play discourse, and focus closely on specific conversational exchanges. Despite the widespread acceptance of the idea that play develops in interactional complexity and sophistication, there are very few studies of how this development affects play conversation.

The Collective Creativity of Interaction

How can children collectively create coherent dramatic situations? This is a question about children's developing intersubjectivity: How do children learn to arrive at shared understandings about social realities? The cybernetician and anthropologist Gregory Bateson observed that before children can engage in play they must first communicate a shared agreement that their actions in play don't mean what they would normally mean. Children have to be able to first frame what they are about to do as pretend. Bateson called this communication about the interaction itself *metacommunication*. The statement "This is play" is metacommunicative because it says, "These actions in which we now engage do not denote what those actions *for which they stand* would denote" (Bateson, 1955/1972, p. 180).

The message "This is play" is usually unnecessary in the preschool because children are in a context in which play is the expected activity. However, once play has begun, metacommunication is still necessary, because children need to collectively regulate the emergence of the play drama, and to integrate their distinct ideas about what is going on. This regulation is metacommunicative because it serves to provide a framework for interpreting each child's utterances.

Actors performing an improvisation do not need to send the message "This is staged," because they know they are on a stage and are expected to perform. Yet in both improvisational theater and children's play, metacommunicative processes define and regulate an emerging performance. The following transcript of an improvised performance is an example of how metacommunication is used to create new dramatic situations.

Example 3. Four actors stand at the back of the stage. Andrew begins the scene.

(1)   (Andrew steps to stage center, pulls up a chair and sits down, miming the action of driving by holding an imaginary steering wheel)
(2)   (Ben steps to stage center, stands next to Andrew, fishes in pocket for something)
(3)   Andrew   On or off?
(4)   Ben   I'm getting on, sir (continues fishing in his pocket)
(5)   Andrew   In or out?
(6)   Ben   I'm getting in!
               I'm getting in!
(7)   Andrew   Did I see you tryin' to get in the back door a couple of stops back?
(8)   Ben   Uh...

At the end of this exchange, the actors have established a reasonably complex drama. They know that Andrew is a bus driver, and that Ben is a potential passenger. Andrew is getting a little impatient, and Ben may be a little shifty, perhaps trying to sneak on. But how do the audience and the actors know this? How was it decided? There are two points to emphasize about this example: one is the *contingency* of interaction at each utterance. For example, at turn (2), Ben had a range of creative options available. Ben could have pulled up a second chair and sat down next to the driver, and he would have become a passenger in a car. At turn (3), Andrew had an equal range of options. He could have addressed Ben as his friend, searching for theater tickets. This doesn't begin to address the range of dramatic options that can occur on stage. For example, at

(2), Ben could have addressed Andrew as Captain Kirk of "Star Trek," creating a TV-show parody. A few minutes of examination of an improvisational transcript indicates many plausible, dramatically coherent utterances that the actors could have performed at each turn. A combinatorial explosion quickly results in hundreds of potential performances, branching out from each actor's utterance.

The other point to emphasize is the *implicitness* of metacommunication. None of the actors said what was going to happen explicitly. This is one of the basic principles of improv: Show, don't tell. The actors are abiding by Goffman's (1974) observation that "breaking frame," stepping outside the interactional definition, is unnatural and socially sanctioned. Actors refer to this as "crossing the fourth wall," a wonderful metaphor. In improvisational theater, by design, metacommunication about how the drama will proceed is both *implicit* and *within frame*; Bateson referred to this as *implicit metacommunication*, and like Goffman, argued that most communication about the flow of interaction is implicit.

Of course, most social life is like this. In most everyday interactions adults metacommunicate implicitly, and they stay within frame. Adults are adept at using these interactional techniques. However, with children, the component functions of interaction are not as integrated, because they are being learned at different stages and different rates. The following transcript demonstrates the contrast between children's play discourse and adult metacommunication:

Example 4. Jennifer and Muhammed are playing with toy animals at the sand table. Jennifer has a little duck, and Muhammed has a dinosaur.

(1)	Jennifer	Oh big dinosaur	high-pitched voicing, as duck
(2)		I cannot	
(3)		(screams)	
(4)	Muhammed	No, you can get on me	in deep, gruff voice
(5)		I just won't care	
(6)			J puts her duck on the dinosaur's back.
(7)	Jennifer	He said, he said	
(8)		You bad dinosaur	in deep voice
(9)		Quickly, she hided in the sand	pushing the duck into the sand
(10)		so the dinosaur	
(11)	Muhammed	No, pretend he killed her	
(12)		Ow!	
(13)		He's already killed	

The main difference between this transcript and the improvisational theater transcript of Example 3 is that these children break frame frequently, and their metacommunications are frequently explicit. Although they spend a lot of time enacting a play role, within the play frame, they often step outside the frame for metacommunicative statements, what Bateson would call *explicit metacommunication*. Children use a complex blend of implicit and explicit, in-frame and out-of-frame metacommunication when they play. Out-of-frame or explicit metacommunications in Example 4 include lines 7, 9, 10, 11, and 13. This mixture of metacommunicative strategies provides the opportunity to examine how children choose between strategies, and what types of strategies are effective. By deconstructing the different functions of adult interaction, play provides a unique window onto its study.

These transcripts demonstrate a second difference between children's play and improvisational theater. A basic principle of improv which actors learn early in training is the rule "Don't deny." This means that anything that is suggested or proposed by an actor must be accepted by the other actors, and integrated with the unfolding drama. But children's play is quite different. They deny each other all the time, for example, in utterance 11 of Example 4. This difference suggests several interesting questions about children's play: When are metacommunications successful? What makes a child's suggested modification to the play frame be accepted by the other children? How do children choose between strategies? How do contexts of play affect the success of different interactional strategies?

As the previous discussion demonstrates, the improvisational analogy is useful not only in highlighting the ways that children's play is like adult improvisation, but we also learn from the differences between the improvisational interactions of children and adults. Children's play is fundamentally improvisational because each unfolding moment of the emerging play drama is contingent; there is no script or set of rules specifying what each child is to do. Like adult improvisation, children's group play is a collective social product in which several participants contribute to the creation of the drama. At the same time, we have identified several aspects of children's play which are distinctly different from adult improvisations. Children combine both explicit and implicit metacommunication, both in-frame and out-of-frame voices, and children deny each other. Both these similarities and differences have implications for the broader study of interaction.

Up to this point, I have argued that the improvisational analogy can provide psychologists with a useful perspective on how children's play contributes to the development of pragmatic and social skills, by suggesting that it is a context for practicing how to collectively manage an ongoing interaction. There is a second way in which the improvisational analogy can help us understand adult interactions. A wide range of social-science theorists have proposed that social and cultural contexts are closely interrelated with behavior in specific social interactions. The improvisational analogy suggests a new way of working through the social constructivist argument that people and contexts mutually create each other. In play, children constantly create and then inhabit temporary interactional realities, Bateson's "frames." They are constructing their social microworld at the same time that they are enacting it. The transcript examples already presented give a feel for the variety of temporary social worlds children create in play. Several developmental researchers have argued that pretend play is an important factor in socialization during preschool (Corsaro, 1985; Gaskins, Miller, & Corsaro, 1992; Hartup, 1983). The unique role of play in socialization could result from its framed nature. When we study improvisational interactions, we can see more easily how social worlds are created, and how they in turn influence individual participants.

Thus we have two motivations for applying the improvisational analogy to children's play: It can help us understand the processes of interaction, and it can help us understand the relationships between social context and interactional behavior. Of course, these two issues may be related: Different social contexts may be associated with different interactional processes. In the following chapters, I consider both interactional processes and social contexts, and their potential relationships. If there are relationships between particular blends of interactional strategies and specific contexts of play, it could suggest that these strategies are indexes of their associated social contexts. But it is equally possible that these distinctive processes of interaction serve to create and maintain social contexts. In play, children may be learning how to use implicit metacommunication both to reflect and to constitute social relations. These metacommunicative skills seem to be important components of social skill in adults (see chapter 1). Learning about indexical and constitutive relations between language and social context may be an important factor in the socialization of children into peer groups, and indirectly, into adult social life.

The issues which I've previously discussed using the improvisational analogy have been explored by researchers in many fields, including pragmatics, sociolinguistics, action theory, phenomenology, and symbolic interactionism. However, developmental psychology has rarely addressed the improvisationality of social play. Many developmentalists instead focus on solitary play. When social play is studied, it is usually a method for studying individual-level variables, rather than an examination of intersubjectivity and collective action. Developmental research in psychology has proceeded largely in isolation from research in disciplines such as pragmatics, sociolinguistics, and social psychology, which address these issues theoretically. In chapter 1, I discuss the current state of children's play research, which I propose has advanced to a point at which improvisation becomes a valuable analogy. I argue that the lack of an adequate theoretical framework has prevented psychologists from fully elaborating an integrated sociocultural approach to children's play. Following this discussion, I examine a range of theoretical approaches to the study of conversation, and conclude that none of them fully explain improvised play conversations.

In chapter 2, I propose a theoretical model of improvisational performance, which suggests several analyses of linguistic interaction at the social and pragmatic level. This model draws on research in the child's acquisition of pragmatic skills (conducted in psychology and developmental linguistics); studies of the implicit, regulatory level of interaction (conducted in sociology, linguistics, and semiotics); the study of creative verbal performance (conducted in linguistic anthropology, folkloristics, and performance theory), social-scientific manifestations of action theory (phenomenology, ethnomethodology, and symbolic interactionism), and several concepts developed by the Russian literary theorist Mikhail Bakhtin, including *voice, dialogism,* and *heteroglossia.*

To explore this theoretical model empirically, I chose to conduct an extended observational study of children playing in a familiar context: their preschool classroom. I spent 8 months in a preschool classroom containing 24 children between ages 3 and 5. This resulted in a wealth of ethnographic materials and 29 hours of transcribed children's fantasy play talk. Chapters 3 through 7 are applications of the theoretical model to the analysis and interpretation of these data:

Chapter 3. *The preschool classroom.* Description of the research site, and the methodology that I used to study preschool conversation.

Chapter 4. *Play performances.* Descriptions of social context variables, summary statistics of the corpus and relationships among context variables. I introduce and define a new concept, *performance style,* and show how it affects play interaction.

Chapter 5. *Play entry.* A study of the strategies children use to gain entry to a play group. I examine relationships between the strategies used and social context, focusing on friendship.

Chapter 6. *Improvisational exchanges.* These are negotiations of changes to the play frame. I explore the relationships between interactional strategies and social context.

Chapter 7. *The performance of play.* How do children integrate proposals and counterproposals to collectively create a shared performance? I use the results and analyses of the prior chapters to analyze several play episodes.

In these chapters, I hope to demonstrate that an interactional analysis can show how children's peer play contributes to development in the two areas just discussed: (a) the development of interactional skills, such as implicit metacommunicative framing; (b) the development of the ability to use language to reflect and constitute social relations. These are also key issues in the study of adult conversation and in the study of a wide range of performance genres. However, compared to similar studies of adult conversational interaction, the study of children's play has theoretical and methodological advantages. On the theoretical side, the explicitly framed nature of sociodramatic play makes it an ideal medium for studying interaction more generally. Because children are first learning how to engage in peer interaction during the preschool years, the researcher can observe different skills, and different skill components, being acquired. These skills are analytically more accessible, because in adult conversation interactional strategies are blended in complex and sophisticated ways. On the methodological side, it is easier to acquire naturalistic audiotapes of children's play interaction than of adult interaction. As I demonstrate in chapter 3, the children quickly became used to the presence of a researcher and recording equipment. Another methodological benefit is that the children's social world is much more bounded than adult social networks; for many children, the preschool classroom provides their only peer interaction outside the home, and certainly their only interaction in a large, socially complex group of peers.

In this Introduction, I suggest that the improvisational analogy can contribute to our understanding of two aspects of play which are often ignored. The first aspect is the importance of discursive action in maintaining and constituting social life. Improvisation is characteristic of most small-group interaction, including classrooms, psychiatric encounters, and business meetings. The second aspect is how interaction is influenced by, and in turn constitutes, the social and cultural context of that interaction. Because these two processes among adults seem to happen through implicit metacommunication, this study has the potential to identify developmental links between play talk and adult social skill.

The analogy with improvisational theater is informative both for the similarities it highlights and for the differences it makes plain. I draw on examples from improvisational theater throughout this book, as a form of thought experiment. I will try to demonstrate how the improvisation of children's play is similar to, and different from, the improvisation of adults. In this sense, improvisation is more than an analogy: By working out what improvisation is, one necessarily develops a theory of situated social action. In this Introduction, I have attempted to demonstrate the plausibility of the analogy. I hope that this discussion has convinced the reader that the sometimes-difficult theoretical discussions contained in chapters 1 and 2 are worth getting through; these chapters provide a theoretical argument for improvisation as a model of situated social action. The empirical analyses presented in the subsequent chapters are formulated to test hypotheses suggested by the improvisational model, and their results can be viewed collectively as an evaluation of the usefulness of that model.

1

Play and Conversation

In our view a static analysis of discontinuous, stratified levels is unacceptable, whereas the functional dynamism of assimilation and accommodation, while respecting structural variety, makes it possible to trace the evolution towards equilibrium and thus to grasp the specific role of mental life.

—Jean Piaget (1962, p. 291)

Many social scientists have used performance as a metaphor for social life. Such metaphors are often associated with the writings of Erving Goffman, whose dramaturgical perspective first appeared in *The Presentation of Self in Everyday Life* (1959). Goffman characterized face-to-face interaction as "interpersonal ritual behavior" (1967, p. 22). He referred to temporary situational definitions as *frames*, using a term that Bateson originated to characterize pretend play (1955/1972, 1956/1971). A frame provides a way for participants to interpret each other's actions. Many actions cannot be properly interpreted without understanding that a special frame is in effect. Goffman's examples included jokes, dreams, mistakes and misunderstandings, deceptions, and theatrical performances. In a staged play, the performers know that their actions are not real actions—the dramatic frame is in effect. Pretend play is also framed: Children understand that their actions are the pretend actions of play characters. In a performance genre such as improvisational theater, performers consciously frame their performance as distinct from normal social life. They all know that they are on stage; the professional conventions of the theater require that the boundary between reality and the dramatic illusion be maintained. Among children at play, the boundary between the play frame and everyday social life is fluid and permeable. Instead of the fourth wall that actors imagine to be between the stage and the audience, there is only a nebulous boundary between fantasy interaction and its ongoing maintenance and regulation.

In recent years, several psychologists have commented on the performative and improvisational nature of children's pretend play. Some developmental researchers have drawn inspiration from Burke's dramatism (Burke, 1968, 1969) to conceive of children's play as performance (Franklin, 1983; Forbes & Yablick, 1984). Singer and Singer (1990) suggested that symbolic social play provides children with a flexibility that allows them to move beyond ritual interaction patterns, toward more improvisational behavior. In the preschool classroom, the improvisations of dramatic pretense mediate this social development. Many other researchers have commented on the improvisational character of children's interaction. For example, Griffin and Mehan (1981, p. 205) characterized classroom discourse as "spontaneous improvisations on basic patterns of interaction." In Baker-Sennett's work, children's creative planning of a stage play was found to incorporate both explicit and implicit direction; this implicit direction is like improvisational performance, because new script ideas are proposed by a child enacting the new suggestion within the dramatic frame (Baker-Sennett & Matusov, in press; Baker-Sennett, Matusov, & Rogoff, 1992). Rather than being taught this technique, these improvisational strategies of implicit planning emerged spontaneously among the child actors. Many of Corsaro's analyses focused on the ways that children embellish play routines (e.g., 1992). He argued that most types of embellishment in children's peer routines are collective rather than personal. They are cooperatively orchestrated acts that result in novel, improvisational performances (1992).

In a classic paper, Schank and Abelson (1977) presented the *script* model, a performance analogy that has been influential in studies of children's play. Schank and Abelson compared social action to a script, intentionally invoking the parallel with a dramatic text. They proposed that scripts were mental representations for culturally prototypical action sequences. Developmental psychologists soon picked up on the script metaphor. Applications of the script metaphor to children's play include Bretherton (1984, 1989), Nelson and Gruendel (1979), Nelson and Seidman (1984), and Goncu (1987). Other theories that propose that actions are structured temporally include Mandler's event schemas (Mandler, 1979) and the interactional routines of conversation analysis (Peters & Boggs, 1986). Nelson and Gruendel (1979) characterized the script as a shared context:

> To sustain a dialogue the participants must each assume a shared topic context within which that dialogue is structured. This shared context determines such things as what is expressed and what is left to inference, the particular answers that follow from a given question, and the particular semantic and syntactic links that will be established between utterances. (p. 76)

Frames and scripts are both static structural descriptions of the play drama, situational definitions that must be shared by children before play can proceed. Because these models emphasize static situational definitions, they may not adequately characterize play sessions in which a stable frame is difficult to identify. The problems with the script model were evident early on: How does one represent variation from a script? How do people know how to react when an odd event happens? Does another script get instantiated? Is a subscript invoked? Bretherton (1989) argued that Schank's more recent formulation of script theory (1982) was better able to represent such improvisational, embel-lished schemes, although Schank himself did not work out how individuals could create novel schemas. Bretherton's interpretation has the effect of making script theory more amenable to improvisation. Many improvisations indeed make use of rehearsed sequences that have a script-like sequential structure. For example, jazz musicians say that they use common melodic patterns, or *licks*, during improvisational solos (Sawyer, 1992). Conversation analysis has focused on structured interactional routines, and how they are embellished in situated use. But in practice, script models tend to emphasize the structures of social life, and to neglect the improvisational creativity of interaction.

Many key questions remain unaddressed by structural, scriptal models: To what extent is social life structured versus improvised? What is the nature of the structures which guide social action? If they are frames or scripts, what are the mechanisms whereby such social facts become intersubjectively shared? What constraints do structures place on action in specific instances? What opportunities are there for creative variations among similar event sequences? What, in fact, is the definition of "similar"? These questions predate cognitive psychology, because they are new versions of old questions: What is the nature of social action? What is the nature of human experience in the world? Are there static structures (reified, essentialized) or is there simply a never-ending flux of possibilities? Like most cognitive-science theories of the 1970s, script models are based on a structuralist view of the social world, a view that is increasingly difficult to maintain as structuralist theories have been attacked by social science theorists (e.g., Bourdieu, 1977; Cicourel, 1974; Derrida, 1978; Gadamer, 1975; Schutz, 1932/1967). Of course, there is structure to social life; the script metaphor appeals to our common-sense understandings about the world. Of course, there is variation from one script performance to another. There is truth in both: This opposition is one between ideal types.

Some sociolinguists and linguistic anthropologists have approached the issue of social action without invoking script-like event sequences. This approach involves a focus on speech genres, speech styles, and their relationships to the microcontext of interaction. There is a spectrum of genres of interaction in each culture, with each genre considered appropriate for a particular cultural con-text. Some of these contexts have very structured, scripted styles of interaction associated with them: For example, religious rituals tend to use highly scripted texts. Schank and Abelson's classic example, the procedures for entering a restaurant, ordering, and eating, is a relatively scripted example of everyday social action. In contrast to these structured situations, many interactional contexts are relatively unstructured. These include gossip, bar and mealtime conversations, and party small talk. In these situations, the script model seems less plausible as a model of social action. To understand unstructured interaction, we need a model of improvisation, a theory of how situations become associated with styles, and a way of linking the process of improvisation with its moment-to-moment structure.

This chapter explores different ways of discussing these issues in children's play, and discusses theories of adult conversation that might help us resolve these key issues:

1. When interaction is unscripted, how is it collectively created and maintained? How do children learn to improvise with each other in social play?
2. Does play become more scripted in certain contexts, and more improvisational in others? What is the influence of play context on improvisational processes?

Children's play often seems quite scripted and stylized. For these types of play, script models can be accurate and informative. Yet equally often, children's play is a creative, novel improvisation, in that children collectively create and perform a new drama, one which must be considered to be unscripted. Theories that propose that interaction is structured in advance are not able to adequately account for children's improvisational play.

The Development of Interactional Skills in Children's Play

Between the ages of 3 and 5, children learn a wide range of cognitive and social skills. Psychologists have found that these are important years for the development of theories of mind (Astington, Harris, & Olson, 1988), the development of the ability to represent and construct narratives (Galda, 1984; Scarlett & Wolf, 1979; Trabasso, Stein, Rodkin, Munger, & Baughn, 1992), the development of social cognition (Shantz, 1983), the development of the personality (Bronfenbrenner, 1979; El'konin, 1969; Lewin, 1935), the development of intersubjectivity (Goncu, 1993a, 1993b), and the development of complex fantasy play (Iwanaga, 1973; Parten, 1932; Smilansky, 1968). This book focuses on play conversations during this same age range. Conversational skills are important components of many of the skills acquired during this period, particularly narrative representation, social cognition, intersubjectivity, and fantasy play.

Children's relationships with same-age peers during the preschool years seem to contribute to social development independently of relations with the parents (Corsaro, 1985, 1992, 1993; Damon, 1977; Field, 1981; Gottman, 1983; Gottman & Parkhurst, 1980; Guralnick, 1981; Hartup, 1979, 1981, 1983; Howes, 1981, 1983, 1987a, 1987b; Lewis & Rosenblum, 1975; Rogoff, 1990). These studies suggest that children learn some things better with peers than with their parents. Peer play seems to be more improvisational than play with parents, and to involve a more complex blend of improvisational strategies. Play with peers is different from play with adults in many ways (Barker & Wright, 1955; Whiting & Whiting, 1975). The most obvious distinguishing characteristic of peer interaction is the coequal status of the participants. Hartup, who argued this point most forcefully, noted two unique elements in peer interaction (1979): the egalitarian nature of interaction between children of similar ability, and the relative lack of constraints on interaction, because the child's relationships with adults are constrained both by attachments and hierarchies. Many studies have found that mothers almost never engaged in pretend play with children; mothers tend to observe, rather than participate in, children's fantasies (Bloch, 1989; Dunn, 1986; Field, 1981; Howes, 1992). They rarely enter the game as full partners. Peer interaction has more negotiation, and it is more improvisationally creative. Fein and Fryer (1995) recently concluded that there is no evidence that mothers contribute to the quality or sophistication of peer play.

One of the primary ways that peer relationships contribute to development is through social pretend play. For example, there are correlations between the amount of peer play and role-taking ability (Connolly & Doyle, 1984; Doyle & Connolly, 1989; Rubin, 1976), general people orientation (Jennings, 1975), cooperation with adults and peers (Singer, 1979), and friendliness and popularity with peers (Black & Hazen, 1990; Connolly & Doyle, 1984; Corsaro, 1985, 1988; Doyle, 1982; Hazen & Black, 1989; Howes, 1987a; Marshall, 1961; Marshall & McCandless, 1957; Rubin & Maioni, 1975; Singer, 1979). In addition to these correlations between the quantity of play and social skills and social context, other studies have found relationships between different styles of play and social context. Children play differently with familiar and nonfamiliar peers (Doyle, Connolly, & Rivest, 1980; Garvey & Hogan, 1973; Gottman & Parkhurst, 1980; Matthews, 1977; Mueller, 1972; Schwarz, 1972); children of high and low sociometric status play differently (Connolly & Doyle, 1984; Hazen & Black, 1989; Marshall, 1961; Rubin & Maioni, 1975); and children who are friends play differently from children who aren't (Corsaro, 1985; Gottman & Parkhurst, 1980; Howes, 1983). Other factors hypothesized to affect peer play include cultural differences and socioeconomic status. There have been many studies comparing play in different cultures, originating with the Whiting study of six cultures (Whiting & Whiting, 1975) and the cultural-ecological model presented in Whiting (1980). Most of these studies have found no significant differences in the amount, type, or developmental pace of social pretend play. When differences have been found between U.S. groups and other cultures, social peer play tends to be of more importance in the non-American culture. For example, Bloch (1989) conducted a comparative study of 2- to 6-year-olds in midwestern U.S. families and Senegalese families, and found that in both cultures and at all ages, 25% to 30% of waking time was spent in play, and that this play time was evenly split between social and solitary play, with one exception: 5- to 6-year-old Senegalese children engaged almost exclusively in social play. In the U.S. sample, the children played three times as much with peers than with parents; in the Senegalese sample, 94% of the children's social play was with other children. These results are consistent with the studies previously referenced, that found that U.S. parents rarely engage in pretend play with their children. One of the most important studies of cultural differences in play was Helen Schwartzman's *Transformations: The Anthropology of Children's Play* (1978). Slaughter and Dombrowski (1989) reviewed the cross-cultural work since this 1978 volume. These recent studies have consistently shown the same levels of social pretend play among cultures: Israel and South Africa (Udwin & Shmukler, 1981), United States and Kuwait (Al-Shatti & Johnson, 1984), United States and Puerto Rico (Yawkey & Alverez-Dominques, 1984), and Turkey and Iran (Bower, Ilgaz-Carden, & Noori, 1982). A contrasting set of studies has found that in some cultures, symbolic play either does not exist or exists only in stereotypic forms, and represents a much smaller percentage of children's activity (Ariel & Sever, 1980; Feitelson, 1977; Feitelson, Weintraub, & Michaeli, 1972; Gaskins & Goncu, 1988; LeVine & LeVine, 1963; Smith, 1977). Making a strong claim that social play is a modern Western phenomenon, Konner (1975), observing !Kung San infants between the ages of 1 and 2 years, found that only 10% of their contacts was with other children. He argued that multiage groups must have been more common for children in the history of mankind, since in small hunter-gatherer bands there aren't many same-age peers available (defined as ± 3 months). Gaskins and Goncu (1992) found that Mayan children's play was not like the creative and free-form play of U.S. children. In the Mayan culture, play seemed to be more scripted and less improvisational.

Other studies have explored differences in sociodramatic play as a function of socioeconomic status; perhaps the best-known of these is Smilansky (1968). A prevailing assumption in the literature is that economically disadvantaged children, compared to middle-income children, engage in less frequent and lower quality sociodramatic play, and play that is characteristically unimaginative, repetitive, and simplistic (McLoyd, 1982). McLoyd (1982, 1986) noted a wide variety of problems with this literature, including flawed methodologies, confounding of classroom- and school-related variables, conflicting results, and (particularly important to our study) insufficient consideration of how verbal behavior is affected by socioeconomic class. She concluded that these studies were so heavily flawed that they tell us nothing about social class differences in play. Other researchers (Fein, 1981; Rubin, Fein, & Vandenberg, 1983) have made similar criticisms.[1]

The balance of this research suggests that cultural and social class differences in play remain to be identified. A few cultures, including the !Kung San and the Maya, manifest relatively little pretend play; however, such examples seem to be rare. When there are cultural differences, it seems that peer play is more salient in the non-Western culture. The consensus of the literature seems to be that peer play is a key contributor to development in the majority of the world's cultures, and that it is certainly not limited to industrialized or Western cultures. These studies have demonstrated the importance of peer play, and its near-universal presence during the preschool years. However, such studies have rarely explored the conversational processes through which play interaction contributes to social development. I propose that these relationships are mediated through the collective improvisational processes required to negotiate an intersubjective play frame. This book builds upon these studies by focusing closely on play conversation, and on how conversation varies in different contexts.

Classic Psychological Perspectives on Play

There is a strong tradition in developmental psychology of studying play, extending back to Piaget. Piaget's method of focusing on developmental stages, developed in the 1920s, is still influential in developmental psychology. All children, it is hypothesized, pass through these stages in the same order. In taxonomies of social play, the stages are usually defined as configurations of children. The most basic division is between solitary play and social play, and some theories identify three or more configurations of social play, based on the nature of the relationships between the play characters. Theories that define developmental stages in terms of the configurations of children are structuralist, and can be contrasted with theories that focus on the interactional processes of play.

Piaget.   Drawing on his psychoanalytic training and the semiotic theories of de Saussure (1915/1966), Piaget identified play as critical in the development of symbolic skills. In his first book, *The Language and Thought of the Child,* he proposed a continuum from egocentric language to adult conversation, in which the child passes through four stages: (a) egocentric talk; (b) collective monologue; (c) collaboration in action, in which the conversation focuses on an

---

[1]The debate continues. Sutton-Smith (1983) responded formally to McLoyd's 1982 article, and argued that the combined weight of 50 years of research provided strong indications of an effect of social class, despite their particular methodological deficiencies. McLoyd (1983), in a rejoinder, claimed that the older studies of social class cited by Sutton-Smith do not address pretend play.

activity which the children are doing together, but each child speaks only of his own actions; and (d) collaboration in thought, in which the conversation focuses not on the immediate activity, but on explanations, memories, or the order of events (1923/1955). This highest conversational level is collaborative and intersubjective, and concerns an abstract topic.

Reflecting the influence of both Freud and de Saussure, Piaget's most involved treatment of play was in the book *Play, Dreams, and Imitation in Childhood* (1946/1962). Piaget believed that symbolic play was the context for the child's developing semiotic capacities. He argued that symbolic thought resulted from the tension between two strategies for interacting with the physical world: accommodation and assimilation. In accommodation, the child modifies his behavior and thought to be consistent with his perceptions. The activity Piaget associated with accommodation was *imitation*. Piaget used terms borrowed from de Saussure in describing imitation as the child acting on the signified, but without making a distinction between signifier and signified.[2] In contrast, in assimilation, the child modifies his perceptions of the external world to be consistent with his own internal cognitive schema. The activity Piaget associated with assimilation was *symbolic pretend play*. In symbolic pretend play, the child distinguishes between signifier and signified, but is still operating at an immature level because he or she is assimilating reality to the ego. Piaget called this assimilation *egocentric thought*, and argued that symbolic play was a manifestation of its purest form (1946/1962). The egocentric tendencies of the child to assimilate reality to the ego lead the child to begin to distinguish between signified and signifier. The final stage of development comes after symbolic play, when the competence for symbolic thought, developed through play, begins to be used for *adaptation* to reality.

> [Children's play] occurs when assimilation is dissociated from accommodation but is not yet reintegrated in the forms of permanent equilibrium in which, at the level of operational and rational thought, the two will be complementary. In this sense, play constitutes the extreme pole of assimilation of reality to the ego, while at the same time it has something of the creative imagination that will be the motor of all future thought and even of reason. (Piaget, 1946/1962, pp. 161–162)

---

[2]Piaget's terminology, although following Saussure, differed in a fundamental way. For Saussure, *sign* and *symbol* are terms for two kinds of signifier–signified relationship: The sign is an arbitrary relationship, the symbol is a motivated relationship. Piaget used the same terms to refer to two kinds of signifiers, rather than to the signifier–signified relationship. *Signs* were the signifiers of language and formal systems; *symbols* were images and imitations (see also Krampen, 1981, pp. 200–203). This shift results from Piaget's psychoanalytic origins: Signs are associated with the reality principle, the ego, whereas symbols are associated with the pleasure principle, the unconscious; both are psychological entities.

We often see pejorative terms like *distortion* and *extreme egocentrism* in Piaget's discussions of play. According to Piaget, children engage in pretend play because they aren't yet capable of "immediate assimilation of the universe to experimental and logical thought" (p. 166). Piaget viewed pretend play as a developmental stage preceding the development of mature symbolic thought, when assimilation and accommodation operate in equilibrium. Piaget argued that rule-governed games are the final, third stage of symbolic development, when the egocentric tendency to assimilation is balanced by the need to accommodate to group-specified rules. In his early book on conversation, Piaget claimed that children remain egocentric until age 7, well after the peak ages for pretend play (Piaget, 1923/1955).

Piaget only briefly discussed sociodramatic play, which he called *collective symbolism* (1946/1962). In collective symbolism, children take on different, complementary roles. This is the most improvisational stage described by Piaget. He did not discuss how social pretend play could be interpreted within the assimilation/accommodation framework; he rarely discussed accommodation to other children, instead focusing on accommodation to physical reality. On those few occasions when Piaget mentioned accommodation to the social world, he was referring to accommodation to a rule-governed game activity.[3] But even when children engage in games with rules, there are often improvisational, creative elements to the play, as they attempt to modify the game (Baker-Sennett & Matusov, in press; Baker-Sennett, Matusov, & Rogoff, 1992; Bearison, 1994, 1995; Singer & Singer, 1990).

I chose the epigraph to this chapter to emphasize that Piaget's general approach to constructivism is not at issue. The problems, rather, result from neglect: Piaget showed little interest in sociodramatic play, and his choice to focus on rule-governed games led to a view of play as overly structured and scripted. Piaget's model, although dynamic and constructivist in many ways, is rather static and structuralist with respect to children's sociodramatic play. Thus, his model must be extended and elaborated to account for improvisational play.

I suggest that group play represents the tension between assimilation and accommodation to a social reality. With an object, the child is free to be purely assimilating, purely egocentric, as Piaget claims. But when playing with another child, there are additional constraints. To play collectively, the child must

---

[3]Some Piagetians might argue that the child's interaction with the social world is no different from his interaction with the physical world, but this is harder to maintain in light of sociocultural perspectives. The improvisational metaphor supports a sociocultural perspective: Jazz musicians say that improvising with a group is quite different from improvising at home alone, or from improvising along with a record (the so-called *music minus 1*). There is a fundamental difference between interaction with an inert physical environment, and interaction with other people who have their own creative contributions. Issues of subjectivity and intersubjectivity become fundamental. Also see Hirschfeld (1994), who argued that accommodation to a social reality is qualitatively different than accommodation to physical reality, and thus was neglected by Piaget.

accommodate to the other children, to their own assimilations. Each child seems to have a unique, idiosyncratic play frame. Each child attempts to assimilate the other children to his frame, while accommodating to their frames.

To account for improvisational play, Piaget's model must be extended in two ways: by focusing on the relationship between a child and another child, rather than between the child and an object, and by focusing on the necessary balance between assimilation and accommodation to interlocutors, rather than to objects. A microinteractional approach allows the identification of specific techniques of assimilation and accommodation to a social reality. This approach focuses on the pragmatic usage of symbols, how symbols are used in mediated action (Wertsch, 1985b).

From this perspective, children don't engage in symbolic play merely because adaptation is too hard, as Piaget claimed (1946/1962); it is an essential stage in the development of the pragmatic use of symbols. Piaget's theory may be adequate to the development of symbolic mental abilities; however, he did not address issues of how symbols are used in interactional contexts. Because I believe this is the fundamental contribution of group play between the ages of 3 and 6, I believe that Piaget missed the importance of this phenomenon. As Bretherton (1986) noted in her critique of Piaget, Piaget believed that thought about everyday events became coherent only at the end of the preschool period, after the child had mastered operations such as classification, ordering, and conservation. Pretense was not a contributor to cognitive development. However, research on social play suggests that everyday event representation (in the form of scripts or event schemata) is a fundamental component of play, and that play with event representations may form a basis for operative thought.

Structuralist Taxonomies of Play. Piaget's categorizations of children's play and of children's conversation were developmental: Types of play and types of conversation are correlated with the age of the child. As children get older, they pass through stages associated with distinct types of play. Like Piaget, other developmental psychologists have usually categorized play by developmental stage.

Mildred Parten was the first American psychologist to develop a taxonomic scheme for social play between the ages of 2 and 5 (Parten 1932, 1933/1971; Parten & Newhall 1943). Although Parten did not reference Piaget's 1926 English translation, their schemes share many similarities. She proposed six levels of participation in play, ranging from the least participatory, *unoccupied behavior*, where the child watches whatever happens to be in the environment but does not play, through *parallel activity*, where the child plays independently, but with similar toys and in similar ways to children around him, to the most participatory, *cooperative play*, where the children work together to dramatize a situation from real life (Parten, 1932). Parten's data suggest that solitary and parallel play decrease between the ages of 2 and 4½ years, whereas cooperative play increases: All six of the children who frequently engaged in cooperative play were over 3 years old.

Parten's study established an influential paradigm for play research. Her methodology, involving observational coding and analysis of undirected children's play, has been the predominant approach in psychology, and is the basis for this book's methodology. Her theoretical framework, involving a set of sequential developmental stages, has also been standard in developmental research. Later studies that were influenced by Parten and by Piaget's early work include Garvey (1974), Iwanaga (1973), Rubin (Rubin, Maioni, & Hornung, 1976; Rubin, Watson, & Jambor, 1978), and Smilansky (1968). Each of these studies presented a taxonomy of structurally defined play stages, and analyzed play data to determine the validity of the taxonomy. Many of these studies, including Parten's and Iwanaga's, found that children began engaging in non-egocentric behavior between the ages of 3 and 5; in contrast, Piaget claimed that this did not occur until age 7 (1923/1955).

Despite the variations among the previously discussed taxonomies, all of them can be considered to be structuralist theories of development, because the categories are defined in terms of the number of children and the types of their relationships. They are also synchronic characterizations of children's play. Rather than describing how a play episode changes over time, or describing the processual characteristics of play, these taxonomies focus on aspects of play which are stable throughout a play episode. These approaches don't examine the moment-to-moment processes of play improvisation. A closer focus on play interaction would allow us to better understand the changes that take place within a structural stage, and how play interaction at one developmental level leads to a transition to the next level.

Russian Psychology: Vygotsky and El'konin. The Russian developmental tradition focused on the role-taking aspects of play. These writings began to appear in English in the early 1960s. In 1969, an English-language review of Russian psychological research appeared, compiled by the psychologist El'konin. El'konin emphasized that post-war Russian work in developmental psychology had focused on social play, in contrast to the Western focus on solitary object play inspired by Piaget's theories. These Russian psychologists believed that social play was critical in child socialization, a view that did not become common in American developmental research until the 1980s. "Play—specifically, topical dramatic play—has been recognized as the preschooler's most important activity. ... Soviet psychologists have viewed topical dramatic play as a form of activity arising out of the child's life in society and representing a special type of liaison between the child and society" (El'konin 1969, p. 172).

Of well over a dozen Russian researchers cited by El'konin, Piaget's Russian contemporary, Vygotsky, has had the most influence on American psychology.

He has been a recent influence on American psychologists who are interested in studying the social factors active in child development. Vygotsky's writings are often interpreted to be a contrast to or critique of Piaget's developmental model. For example, whereas Piaget argued that development proceeded from egocentric speech to socially oriented thought, Vygotsky argued that social interaction was prior to egocentric speech (1978). Likewise, where Piaget perceived inexorable staged development, Vygotsky focused on the importance of the child's interaction with the symbolic world, and the contingency of that development on social interaction.

Two volumes contain the majority of Vygotsky's English translations, *Thought and Language,* published posthumously based on lectures (Vygotksy, 1986; originally published in Russian, 1934, and translated into English in 1962), and *Mind in Society,* a combination of two monographs selected by his student Alexander Luria for publication in English (1978). James Wertsch has perhaps been the preeminent interpreter of Vygotsky for American academics, having edited the influential volume *Culture, Communication, and Cognition: Vygotskian Perspectives* (1985a), and written two books based on Vygotskian theories, *Vygotsky and the Social Formation of Mind* (1985c) and *Voices of the Mind* (1991). I refer the interested reader to these excellent volumes. My review here only summarizes these theories, to the extent that they impact the study of improvisation.

Vygotsky, in contrast to Piaget, argued that social interaction comes prior to the development of both thought and language, and that both thought and language are internalizations of interaction with physical objects and with other people. In a much-quoted passage, he wrote "Every function in the child's cultural development appears twice: first, on the social level, and later, on the individual level" (1978, pp. 56–57). Consistent with Marxist theory, Vygotsky argued "The internalization of socially rooted and historically developed activities is the distinguishing feature of human psychology" (1978, p. 57). Vygotsky's focus on social role enactment is more compatible with a performance analogy than Piaget's theories. Yet Vygotsky characterized group play as rule-governed, arguing that the rules were covert, deriving from the imaginary situation rather than being explicitly specified: "The notion that a child can behave in an imaginary situation without rules is simply inaccurate. If the child is playing the role of a mother, then she has rules of maternal behavior" (1978, p. 95). Development is a progression from covert rules to overt rules (1978, p. 96). The child must begin to learn the meaning of the situation because this is what guides play behavior. Like script theories, Vygotsky argued that play is structured by expectations and conventions derived from adult society. In contrast to script theories, which propose that play is structured by a cognitive representation of a temporal ordering of events, Vygotsky argued that play is structured by a cognitive representation of role-appropriate behavior. Both approaches fail to account for the creative, improvisational aspects of children's play.

Parallel to Piaget's dialectic of assimilation and accommodation, Vygotsky recognized the tension in social play between creativity and the rules of the game. Vygotsky argued that the child would subject himself to the rules, and renounce impulsive action (1978). In other words, the child instinctively chooses against improvisational behavior.[4] Nonetheless, this is an important developmental step, because the rules of play are easier to conform to than the rules of real life: "This strict subordination to rules is quite impossible in life, but in play it does become possible: thus, play creates a zone of proximal development of the child. In play a child always behaves beyond his average age" (1978, p. 102). Thus, the developmental function of play is to teach the child how to conform to rules. Vygotsky's position is in dramatic contrast with the improvisational analogy, which suggests that the developmental function of play is to teach children how to be collectively creative, within the unique constraints of the temporary fantasy reality.

Despite the greater role Vygotsky attributed to social play, he still viewed the interactional aspects of sociodramatic play much as Piaget, focusing on the rule-governed nature of the play. Neither theorist addressed the collective, improvisational processes of play. Of course there are constraints on play behavior, just as there are always constraints on social action. The key questions, presented at the beginning of this chapter, remain unanswered: What is the nature of these constraints? How can we conceptualize microsocial context? Given a particular context, what are the opportunities for improvisationality? How do children collectively determine what the context—that is, the play frame—will be?

Solitary and Social Play:
Evaluations of Piaget and Vygotsky

There is much agreement between Piaget and Vygotsky: They both perceived children's social play to be fundamentally rule-governed (for other similarities, see Gaskins & Goncu, 1988; Lucy, 1988). Yet, they contrast in a fundamental way. Piaget, Parten, and other structuralists argued that play is first solitary and then becomes social; in contrast, Vygotsky argued that play is first social and then solitary. Recent developmental research by both Vygotskians and neo-Piagetians has suggested a synthesis between the two positions. This research demonstrates that play is both solitary and social at all preschool ages. As I have suggested, both the structuralists and Vygotsky looked for play development in

---

[4]El'konin (1969) claimed to have unpublished experimental support for Vygotsky's "rule-role" theory. He created play situations in which actions that were attractive to the child conflicted with the child's role's expectations; the children tended to act in accordance with the role, rather than "give way to momentary desires" (p. 176).

the structural properties of interaction. Instead, this recent research suggests that what develops are the processual and interactional characteristics of the interaction.

Most of these studies were attempts to evaluate whether Parten's and Piaget's structuralist models of play stages were accurate. Some studies were conducted before Vygotsky's theories were widely available in English, and were attempts to evaluate the construct validity of the various stages of structuralist models; other studies, influenced by Vygotsky, were more clearly attempts to discredit the solitary-to-social trajectory. Parten argued that play is first solitary, then parallel, and then social. Piaget suggested that social play did not emerge until after solitary levels of play were mastered. In contrast, Vygotsky and the Russian developmentalists claimed that social play was developmentally prior. Supporting Piaget, some studies indirectly suggested that there is a shift from solitary to social pretend play around 3 years of age (Emmerich, 1977; Reuter & Yunik, 1973; Rubin, Watson, & Jambor, 1978; Sanders & Harper, 1976). Other studies seemed to contradict these results, finding that the solitary-social shift model is, at best, overly simplistic. For example, many studies have found that solitary play continues through preschool, and may even be indicative of independence and maturity rather than immaturity (Hartup, 1983; Howes, 1980; Moore, Evertson, & Brophy, 1974; Smith, 1978).

Both Rubin et al. (1978) and Fein, Moorin, and Enslein (1982) argued that Parten-derived social taxonomies must be combined with cognitive stages to accurately describe play development. Both found evidence that development does not proceed in the fashion suggested by Piaget and Parten. Instead of a smooth transition from solitary to parallel to social play, Fein et al. (1982) found evidence for a combined cognitive-social model, in which the transition to the next stage of cognitive difficulty resulted in a downward shift from social to solitary play. Interestingly, in their 11-stage model, the three most developmentally advanced levels were the most creative and improvisational types of play; Levels 9, 10, and 11 were metacommunication, and dramatic pretense with toy figures. Their data suggested that when children enter preschool, around 36 months, they are just acquiring these improvisational skills.

Among researchers who accept the basic outline of Parten's or Piaget's model, there has been debate about the characteristics or construct validity of one or another stage. Many researchers have chosen to use a three-stage model of play development: solitary, parallel, and sociodramatic (Bakeman & Brownlee, 1980; McLoyd, Thomas, & Warren, 1984a; Rubin, Watson, & Jambor, 1978; Smith, 1978). Bakeman and Brownlee (1980) found parallel play among all children ages 32 to 42 months, and with a sequential analysis methodology, found that parallel play served as a transitional state to sociodramatic play. They concluded that parallel play is used as a strategic bridge into dramatic role play.

Other researchers have criticized the solitary–parallel–social developmental trajectory as fundamentally incorrect. Carrollee Howes is perhaps the best known; in a series of publications (1979, 1980, 1981, 1987a, 1987b, 1992), she argued that all play is social to some degree. For example, Howes (1980) criticized Parten's scale by noting that (a) infants participate in peer interaction; (b) pre-schoolers do not progress from solitary, through parallel, to group play. Howes suggested five levels of play, arguing that all five are social to some degree. She argued that development is characterized not by a transition from solitary to social play, but by the changing characteristics of the social play itself. Play is always social, and with age, play interactions become progressively more complex.

Other studies of infant play have found that a majority of their play is social, not solitary. Such studies are often viewed as validations of a Vygotskian position. In one of the earliest such studies, a test of egocentrism in a sample of 3½- to 5½-year-olds, Mueller (1972) coded utterances for 10 interactional characteristics, including whether it resulted in a response by the addressee. In 94% of all utterances, children displayed social interest, and they received replies 62% of the time. Mueller found no relationship between either measure and age, suggesting that 3½-year-old children have already reached compe-tence at the maintenance of verbal exchanges. These data suggest that children have already left the egocentric stage by preschool age. In a longitudinal study of children from 12 to 48 months, Haight and Miller (1993) found that social play was between 68% and 75% of all pretend play, with no increase in the proportion of social play with age. In Bloch's (1989) study of 2- to 6-year-old U.S. and Senegalese children, half of the U.S. children's play was social, and the oldest Senegalese children engaged in social play six times as much as solitary play. Note that these studies do not convincingly prove Vygotsky's position, either; infant play is both solitary and social, rather than being completely social, as Vygotsky's theory suggested.

Regardless of the relative percentage of social play, there is substantial evidence, using a variety of taxonomic schemes and methodologies, that interactive pretend play becomes progressively more complex and sophisticated between 3 and 6 years (Corsaro, 1979b; Howes, 1980; Iwanaga, 1973; Rubin, Watson, & Jambor, 1978; Sanders & Harper, 1976; Smilansky, 1968). What are the social and conversational skills that accompany and support this develop-ment? Psychologists have not yet proposed a comprehensive theory of what these social skills are, and exactly how the unique context of fantasy play contributes to the development of these skills. This is one of the key tasks presently facing play researchers.

Developmental Pragmatics

Linguistic interaction is a defining feature of children's sociodramatic play. Like adult conversations, children's play talk is framed and contextualized. Studies of adult conversation can offer theoretical insights that help to characterize two aspects of children's interactional skills during play: the influence of sociocultural context, and the constantly changing, negotiatory nature of play. Adult conversation is studied from many different perspectives and in many disciplines, including linguistics, conversation analysis, and sociolinguistics.

The field of linguistics is traditionally subdivided according to the structural levels of language. The canonical subdisciplines are *phonetics, morphology, semantics, syntax,* and *pragmatics.* Pragmatics is the research area that focuses on how language is used in context. Unlike semantics and syntax, which study words and sentences in isolation from any specific context of use, pragmatics is concerned with how the meaning of an utterance is related to its context of use: To what extent is meaning dependent on context? Can the interactional meaning of the same utterance be different when used in different contexts? Regardless of specialization, most linguists would agree that in most cases, the context of use is important when interpreting the interactional meaning of any given utterance. As with other linguistic research, pragmatics has been theoretical and introspective, rather than empirical. Although many definitions of pragmatics have been proposed, I prefer Levinson's definition: "Pragmatics is the study of those relations between language and context that are *grammaticalized,* or encoded in the structure of a language" (1983, p. 9). This definition incorporates the study of deixis, presupposition, and speech acts. Each of these aspects of pragmatic theory has influenced studies of children's talk, particularly in the interdisciplinary field called *developmental pragmatics* (e.g., Ochs & Schieffelin, 1979).

Most language acquisition research through 1980 focused on how the child achieves full adult grammatical competence (Cook-Gumperz, 1986). This work also focused on the cognitive abilities underlying language development (Slobin 1973, 1978), since linguistic development was theorized to derive from cognitive development. In the mid-1970s, a minor paradigm shift began, with a focus on the early acquisition of pragmatic skills. This line of research attempted to identify continuities between prelinguistic interaction patterns between child and parent, and subsequent language acquisition. Much of this was in response to the Chomskian claim that language acquisition followed an innate developmental path. This paradigm shift can be traced to Bruner's 1975 paper "The Ontogenesis of Speech Acts," which demonstrated how two fundamental aspects of grammar, subject–verb constructions and case grammar, could be seen to emerge developmentally from prelinguistic play interaction between child and parent. In this and other papers, Bruner (1981, 1983) argued that pragmatic skills were a prerequisite for syntactic development.Other developmentalists also explored the pragmatic origins of language. In a longitudinal study from 3 months to 2 years, Freedle and Lewis (1977) found evidence to support Bruner's claim. Bates (1975, 1976; Bates, Benigni, Bretherton, Camaioni, & Volterra, 1977) explored the dependencies, relationships, and prerequisites between language, cognition, and social development. Camaioni

(1986) elaborated on Bruner's writings by suggesting that language skills emerge from special forms of conventionalized, or ritualized interaction—multiple-turn interactional sequences. In this, she followed Bruner's (1975) focus on play games, and anticipated Boggs' (1990) later work in conversation analysis (discussion following). Note that this is an inversion of Piaget, who claimed that rule-governed games were the endpoint of play development. In contrast, Camaioni argued that prelinguistic rule-governed games were an early stage.

This research has been influential in developmental psychology, and contributed to the resurgence of Vygotsky during the 1980s. However, for the most part, this work has not directly influenced research on children's play. Psychologists who study children's play have generally not focused very closely on the pragmatics of play talk. Note that almost all of this research focused on children much younger than preschool age; often, the children were in the first year of life. As a result, this research focused on caregiver–child interaction, rather than peer interaction. Most developmental pragmatics focused on specific types of acts by children, rather than action sequences, or the collective action more characteristic of preschool play. Thus, this research leaves our key questions unanswered: What is the nature of the structures and contexts guiding children's social play? How do children collectively regulate this improvisational performance?

Speech Act Theory

Speech act theory was first developed by John L. Austin (1962) in a now-classic volume titled *How to Do Things With Words*. Although the theory has been elaborated by many others, notably the philosopher John Searle (1969), a review of Austin is sufficient for understanding the theory's influence on the study of child discourse. Austin attempted to understand a special class of sentences which are used not only to say things, but also to do things; sentences that are inherently "actions." An example is the sentence "I apologize." The sentence itself constitutes the act of apologizing. Austin called these sentences, and the special class of verbs used in them, *performatives*. The interesting thing about performatives is that they have a dual character; they have both a denotational meaning and an interactional effect. In the terminology of play researchers, they are both enacted and metacommunicative. In addition to "saying something," they serve the metacommunicative function of "saying what they are saying." For example, when a person says "I apologize," he is actually apologizing (the denotational content), while at the same time saying that he is apologizing (the interactional effect). The latter sense of the usage is metacommunicative, in that it comments on the denotational content; the metacommunicative message is "I am apologizing now." These performative verbs communicate their interactional effect explicitly, and reflexively regulate the utterance itself. Before these interactional effects can be interactionally effective, Austin noted that they must be *felicitous*. For example, before "I apologize" can constitute an act of apology, the utterance must satisfy the situational conventions, or pragmatic presuppositions, required of an apology. To be felicitous, the state-ment "I apologize" requires that the speaker has done something to the addressee that requires an apology; the act's interactional effect is that an apology has been made. Performatives, unlike propositions, cannot be true or false; however, they can be inappropriate, if they don't satisfy the pragmatic presuppositions. Austin used the term *infelicitous* for a performative that is used without the proper presuppositions present.Austin identified a special class of English verbs that are explicitly performative, verbs such as *promise, wish, baptize, apologize*, and *warn*. He called these verbs *explicit primary performatives*. However, many utterances with the same presuppositions and interactional effect as these verbs do not have the explicit form of a performative: for example, "I'll never do that again," may have the performative effect of an apology. Austin referred to these types of speech acts as *implicit*, and claimed that all implicit acts could be translated into an explicit primary equivalent.

Austin separated the performative nature of an utterance into three kinds of effects: (a) *locutionary*, the denotation of the utterance; (b) *illocutionary*, the conventional "force" associated with an explicit performative (or, if implicit, its explicit paraphrase); (c) *perlocutionary*, the effects of an utterance that are not inherent in its performative verb, but that are special to the circumstances of the utterance. The illocutionary act is Austin's focus, and indeed the focus of all contemporary researchers using this model. The analysis of illocutionary force allows the specification of regularities between grammatical structure and interactional effect, allowing researchers to bracket the more complex issues of contextualization, by narrowly defining context to be conventional situations. Perlocutionary forces, not being conventional, cannot be analyzed in terms of the regularities between grammatical structure and interactional effect. As such, their existence undermines the legitimacy of speech act theory (and more generally undermines the basis for the endeavor of pragmatics as a purely linguistic discipline).

Like other theories in pragmatics, speech act theory is a theory about utterances. As such, it is not a theory of conversation per se. Nonetheless, it has been influential in recent studies of children's discourse, particularly in studies of language acquisition (Bates, 1976; Bates et al., 1977; Bruner, 1975) and classroom interaction (Cazden, 1988; McTear, 1985; Mehan, 1979; Sinclair & Coulthard, 1975). For example, Corsaro (1979b) showed correlations be-tween the relative role relationships being enacted during play and the percentages of speech acts used. Children's use of speech acts during play indicated their developing knowledge of status and role.

When we attempt to apply speech act theory to improvisational perform-ance, we find that it fails in several ways. First, speech act theory is based on a notion of speaker intentionality. A speaker is performing an act through the use of a performative utterance. However, in group improvisation, intentionality is distributed; it is often unclear what the denotational meaning or the interactional effect of a single utterance is, apart from its performance context, because of the contingency of the ongoing interaction. Second, speech act theory focuses at the utterance level. It does not provide a theory for how social action may be found in broader interactional structures. When we expand the analysis above the level of the utterance, we are analyzing interactional structures with multiple participants. Speech act theory fails to account for those cases when meaning and intentionality are collective, emergent phenomena. Third, speech act theory focuses on lexicalization (although recent adherents have been more flexible on this than either Austin or Searle). The assumption is that the explicit performative is normative, and represents the deep structure of even implicit acts. In contrast, Bateson, Goffman, and others have argued that the normative case is implicit metacommunication. From this perspective, performative verbs are a unique example of in-frame speech becoming explicitly metacommunicative. The fourth, and perhaps most important reason that speech act theory cannot explain improvisation, is that performatives are effective precisely because they are reliably uncreative, since their effectiveness is a function of their conventional, explicit form. Because of these problems, speech act theory cannot be extended to become a theory of improvisation in discourse.

Speech act theory has been criticized by other researchers on similar points (Cook-Gumperz, 1986; Silverstein, 1979, 1993). Cook-Gumperz argued specifically against the application of speech act theory to child development. The theory assumes that context and presupposition are nonproblematic for children. She pointed out that the theory does not address what these interactional events mean to the children, and thus, cannot adequately represent the intentionality of children. There are several other problems related to the difference in perspective of the adult analyst and the child: For example, children's notions of the range of contexts to which the presuppositions of any single speech act apply may differ from the adult's nonsituated judgment. In place of speech act theory, the key questions should be: How do children draw on their own knowledge of the world to do things with words? How do their perceptions of social setting and context shape their verbal exchanges? In Cook-Gumperz's interpretive approach, speech acts are seen as occurring within activities that have a social meaning for the participants; the contextual presuppositions are renegotiated in the course of conversation, and this improvisational process of negotiation is the central aspect of language socialization. Despite these problems, speech act theory has been important in showing that language is a form of social action. Prior to the introduction of speech act theory, most of pragmatics was distinctly unhelpful to developmental psychology. Speech act theory became influential primarily because it was the first pragmatic theory connecting language form to social context. It addresses many of the same concerns that led psychologists to propose the metacommunicative model of children's play. It is an attempt to connect the denotational and regulatory levels of interaction, by focusing on a special class of grammatical forms that seem to fix this relationship.

Discourse Analysis

Like speech act theory, most of pragmatics has studied isolated sentences and their relationship to their contexts of use. The branch of pragmatics that studies two or more utterances in sequence is called *discourse analysis*. Discourse analysts develop models to represent the sequential structure of written text and of conversations. In practice, this involves developing sequencing rules that look a lot like the grammatical rules that structure sentences. In the same way that words are linked through rules of syntax, sentences are linked through rules called *text grammars* or *discourse grammars*. In the same way that words can be categorized as nouns, verbs, and adjectives, the sentences, or speaker's utterances, are assumed to be identifiable as one of a set of basic discourse categories. If a text, or a conversation, follows these rules, the discourse is said to be coherent; if the rules are not followed, the discourse will not be coherent. Developing this kind of "grammar" requires that the analyst develop a set of basic categories, or units of discourse.

In the application of speech act theory to discourse analysis, the general idea has been to develop discourse grammars in which the basic categories of discourse are speech acts. For example, Mehan (1979) analyzed teacher–child interactions into sequential patterns of speech acts; the most common one was called Initiation–Response–Evaluation(IRE), a three-act sequence. Mehan also proposed a higher level unit of discourse, the Topically Related Set (TRS), a sequence of connected talk focused on a single topic. In similar fashion, McTear (1985) considered the most basic unit actions to be initiations and responses; his innovation was to suggest that many utterances combine a response (R) with a new initiation (I). These moves were coded as R/I. McTear also coined a phrase to refer to the creative interactional effect of an utterance: its *prospective extent*. Utterances with *low prospective extent* (relatively uncreative) were coded as R/(I), indicating that they have less of an initiating component (McTear, 1985). This approach has the benefit that it acknowledges the moment-to-moment creativity of an improvisational interaction. Hazen and Black (1989) used McTear's (1985) model to analyze several skills required for coherent discourse: the ability to direct initiations clearly to an addressee; the ability to respond contingently; and the ability to combine a response with a new, creative initiation. These three skills are improvisational skills, because they allow each child to manage the contingency and uncertainty of the ongoing play drama. Their results suggest that children who are more skilled at improvisation are more popular. Halliday (1984) elaborated similar notions to develop the *systemic-functional* approach to the acquisition of conversational skills.

Halliday characterized the child's developing interactional skill as a progressive differentiation of types of moves possible. Halliday suggested the following set of basic moves: initiate, respond, offer, statement, command, and question (1984). With development, the child acquires the ability to distinguish between different types of basic moves.

When we consider children's play as a form of improvisational performance, we realize that many aspects of the interaction are contingent, and are constantly being renegotiated. These aspects include the roles of the children, the role relationships, the events taking place, the actions of each play character, and the current plot of the drama. In the study of linguistic interaction, discourse analysis has restricted its analyses to concepts such as the *topic structure* of the conversation, the collection of topics in play as well as those forbidden or taboo. But note that *topic* and the usual discourse analyses of topical coherence, topic shift, and the like represent only one facet of the complex performances created by children. Topic refers to a denotational and referential aspect of the ongoing conversation; for discourse analysts, topic is often considered to be a noun phrase, and is distinguished from the *comment*, a dichotomy parallel to Clark and Haviland's (1977) *given–new* distinction. For Keenan and Schieffelin (1976/1983), *discourse topic* is a proposition, associated with the presuppositions of the prior discourse and its context. These definitions of topic only represent a small portion of what children have to negotiate in play. Other aspects of play that are negotiated include social role assignments, relative role relationships, and other sociological situational factors, such as how long the play session is expected to last. Like speech act theory, discourse analysis is ultimately unable to provide a theory of improvisational performance, because of its exclusive focus on lexical and grammatical forms, and its failure to account for social and interactional processes. Discourse analysis does not account for the creative contingency of improvisation, because it assumes that discourse is highly structured. A grammar of discourse is, ultimately, a formal representation of a script or event schemata. This sort of analysis is relatively easy to conduct after the fact, when the analyst is examining a fixed transcript on a page. Yet representations of discourse such as hierarchical trees of moves or speech acts, as broad structures of a complete interaction, cannot help us understand the moment-to-moment contingency of improvised interaction. Other fundamental problems with discourse-analytic approaches include their appeal to intuitive judgments and their nonempirical nature, typical of linguistics at large (Levinson, 1983). Conversation analysts attempted to address both of these weaknesses through a rigorously empirical study of naturally occurring conversation.

Conversation Analysis

Conversation analysis (CA) involves the microanalysis of naturally occurring conversation. In contrast to the often-intuitive appeals of discourse analysis,

CA is a naturalistic observational discipline (Schegloff & Sacks, 1973) that analyzes audiotapes and transcripts of naturally occurring conversations. CA began by focusing on the most basic mechanics of conversation: *turn-taking*. Turn-taking refers to the transitions between speakers: How do listeners know when a speaker is finished, and that they can start talking? A classic early paper (Sacks, Schegloff, & Jefferson, 1974) established the core of the CA methodology: a close focus on extremely detailed transcripts. These transcripts included information that is often filtered out of transcripts: pauses, false starts, stutters, intonation contours, and representations of speaker overlap. Sacks et al. (1974) demonstrated convincingly that participants in interaction attend to this level of detail, albeit subconsciously, in determining when a speaker's turn is complete. Ervin-Tripp (1979) argued that children are competent turn-takers by the age of 2, and suggested that these skills may emerge from peer interaction, and do not have to be taught by the caregiver.

In addition to the study of turn-taking, CA explores how the cross-utterance structure of interaction can contribute to the regulation and coherence of the interaction. These routines seem to be particularly important aspects of children's pretend interaction (Boggs, 1990; Camaioni, 1986; Corsaro, 1985; McTear, 1985; Peters & Boggs, 1986). Following Schegloff (1968), conversation analysts usually define the routine to be a *pair-part* sequence of two turns, in which the second turn is constrained by, and follows from, the first (Peters & Boggs, 1986). Canonical exchanges, such as a question followed by an answer, or a greeting followed by a response, were referred to as *utterance pairs* or, later, *adjacency pairs* (Schegloff & Sacks, 1973). CA has focused on three types of relatively complex routines: *openings* (Schegloff, 1968), a sequence that initiates a conversation; *repairs* (Schegloff, Jefferson, & Sacks, 1977), or the ways that speakers self-correct their mistakes; and *closings* (Schegloff & Sacks, 1973), sequences that terminate a conversation.

Some researchers define the routine more expansively. For example, Corsaro (1986) defined a routine to be any activity that is both predictable and adaptable. For Corsaro, a routine is a recognizable, repeatable game with a loose framework, which the children collectively understand, but with room for embellishment and improvisation. Schegloff (1990) argued that these routines serve the metacommunicative function of providing coherence to interaction. McTear (1985) argued that most of the coherence in children's talk is provided by interactional routines, and that these routines have a metacommunicative effect, helping to manage the flow of interaction. This position is similar to the argument that children use scripts to organize their pretend play; in conversation-analytic terms, a script is an extended stereotypical interactional routine.

Although some conversation analysts have argued that talk must be viewed as fundamentally in play during interaction, these theorists have rarely analyzed the interactional techniques that conversationalists use to negotiate what is going on in a conversation. CA has, in practice, focused on relatively static interactional routines, in formalization almost as static as discourse grammars, rather than exploring how routines are co-constructed in interaction, or how the selection of a given routine is negotiated. The benefit of this approach is that it counters the reductionist tendency of linguists to focus on the utterance level as the source of all conversational structure. Whereas most linguists expect conversational coherence to be found in each utterance's relationship to a hypothesized topic structure, Schegloff (1990) argued that interactional sequences often provide coherence in interaction, more so than topic. Boggs (1990), in a developmental variant of Schegloff's argument, suggested that children use routines for coherence only up to the point when they become capable of using topic constraints; he hypothesized that this switch occurs between the ages of 7 and 11. In Boggs' view, routines provide a form of scaffolding that helps children maintain conversational coherence up until the age when they are capable of topic-based structuring.

This research suggests that multiple-utterance structures of interaction can be used strategically by children to implicitly negotiate the play drama. The position of a turn within the ongoing flow of interaction may itself influence how the child's turn is interpreted. This influence is implicit, because the flow of the overall play conversation has implications for the speaker's actions, and these implications do not need to be explicitly stated. Creative actions during play may be more or less effective, depending on how they interact with the ongoing flow of discourse. The aforementioned research in psychology, discourse analysis, and CA suggests that these routines are at least as important among children as among adults.

The problems with this approach are similar to many of the critiques already discussed. It's unclear how the interactional routine of CA is different from script or frame theories of play. CA doesn't incorporate a theory of play improvisation: It argues that the regulatory level of interaction is derived from the (predefined) structure of the routine, especially among children. Although this suggests an approach toward understanding the implicit metacommunication of play improvisations, at the same time it fails to fully account for the improvisationality of children's play. As such, CA doesn't yet provide us with a complete theory of improvisational interaction.

Sociolinguistics and Role Play

Several researchers have studied how children learn to understand what others are thinking and feeling through the role playing of sociodramatic play. These developing abilities to understand others are called *metacognition* or *theories of mind*. In contrast to researchers who define play stages in terms of the static structural relations between play participants, those who study role playing focus more closely on how a child's ability to enact a play role changes through development. These researchers have identified relationships between role-playing ability and the development of social cognition, metacognition, and moral development. Role playing requires that children be able to enact roles compatible with a dramatic play theme. This research has proceeded under several different names and within different theoretical frameworks. A focus on *role taking* is associated with the work of Selman (1971, 1976). Selman argued that social skills are based on the child's increasing ability to conceptualize role taking in oneself and in others, which he referred to as social perspective taking. In conversation analysis, roles have been analyzed in terms of their positions within participant structures (Phillips, 1972). Fein (1985, 1987), in a more personality-focused approach, proposed that children's play is guided by affective representational templates, which she explicitly opposed to script models. Other researchers who have explored role playing include Bretherton (1986), Garvey (1982; Garvey & Berndt, 1977), and Smilansky (1968).

Role-taking views of play emphasize that play is a way of learning about social roles and their interrelationships. A play situation arises from the interaction of a set of role assignments. Some roles require that complementary roles be taken by another child; for example, if one child acts as the "baby," another child must take on the "mother" role. Iwanaga (1973) found that at least 25% of preschool play is role play, and suggested that the time spent in this type of play increases from ages 3 to 5. Garvey and Berndt (1977) showed that role play becomes more improvisational between ages 3 and 5. Among 3-year-olds, relationship roles were always based on the child's experience (e.g., mother and child), and the play activities were based on real-life experience. If one of the children departed from the real-life standard, the play role was subsequently abandoned; in other words, there was a low tolerance for creative variation. In contrast, for the 5-year-olds, the roles extended beyond the child's personal experience, and incorporated relationships observed in others (such as wife to husband). The 5-year-olds engaged in role activities that were not family related (gunfighting); often an imaginary third party was involved. Older children had a higher tolerance for departures from role-appropriate behavior, but the integrity of the relationship itself was never violated.

This research suggests that children become more creatively improvisational between ages 3 and 5. Play among 3-year-olds is imitative and more obviously scripted; these children show a low tolerance for variation from the script. In contrast, 5-year-olds are less imitative and are more adept at proposing and incorporating novel variations in their play. Although all of the children in this age range seem capable of some sort of role play, children seem to be learning how to be more creative and more improvisational. Because role play is inherently social, these children are also learning how to be improvisational within a highly social context; their improvisational role-playing skill is essentially a social skill.

Role enactment and role assignment are critical to the initiation and maintenance of social play. Although role assignment is often done explicitly, through a metacommunicative statement like "You be the mommy and I'll be the baby," children also implicitly assign roles (e.g., Giffin, 1984). Implicit assignments can be accomplished through speaking in a certain manner, indexing the social role that the speaker wishes to enact, for example, by using a deep, scary "bad guy" voice. Sometimes a style of speech serves to assign roles to the addressee as well as the speaker; for example, by speaking as a mother addressing a baby. Implicit role assignment can also be accomplished through the use of deictics, such as proper names and personal pronouns. The study of how individuals assign themselves relative social roles through implicit ways of speaking is an important part of sociolinguistics. Like conversation analysis, sociolinguistics focuses on empirically observed occurrences of language in social situations.

Several writers in sociolinguistics have analyzed how ways of speaking, or *speech styles*, are used to accomplish role assignment and other interactional goals (e.g., Andersen, 1986, 1990; Ervin-Tripp, 1972; Gumperz, 1972, 1982; Hymes, 1974). A speech style is a combination of lexical selection, characteristic syntactic patterns, and prosodic features. Each speech community has a variety of speech styles familiar to its members, its communicative repertoire (Gumperz, 1977). Sociolinguistics has focused on how these speech styles are associated with specific roles, traits, attitudes, or social groups; thus, their use has the effect of assigning a social role to the speaker. The term *register*, often used incorrectly to refer to a speech style, refers to speech styles that stand in a one-to-one relationship to a situation, rather than to a role or a group (Halliday, McIntosh, & Strevens, 1964). A speech style, unlike a register, is a way of speaking that can be used outside its defining context. Each culture has styles associated with, for example, classes, ethnic groups, regions, and formality (Hymes, 1974). Many researchers have settled on the term *register* as a generic term for all ways of speaking, and in some contexts I've continued this usage.

A child can assign a play role to herself by speaking in the style appropriate to that role. Andersen (1986, 1990) has demonstrated that by age 4, children are able to speak in different registers, and to respond appropriately when their partner chooses a register. For example, rather than explicitly state:

(1) Let's say I'm the mommy.

a child can say, using appropriate prosody and tone of voice:

(2) Quiet in here! I said it was bedtime.

In similar fashion, a child can implicitly assign a play role to another child, by addressing that child using a speech style associated with a social relationship. Utterance (2) assigns the addressee the play role of a child of the speaker, who is speaking as the mother. When an implicit like (2) invokes a social relationship, it can be a more efficient way of proposing a change to the play frame, because it proposes two play role transformations in a single statement. To accomplish this goal explicitly, a child would need two statements:

(3) Let's say I'm the mommy
(4) and that you were the daughter.

Also note that the implicit version is somewhat more ambiguous than the explicit version: Although the speaker is probably the mommy or daddy, depending on the child's gender, (2) could also be spoken by an older sibling or a babysitter. This increased ambiguity seems to be a general characteristic of implicit play speech.

In languages with complex pronominal systems that reflect social status and formality of speech, role assignment in adult conversation is often accomplished through the selection of personal pronouns. One of the classic treatments of such pronoun usage is that of Brown and Gilman (1960). Brown and Gilman suggested that, in languages with a unidimensional contrast set of pronouns (usually, on a dimension from informal through formal), each speaker's pronoun selection will be based on two variables: the power differential between the speakers, and their degree of solidarity. However, selection is not always fully determined by these pragmatic presuppositions. In difficult or ambiguous situations, the actual use of a particular mode of address can serve to creatively metacommunicate the relationship between speaker and addressee. This type of creative metacommunication has rarely been explored by sociolinguists, who have instead focused on how ways of speaking are chosen based on the indexical presuppositions deriving from the social context of the speakers. Creative metacommunication is a prominent feature of improvisational interaction, and it is a core topic of this book.

In some languages, pronoun selection provides a large and complex range of choices to speakers, the range depending on the language and the degree of differentiation of the social structure. Friedrich (1971) analyzed how the usage of the polite/familiar pronomial distinction in Russian can be strategically used by speakers to place the addressee in a socially inferior role. Modes of address are not limited to pronouns, but also include choices such as whether to use an honorific title (e.g., Dr. or Mrs.). In those cultures that assign multiple names to each individual, with restrictions on which speakers may use each name, the choice of a name can be implicitly metacommunicative because it suggests one way that the interaction might be framed. Children frequently use names and titles as an implicit technique of role assignment. Ervin-Tripp (1972) proposed an elaborate decision tree to represent how U.S. speakers determine the proper mode of address in a given situation. Even though English has a relatively simple pronoun set, modes of address can be strategically manipulated in complex ways. Some languages have several distinct "politeness registers" that can be used with similar effects. For example, Errington (1985) analyzed how the Javanese use a scale of nine linguistic registers, varying in formality, to assign relative status to both speaker and addressee.

This type of linguistic action is problematic for speech act theory. When a speaker uses a term of address or a style of speaking that places the addressee in a subordinate role, to the strategic advantage of the speaker, clearly a social act has been performed. In languages with complex pronominal systems, the social act must be considered to be lexicalized in the pronoun, rather than in any performative verb. In a language like English, these effects are rarely lexicalized at all, instead being communicated in indirect, implicit ways. Although children do this both explicitly and implicitly, adults rarely perform role assignments explicitly. It's difficult to imagine how we could translate a status-positioning manner of speaking among adults into an explicit version equivalent to statements (3) and (4), mentioned earlier. An explicit translation might look something like "We both know you are lower ranking than me, and I will now address you in a corresponding manner." Although speech act theory posits that the explicit performative is normative, such a statement would never be uttered explicitly, and it consequently sounds strange. Although English does not have lexical items for this speech behavior, some languages lexicalize aspects of register. For example, the French use the verbs *tutoyer* and *vouvoyer* to indicate *speaking using the familiar form* and *speaking using the formal form*, respectively. However, these terms do not refer to the overall register of the speaker, but to the verb form used.

Summary

At the beginning of this chapter, I presented two questions that have guided my study: (a) What is the nature of the structures guiding social play, and to what extent are they improvisational? (b) How does social context influence these processes? To explore these two questions, this chapter has reviewed relevant research in developmental psychology and related fields. The studies reviewed in this chapter provide the basis for a study of children's improvisations. From this research, we know that peer relations are important, especially after 3 years of age; social play is the primary social activity between ages 3 and 5; play with peers is different from play with adults; and play is related to the development of pragmatic skills. These studies indicate that the complexity of play increases through development, and that peer play contributes to social development. This research also suggests that much of play's complexity is found in the pragmatics of play conversation.

The improvisational analogy presented in the Introduction provided us with a guiding perspective from which to evaluate these theories of social play development. This research leaves many "how" questions unanswered: How are peers contributing to the development of play and pragmatic skills? Which aspects of sociocultural context affect which aspects of play? How does play contribute to pragmatic development? How do conventional interactional structures, such as scripts and routines, influence specific play interactions? Although conversation analysis and script theories represent these conventional structures quite well, their focus neglects the moment-to-moment interactional work required to negotiate and to effectively use these intersubjectively shared interactional patterns.

An examination of the improvisational processes of pretend play has the potential to provide us with an answer to these "how" questions. For example, metacommunication is used creatively in improvisational play interactions, and it may mediate the development of these social and conversational skills. Yet very few researchers have directly studied these improvisational processes, or the potential relationships between play improvisation and social context. In the next chapter, I present a model of play improvisation, which builds on several contemporary responses to the research previously discussed.

2

An Improvisational Theory
of Children's Play

*Talk is unique, however, for talk creates for the participant a world and a reality that
has other participants in it. Joint spontaneous involvement is a unio mystico, a socialized
trance. We must also see that conversation has a life of its own and makes demands on
its own behalf.*

—Erving Goffman (1967, p. 113)

After reviewing a wide range of approaches to the study of children's play and
conversation, we found that none of them were wholly sufficient to explain
children's play at its most improvisational. Of course, children's play is not
always so creative. Many play episodes are enactments of scripts learned by
watching adults, or fantasy plots taken from TV or movies. Yet, children's play
is just as frequently a novel, creative improvisation, a combination of roles,
characters, plots, and events that has never before been enacted. In these cases,
many models of play seem too structured and they do not account for the
collective creativity displayed by the children. Most adult conversations are also
improvised because many aspects of the interaction are not determined in
advance: The topic, the order of speakers, the formality or style of the interaction. Although children's fantasy play is more creative and more improvised
than most adult conversations, Ochs (1983) noted that the most unstructured
adult conversations were the most like children's play discourse. If the improvisational analogy is valid, it could provide us with a plausible developmental
continuity between children's fantasy play and adult conversational skill.

In this chapter, I present a theoretical framework, which I use in later chapters to characterize, operationalize, and analyze children's play at its most improvisational. I propose that play contributes to development through collective improvisational processes that I call *metapragmatic negotiation*. This theory builds upon prior psychological studies by focusing closely on linguistic interaction during play, and on how language use varies with social context. I examine a range of different metapragmatic strategies that children use to negotiate the play frame. For example, sometimes children step out of their play role, proposing a change to the play frame using a director's voice. At other times, they propose and negotiate the play frame while remaining in character. These are two different strategies, each using a different frame and voice. Children's strategies also range from explicit, when they are relatively direct in stating their proposal, to implicit, when they are relatively indirect. I argue that children use these different strategies to improvise the play drama, and that this metapragmatic negotiation contributes to the development of social and conversational skills.

The Study of Situated Social Action

Children's play improvisation is a form of collective, contextualized social action. Symbolic interaction was a key concern for the American pragmatists, particularly for the branch of social psychology known as *symbolic interactionism*. Symbolic interactionism focuses on *social acts* (Mead, 1934), or *joint action* (Blumer, 1969): "The larger collective form of action that is constituted by the fitting together of the lines of behavior of the separate participants" (Blumer, 1969, p. 70). Symbolic interactionists emphasize that social action is an appropriate level of analysis for study, distinct from the individual level and the macrosocial level: "Both such joint activity and individual conduct are formed *in* and *through* this ongoing process; they are not mere expressions or products of what people bring to their interaction or of conditions that are antecedent to their interaction" (Blumer, 1969, p. 10). Symbolic interactionists, like the pragmatists before them (particularly Mead and Dewey), argued on epistemological and ontological grounds that collective activity is the only appropriate level for social scientific study. As Mead (1932) wrote, "The world is a world of events" (p. 1). John Dewey's related notion of *experience* is also relevant to the study of improvisational interaction. Dewey used the concept of experience to develop an aesthetic theory that is remarkably well suited to improvisational phenomena. He argued that the experience of perceiving a work of art, even a static work such as a painting or sculpture, was essentially the same experience as perceiving a creative performance, such as dance or music. Dewey argued that all art products have a temporal dimension, because they are created by the artist through time, and they are perceived by the audience through time (Dewey, 1934). By defining art as aesthetic experience, Dewey was able to propose a creative unity underlying performance and fixed artistic genres. But Dewey's theory of experience was more than an aesthetic theory; it was a theory of all human experience. Everyday activities, such as gardening, working, or speaking with others, can be considered to have an aesthetic dimension. On several occasions, Dewey (1934) made it clear that he considered conversation to be a form of aesthetic experience:

> In a work of art, different acts, episodes, occurrences melt and fuse into unity, and yet do not disappear and lose their own character as they do so—just as in a genial conversation there is a continuous interchange and blending, and yet each speaker not only retains his own character but manifests it more clearly than is his wont. (p. 37)

Experience, for Dewey, was a way of characterizing how people interact with their physical and social environment. This interaction, like genial conversation, is always improvisational, because human experience is never predictable. Like many pragmatists, Dewey rooted this concept in the writings of William James (1934), in a passage that seems to be a description of an improvisational performance:

> William James aptly compared the course of a conscious experience to the alternate flights and perchings of a bird. The flights and perchings are intimately connected with one another; they are not so many unrelated lightings succeeded by a number of equally unrelated hoppings. (p. 56)

It is beyond the scope of this book to elaborate Dewey's full theory of human experience and its implications for psychology. Yet it is sufficient to demonstrate that a core element of Dewey's theory, the notion of experience, has parallels with the approach to improvisation presented here. Dewey felt that conversation was a particularly useful analogy for all of human experience, and that everyday conversation was particularly improvisational.

A contemporary and colleague of Dewey, George Herbert Mead, developed similar theories about interaction through time. The metaphor of interaction as improvisation shares much in common with Mead's (1932, 1934) concept of the *emergent*. "The emergent when it appears is always found to follow from the past, but before it appears, it does not, by definition, follow from the past" (Mead, 1932, p. 2). Mead was commenting on the contingency of improvisational interaction: Although a retrospective examination reveals a coherent interaction, each conversational turn provides a range of creative options, any one of which could have resulted in a radically different performance. The emergent was the fundamental analytic category for Mead's philosophy, and the paramount issue for social science. He claimed, "It is the task of the philosophy of today to bring into congruence with each other this universality of determination which is the text of modern science, and the emergence of the novel" (1932, p. 14).The difficulty, Mead continued, is that once an emergent appears, the analyst attempts to rationalize it, showing (incorrectly) that it can be found "in the past that lay behind it" (1932, p. 14). For example, a transcript of a conversation is an emergent, a record of the verbal interaction. Once we have the transcript in front of us on the page, it's easier to mistakenly assume that the flow of the conversation was more predictable, more structured, than it actually was for the participants. Dewey referred to this error, in another context, as the "philosophic fallacy": taking the results of an inquiry as having existed prior to that inquiry (Dewey, 1925, p. 389). These observations have an uncanny predictive validity when one examines the ensuing history of research in conversation and discourse analysis. Rather than exploring the improvisational, contingent nature of interaction, most research has focused on structuralizing models of scripts, frames, discourse grammars, or routines. As I noted in chapter 1, these models are structuralizing because they assume that the structure of the interaction existed prior to the interaction. From an improvisational perspective, interactional structure is always potentially novel, varying from any preexisting structure.

Pragmatism's influence has survived in contemporary social science, although one could not say that it has prospered. For the most part, its current influence has been limited to microsociology and education research. For example, symbolic interactionism followed directly from Mead's writings. In combination with action theory, including Parsons (1937) and the phenomenological theories of Schutz (1932/1967), Mead's influence led to the ethnomethodology of Harold Garfinkel, and later, to conversation analysis (see chapter 1). Although psychology should probably be considered the discipline most closely related to the project of pragmatism, the writings of Dewey and Mead have had negligible influence on contemporary psychological practice (some notable exceptions are found in two comparisons of Vygotsky and pragmatism: John-Steiner & Tatter, 1983; Rogoff, in press).

Many psychologists have drawn inspiration from new translations of Vygotsky's developmental writings, which emphasized the social aspects of events during development, and the child's participatory role in those events. These psychologists focus on actions, events, and discourse as the basic units of analysis (Goncu, 1993a, 1993b; Harre & Gillett, 1994; Potter & Edwards, 1992; Rogoff, 1982, in press; Sawyer, 1995a; Wertsch, 1985b; Zinchenko, 1985). Like the pragmatists, these psychologists advocate a focus on collective social action. Wertsch (1985b) based his notion of *mediated action* on Vygotsky's exploration of how signs and symbols are fundamental to cognitive and social action in childhood. Mediated action plays a critical role in development, because the child is learning the mediation system and how to use it appropriately in interactional contexts of use. Goncu (1993a, 1993b) applied these theories in his studies of how intersubjectivity develops during children's preschool play. Goncu studied children's play by closely focusing on transcripts of play talk, and analyzing how children become more intersubjective with age.

Although sympathetic to psychological studies of environmental influences, Rogoff criticized prior approaches for drawing a sharp theoretical distinction between the developing child and that child's context. In a fundamentally pragmatist move, her sociocultural approach to psychological study suggested that the individual and environment are inseparable and mutually constitutive (Butterworth, 1992; Lawrence & Valsiner, 1993; Rogoff, 1982, in press; Rogoff, Baker-Sennett, & Matusov, 1994). This inseparability was a basic tenet of pragmatist philosophy.[1] In an attempt to avoid the individual–environment boundary implied by the term *internalization*, Rogoff (in press) proposed the term *participatory appropriation* to describe how the child, by participating in interactions with the physical and social environment, develops social and cognitive planning skills. The sociocultural approach, like recent work in creativity theory (Csikszentmihalyi, 1988; Csikszentmihalyi & Sawyer, 1995; John-Steiner, 1993; Sawyer, 1992, 1996), focuses on the process, rather than the products, of creative planning. Planning is a creative process that requires improvisational skills (Baker-Sennett, Matusov, & Rogoff, 1992). These researchers propose that the unit of analysis in such a study must be the interactional event (Rogoff, 1982). For example, in the Baker-Sennett et al. study, the unit of analysis was a playcrafting episode.

These approaches are psychological manifestations of a broader change in social science toward interpretive approaches (Bruner, 1990; Gaskins, Miller, & Corsaro, 1992; Rabinow & Sullivan, 1979; Shweder, 1990). This work has problematized the use of language, and the many assumptions about language that underlie several traditional social science research methodologies, including the research interview (Briggs, 1986) and the coding of linguistic data. Gaskins et al. (1992) defined the interpretive approach to child development in essentially pragmatist terms, emphasizing its focus on situated meaning and development, meaning creation as an active process, and the constitutive power of language.

These approaches (interpretivist, sociocultural, pragmatist, Vygotskian) argue for a shift from the individual as the unit of analysis, to a focus on event, process, and action as the unit of analysis. This unit of analysis is essential to

---

[1] In a passage reminiscent of James' discussions of the "material me" and the "social me," Dewey wrote, "Life goes on in an environment; not merely *in* it but because of it, through interaction with it. No creature lives merely under its skin. ...The career and destiny of a living being are bound up with its interchanges with its environment, not externally but in the most intimate way" (1934, p. 13). This is particularly true of heightened experience: "at its height [experience] signifies complete interpenetration of self and the world of objects and events" (p. 19).

study the social and interactional forces that influence play improvisations. To understand the improvisational processes of children's play, to study contextualized implicit metacommunication, one is required to study conversational exchanges, rather than specific utterances or single children. If our goal is to study the relationships between the developing child and the social context of the peer culture of a preschool classroom, we need to focus on the collective linguistic action of pretend play conversation. For example, the unit of analysis could be the *interactional routine*, a sequence of turns or utterances among two or more children. If the focus is on social action, the minimum conceivable unit of analysis is the dyad; and in those cases where more than two children are playing together, that group becomes the unit of analysis, because many conversational events are collectively created and shared by the entire play group.

In chapter 1, I showed how theories that focus on scripts or interactional routines are structuralist models of social action, and are difficult to apply to improvisational behavior. How can we focus on action as the unit of analysis while retaining an ability to represent the improvisational flux of play activity? Some psychologists have recently moved in this direction, by drawing on Bateson's concept of *metacommunication*.

Metacommunication

Several psychologists have used performance metaphors to describe play, describing how children both enact and direct the play drama (Bretherton, 1989; Magee, 1989; Sutton-Smith, 1979). A large percentage of play discourse is occupied by a director's voice, when children work to construct the play frame (Goncu, 1993a; Keenan & Schieffelin, 1976/1983; Sutton-Smith, 1979). Because children speak as both actors and directors, their play speech is dialogic (Bakhtin, 1981). The dialogic combination of the actor's voice with the director's voice accounts for much of the improvisational nature of play, because it allows children to negotiate the play drama while at the same time enacting it.

How do children use this dialogism to negotiate the play drama? To better represent the dynamic, changing nature of the play frame, and how the dual activities of directing and enacting combine to create a play drama, several psychological researchers have applied Gregory Bateson's concept of *metacommunication*. Bateson coined the term *metacommunication* to refer to the ongoing regulation of interaction. He argued that metacommunicative ability was fundamental to interaction, and must have preceded language in the evolution of communication (1955/1972). Many developmental psychologists have applied this concept to pretend play, beginning with the republication of Bateson's 1956 article in the 1971 volume, *Child's Play*. Catherine Garvey (1974; Garvey

& Berndt, 1977; Garvey & Kramer, 1989) is perhaps most responsible for the recent focus in psychology on metacommunication during pretend play. She defined *play metacommunication* to be the regulatory actions children perform during play that maintain, negotiate, and direct the play activity. Garvey emphasized the improvisational and social aspects of metacommunication, noting that each child's actions were contingent on the actions of the other children's (1974). However, she applied the term *metacommunication* only to explicit references to the pretend frame (Garvey & Berndt, 1977), excluding the implicit metacommunication that Bateson argued was so important. For example, an explicit metacommunication would be the following:

Example 2.1. Explicit metacommunication.

(1)   A   Let's play teenage mutant ninja turtles.
(2)   B   OK!

The proposed change to the play frame is explicitly stated. In contrast, in implicit metacommunication, the proposal is indirect and is not explicitly stated. Example 2.2. shows an implicit version of the exchange in Example 2.1:

Example 2.2. Implicit metacommunication.

(1)   A   I'm Donatello!
(2)   B   I'm Raphael!

Because the character Donatello is known within the peer culture to be one of the Teenage Mutant Ninja Turtles (circa 1992), line (1) implicitly metacommunicates that Child A is engaging in pretend play, and is enacting the Donatello character. Child B's response implicitly metacommunicates that he has accepted the proposal to play in this fashion. Bateson argued that most metacommunications were implicit (1955/1972), and often were nonverbal, communicated through gesture or posture (Ruesch & Bateson, 1951).

Several contemporary psychological researchers (Auwarter, 1986; Giffin, 1984; Goncu, 1993a, 1993b; Kane & Furth, 1993) have followed Garvey's lead in combining the metacommunication and the frame concepts to analyze social pretend play. Before children can play together, a play frame must first be created and understood by the participants, containing agreed-upon transformations of objects, persons, locations, and events (Giffin, 1984). Once this frame is created, children can communicate their desires to change the frame by acting within frame, speaking as their play character, or out of frame, speaking as themselves.

Bateson considered metacommunication only to occur at the beginning of play, as a marking of entry into the play frame. However, recent psychological research suggests that this is only true of peer play at the youngest ages, 3 and under (Doyle & Connolly, 1989; Doyle, Doehring, Tessier, & de Lorimier, 1992; Goncu, 1993a, 1993b; Iwanaga, 1973). For example, several studies by Doyle and her students have found that pretend negotiation and enactment are blended and interdependent during play (Doyle & Connolly, 1989; Doyle et al., 1992). At ages 4 and 5, the metacommunicative level is constantly present throughout the play interaction, as children collectively determine what is being played, when changes in the play will occur, and whose versions of "what is going on" will be accepted (Auwarter, 1986; Giffin, 1984). In support of Bateson's claim, Giffin's study found that even though children do occasionally state exactly what they want to happen, most of their proposals are implicit.

Despite these observations, most psychological studies have followed Garvey in restricting the study of metacommunication to explicit metacommunication. Some of these studies suggested that the incidence of explicit metacommunication increases during the preschool years. For example, McLoyd, Warren, and Thomas (1984b) found that 5-year-olds used more explicit metacommunication than 3½-year-olds. Garvey and Kramer (1989) also found that explicit metacommunication increased from ages 3 to 5, and that explicit metacommunication did not appear before age 3. These studies suggest that the amount of explicit metacommunication increases during the preschool years. However, because these studies did not analyze implicit metacommunication, we can't know whether the use of implicit metacommunication increases even more rapidly.

The metacommunication concept is an attempt to analyze the improvisational aspects of children's play. Unlike structuralist models such as script or frame theories, a focus on metacommunication is a focus on the interactional processes whereby children collectively create a play drama. As such, this focus can help us address several key questions: How can we represent variations from a script? If children's play is not scripted, how is it structured and organized? Metacommunicative processes help us understand how children can collectively regulate and maintain their ongoing interaction, in the absence of a prespecified structure. Yet this approach is still relatively new to developmental psychology. Even though most of these researchers have acknowledged, like Bateson, that implicit metacommunication is important, most of them have focused only on explicit metacommunication. Metacommunication is usually defined to be speech in a director's or narrator's voice. More complicated types of implicit metacommunication remain to be theorized and analyzed. For example, couldn't children metacommunicate about their play drama without making any sort of directorial statement? When adults metacommunicate to structure their informal interactions, they are relatively indirect and implicit, and they always remain in the frame of the interaction. Like children's play, adult conversations are dialogic, with two levels present throughout: the enacted performance, and the regulation or metacommunication about how that performance will proceed. Bateson described how dialogic metacommunication results in an improvised psychotherapy session: "The rules are implicit but subject to change. Such change can only be proposed by experimental action, but every such experimental action, *in which a proposal to change the rules is implicit*, is itself a part of the ongoing game. It is this combination of logical types within the single meaningful act that gives to therapy the character...of an evolving system of interaction" (Bateson, 1955/1972, p. 192; italics added).

I suspect that developmentalists have focused on explicit metacommunication precisely because it is what marks play as being different from adult conversational interaction. Adults are almost always implicit, and almost never speak out of frame. It's not surprising that research would focus first on that aspect of play that seems unique to children. However, because explicit metacommunication is rare among adults, an unanswered question in these developmental studies is how explicit, out-of-frame metacommunication during play contributes developmentally to adult interactional ability, which is primarily implicit.

From Metacommunication to Metapragmatics

Several researchers have called for a more intensive focus on the metacommunicative processes of children's pretend play. In the conclusion to their review of the literature on pretend language, Garvey and Kramer (1989) emphasized the importance of metacommunicative strategies for role assignment, and for proposals for new events, actions, and object transformations. They argued that metacommunication had to be studied through a turn-by-turn, sequential analysis of pretend discourse. Goncu (1993a) called for a study of how children negotiate social play, and how metacommunicative processes vary with play theme and with the familiarity of the children. McLoyd et al. (1984b) suggested that future work would have to distinguish among types of metacommunication. All of these researchers saw a need for an elaboration of the metacommunication concept. Unfortunately, researchers have not settled on a shared definition for metacommunication; different studies have operationalized the concept in different ways. This makes it difficult to draw any unified conclusions from prior studies.

Bateson's term, *metacommunication,* refers to communication about communication. Thus, a metacommunication is like a statement in that it has a propositional structure, of which the referent is a denotational communication. Bateson's (1972) classic example was the statement "This is play" (p. 180). But what about the types of adult pragmatics discussed in chapter 1? For example, using a certain speech style, or choosing a particular pronoun of reference, can have the effect of placing the speaker and addressee into a recognizable social relationship. This regulatory act is not really a communication about communication; its referent is not any single denotational utterance. Rather, its referent is the social relationship between the speakers, a pragmatic property of the interaction. Pragmatic characteristics of interaction include the relationships between the speakers and the type of interaction that is proceeding. In children's play, most of the ongoing regulation of interaction is also, strictly speaking, not metacommunicative. The metalevel communications denote pragmatic properties of interaction, such as the play roles assigned to each child, the relationships between these dramatic roles, and the actions that are being enacted. As such, the ongoing regulatory level of play interaction is more properly termed *metapragmatic*.

The term *metapragmatics* originated with Michael Silverstein (1976, 1993). In the same way that Bateson's metacommunication is communication about communication, metapragmatic language comments on the pragmatic level of language use (Silverstein, 1993). Metapragmatic language serves the framing or regulatory function that has often been referred to using the more specific term *metacommunication*. Both Silverstein's metapragmatics and Bateson's metacommunication are attempts to characterize a level of interaction that is parallel to the denotational level of speech, which serves to regulate and frame the interaction. Like Bateson, Silverstein suggested that interaction proceeds on these two levels simultaneously, referring to the levels as the *denotational text* and the *interactional text* (1991, 1993). The interactional text is the regulatory, metapragmatic level of interaction. Although psychologists have preferred Bateson's term *metacommunication*, in practice, they are actually examining the metapragmatic function of children's play speech, because the referents of such speech are not denotational communications, but rather, the properties of the play frame. The properties of the play frame are pragmatic aspects of the interaction, and include the roles of each child, their relationships, and the type of play under way.

Consistent with research demonstrating that pragmatic skills develop before spoken language (e.g., Bruner, 1975), Silverstein suggested that metapragmatic skills develop before denotational skills (1985). Hickmann (1985) summarized the role of metapragmatic skills in child development:

> The metapragmatic capabilities of language transform the child's developing ability to plan, organize, and interpret pragmatic uses of signs in interactive situations: They transform his ability to participate in gradually more complex interactive events with other agents, as well as his ability to reflect on, talk about, and reason about these interaction events. (p. 254)

A common theme in theories of adult language use is that the regulatory level of interaction is largely implicit. For example, conversation analysis locates the regulation of conversation in the structures of interactional routines. Only speech act theory has focused on those rare cases in which metapragmatic effects are lexicalized, in verbs like "promise" that simultaneously work on both denotational and metapragmatic levels (see chapter 1). Although research on play metacommunication has focused on explicit acts, these researchers have usually followed Bateson in acknowledging that implicit metacommunication also plays an important role. Yet the notion of implicit metapragmatics is somewhat paradoxical. How could the complex information found at the metapragmatic level be communicated, if not explicitly? How can we say it without saying it? How do children know what they are playing, if no one has explicitly said so? For that matter, how do adults come to an agreement about what kind of interaction is proceeding, and what their relative roles and statuses are?

The theories of adult conversation discussed in chapter 1 provide us with partial explanations for how play enactment can have metapragmatic effects. The key questions with respect to play are (a) How can enactment be metapragmatic? (b) How can implicit and in-frame statements be effective interactionally? The sociolinguistic research reviewed in chapter 1 suggested that implicit metapragmatic processes are fundamental in adult language use. If they can be linked with an expanded notion of metapragmatics in children's play, we might have a better understanding of how sociolinguistic skills develop through fantasy play.

Indexicality

In analyzing how children collectively improvise a play drama through the use of implicit metapragmatics, I have found it helpful to incorporate several concepts from interactional semiotics, including Peirce's notion of *indexicality* as elaborated by Jakobson (1960, 1956/1985; see also Bar-Hillel, 1954) in his discussion of the *poetic function* of language, and Silverstein's (1976, 1993) discussions of *indexical presupposition* and *indexical entailment*. These concepts can be combined with the conversation-analytic concept of *routine* to help understand how implicit metapragmatic effects are found in patterns of linguistic interaction. The route to an incorporation of semiotic theory into discourse analysis begins with Peirce's concept of indexicality.

In Peirce's trichotomy of signs, an *index* is a sign that requires an association between the sign and its object. The classic example of an indexing sign is the weathervane, which points out the wind direction. A second type of sign is the *symbol*, which is connected to its object only by a conventionally shared rule. For example, most words are symbols, because any sequence of vowels and consonants could refer to a given object. This is not true of the weathervane, because the relationship between the weathervane and the wind direction is not arbitrary, but is determined by the physics of wind flow. Pierce's third type of sign is the *icon*, which is connected to its object by isomorphism or similarity

(Peirce, 1931). An example of an icon is a picture or drawing, which references its object by replicating it.

The index is the most important type of sign for pragmatics research, because many uses of language are indexes of the social context. In the same way that a weathervane points to the wind direction, conversational indexes point to some aspect of the social context. The most studied aspects of the indexical use of language are *deictics*, words such as pronouns, whose meaning is completely dependent on the context (Levinson, 1983). The word "you" only has meaning within the context of a specific interaction: It refers to the person being spoken to. There are many types of indexical relations between language and context. For example, past tense is indexical, since it is relative to the *time* of the utterance. More complex examples can be found in many languages. For example, unlike English, some languages have special ways to mark the topic or subject of a sentence, for example, by attaching certain suffixes to the noun. These syntactic structures indicate that a certain referent has already been identified as the topic currently in play and are indexical of that referent as being the topic of the surrounding stretch of discourse. This general phenomenon has been referred to as *pragmatic presupposition* (Keenan, 1971; Levinson, 1983) or *indexical presupposition* (Silverstein, 1976, 1979, 1993).

Deictics such as personal pronouns are particularly interesting in this regard, because they function indexically on two parallel levels. On a *denotational* level, a personal pronoun such as *you* cannot be resolved to a referent outside of a specific context of use; thus the usage indexically presupposes that the denoted individual is present and is the addressee of the utterance. On an interactional level, some types of personal pronouns also indexically presuppose nondenotational aspects of the context. Keenan's example was pronominal selection in French: The use of *tu*, the informal second-person pronoun, conventionally presupposes that "the addressee is an animal, child, socially inferior to the speaker, or personally intimate with the speaker" (1971, p. 51). As a conversational interaction proceeds, the indexical presuppositions established up to each moment (both denotational and interactional) act to constrain each speaker, because the speaker must maintain some minimum level of coherence with the topic structures, speech styles and registers, and role relations already established.[2] Utterances may also index the future direction of a conversation; Silverstein (1993) referred to this as *indexical entailment*, because the utterance indexes a potential direction that the interaction might take.[3] For example, in

---

[2]Note the distinction between this *interactional coherence* and logical or denotational coherence, which is maintained (in parallel fashion to interactional coherence) through the use of logical/semantic presupposition and semantic entailment.

[3]Although Levinson (1983, p. 174) commented on logical or *semantic entailment*, he did not mention any use of the term *pragmatic entailment* in the literature. Silverstein (1976, 1993) also used the term *indexical creativity*.

languages with a system of politeness registers, for example, the *formal/informal* distinction in Russian, the selection of a given register by a speaker is indexical of one way in which the status relations may play out during the interaction (Friedrich, 1971). Inappropriate use of the informal form may constitute a sort of insult, indexically entailing an interaction in which the speaker is of superior status. Note once again the two-layered indexicality of such pronouns: Indexical entailment of this socially creative sort is a non-denotational form of indexicality, because it has nothing to do with identifying the referent of the pronoun.

Both levels of indexicality are metapragmatic because such utterances refer to the pragmatic structure, the frame, of the interaction. Note that the aforementioned examples for presupposition and for entailment both use the *informal/formal* distinction. This points to a general property of socially creative indexicality: Indexical presupposition and entailment are often found in the same utterance, and utterances can range from relatively creative to relatively presupposing. As Silverstein (1979) noted, "the give-and-take of actual interaction depends on the constantly-shifting communicative negotiation and ratification of indexical presupposition vs. indexical creativity" (p. 207). Although the metapragmatic level combines both indexical presupposition and entailment, at the denotational level indexicality tends to be presupposing, rather than entailing. For example, the use of either *tu* or *vous* presupposes that the addressee is present and is already participating as an addressee. (Entailing exceptions are rare, but they do exist: "Hey you! Yeah, you, I'm talkin' to you.") The fact that both levels of indexicality are often found in the same speech, combined with the fact that the denotational level of indexicality tends to be presuppositional, leads many analysts to identify even the socially creative entailing functions of such signs as presupposition.

This type of analytic error was identified by Mead (1932) in his discussion of the emergent; after an act is performed, everyone assumes it was predicted by the prior flow of the interaction. This analytic error is an example of how emergent structure is, in general, misunderstood to be a metapragmatics of presupposing, denotationally functioning indexical signs. Emergent improvisations are created through the balance of indexical presupposition and entailment. In a discussion of linguistic ideology, Silverstein suggested that this error is cross-culturally universal: Speakers tend to be unaware of the creatively indexical effects of sign forms, instead perceiving those effects as deriving from indexical presupposition (1979).

The Metapragmatics of Dialogic Speech

Children's play talk is often dialogic, combining the play character's voice with the director's voice to propose changes to the play frame. The concept of indexicality suggests several ways that children can metacommunicate about play while remaining in character and implicit. Much of sociolinguistics focuses on how ways of talking have indexical effects, because ways of talking are associated with different types of interactions. For example, speaking informally indexes the social situation as an informal setting. Studies of this kind of indexicality include the study of register as a marker of social status (Hymes, 1972, 1974); the study of politeness as a marker of relative status and solidarity (Brown & Levinson, 1978; Freidrich, 1971); the study of certain lexical sets as a marker of social class (Errington, 1985; Labov & Fanshel, 1977); and the study of contextualization cues as markers of in-group membership (Gumperz, 1982). I've found it useful to connect these models to children's play enactment by using Bakhtin's concepts of *voice*, *heteroglossia*, and *speech genre*. Bakhtin's work suggests that all language use is inherently indexical of social relations and group membership (Bakhtin, 1981, 1986).

These concepts are useful in presenting a developmental model for how the child's enactment of a play role can simultaneously serve a metapragmatic function. Bakhtin argued that the individual participates in a complex, multi-faceted linguistic world, with many different ways of speaking, or *voices*, which are each indexical of a recognizable social role and status. In such a complex heteroglossic, or multiply voiced, social environment, each interaction provides the individual with a wide range of strategies for socially locating themselves relative to their interlocutors. Bakhtin's analysis of dialogue in the novel focused on how members of the society creatively manipulate these voices for particular interactional effects. These creative processes are remarkably similar to many of the improvisational processes I have identified in children's play discourse.

Bakhtin used the term *dialogism* to describe quoted dialogue in the novel that blends the character's voice with the author's voice. The author, while representing the speech of the character, embeds his or her own narrating voice into that speech, sending implicit messages about himself and about that character. This text is dialogic because it contains two voices at the same time. This term can be used to describe children's speech that is enacting and metacommunicating at the same time: When children's play speech is dialogic, they are both enacting the in-frame role, and simultaneously metacommunicating a director's message about that role.

Although Bakhtin's primary purpose was to analyze the novel, his concept of voicing is a useful way of characterizing the processes by which individuals reflexively assign themselves desirable social roles through the use of distinctive speech styles and registers. Because a speech community is made up of individuals speaking from a variety of voices, individuals may have to switch voice when they switch into a different social group, a different professional group, or a group of people much older or younger.[4] Each individual is capable of speaking from a variety of voices, determined by his own location in the social

---

[4]This is the essence of Gumperz's (1982) concept of *code switching*.

matrix; each person's speech contains "heteroglot voices." In the novel, the author must represent each character's many voices in addition to his or her own. Discourse in the novel displays both the heteroglot voices of the characters as well as the author's own voice. Thus the genius of the creative novelist is in understanding the complexity and diversity of dialects and speech communities in his or her society, creating characters who cross group boundaries and thus are subject to heteroglossia. By painting a verbal picture of the different voices of the society and their interaction, the author creates a textual image of the society.

In preschool play, children often enact a play role using a distinctive speech style. These play voices have an implicit metapragmatic function. Example 2.3 is such a case:

Example 2.3. Implicit metapragmatics through voicing. Muhammed holds a dinosaur, Jennifer holds a small duck.

(1)   Muhammed   No, you can get on me   (in deep, gruff voice)
(2)   I just won't care

Muhammed is voicing as the dinosaur figure, which he holds in his hand, and participating in a play conversation with the duck, which his play partner holds. By using prosodic markers characteristic of large animals (a deep, gruff voice), Muhammed sends the metapragmatic message that he is now speaking as the dinosaur, not as himself. His use of the personal pronouns *you* and *me*, which resolve to play frame roles, also metacommunicates that his utterance is in frame. Although voicing as the dinosaur, Muhammed also sends a directorial, metapragmatic message, "Let's pretend that ducks can ride dinosaurs"; thus, his speech is dialogic, combining the dinosaur's voice with the director's voice. This technique of voicing, using a distinctive speech style, allows Muhammed to bypass an explicit metapragmatic step, which we might hypothesize would have taken the form in Example 2.4:

Example 2.4. Explicit metapragmatic equivalent to the implicit metapragmatic proposal of Example 2.3.

(1)   Muhammed   Pretend that your duck could get on the dinosaur
(2)   because he didn't really care, OK?

As I noted previously, many psychologists have noted that children's play speech is frequently dialogic, combining play enactment with metapragmatic negotiation (Bretherton, 1989; Scarlett & Wolf, 1979; Sheldon, 1992). In my observations of children's play, it seems that the majority of play speech is dialogic, embedding directorial, metapragmatic proposals within in-frame, in-character voicing.

In addition to dialogism at the utterance level, I have noticed another sort of heteroglossia that is fundamental to social play: In any given play group, each child maintains a more-or-less idiosyncratic perspective on what is going on. It seems that children are acting with distinct conceptions of the play frame, perhaps because their intersubjective skills are still developing during this age range (Goncu, 1993a, 1993b). Auwarter (1986) noted that the better children become at sharing frames, the less they metacommunicate out-of-frame; by age 6, children are quite competent at establishing a shared frame using dialogic enactment, and therefore do not need to be explicit as frequently. In contrast, when two or more children younger than age 6 play together, they rarely seem to integrate their utterances into a unified situational definition.[5] Cook-Gumperz (1986) observed that children's utterances leave the indexical presuppositions relatively indeterminate, allowing for a wider range of interpretation, and a wider range of subsequent creative options.[6] A developmental analysis of implicit metapragmatic strategies would then be particularly appropriate to children who have not yet achieved skill at maintaining intersubjectivity.

This formulation of play as heteroglossic is problematic for structuralist models of play. These models implicitly propose that each child shares a similar, if not identical, mental representation of some structure. The script model proposes a structure that incorporates a temporal dimension; the frame model proposes a static dramatic structure. But even after children begin social play, it may be inaccurate to speak of a single shared play frame. Children under age 6 engaging in pretend play rarely share a single cohesive play frame, and very young children may not be capable of creating and maintaining a shared structure. Children of this age are not yet expert in enforcing or even recognizing consistency and cohesiveness among the participants, and thus one would expect each child to maintain a distinct perspective of the play frame. Goncu's observation that children have not mastered intersubjectivity suggests that there may be multiple frames in play during children's play (Sawyer, 1993). If we think of these frames as distinct voices in the interaction, we can characterize the play group as a heteroglossic speech environment.

For sociodramatic play to continue in the presence of multiple frames, each child would need some awareness of these frames, and would need the strategic competence to integrate their frame model with the active set of participant

---

[5]Nelson and Gruendel (1979) attributed this to the child's limited number of *routine scripts*: "when there is no shared topic or script—the person doing the assuming ... appears egocentric since he or she proceeds within his or her individual structure oblivious to the fact that the other is operating along a different tact ... preschool children ... have built up few routine scripts and therefore have few to share" (p. 91).

[6]Although in our terms, she seems to be referring to *indexical entailment*. Note once again the tendency to locate entailing effects in presupposition (Silverstein, 1979).

models. We could think of the recognized intersection of individual frames as a "cocreated play frame." This collection of frames, at any given moment in time, is roughly equivalent to the static play structure of the frame and script models. The older and more skilled that children become, the more coincident their multiple frames become; as their individual frame interpretations become more coincident, it would be more accurate to speak of a single play frame. However, during improvisational play, it is always in flux, and it never stabilizes into a fixed structure.

Metapragmatics and the Poetic Function

In chapter 1, I described research in conversation analysis that argued that sequences of discourse could contribute to the coherence of interaction. Maintaining interactional coherence is a metapragmatic function. Several researchers have suggested that children use conventional sequences to serve this metapragmatic function (Boggs, 1990; Bruner, 1975; Camaioni, 1986). Expanding on Jakobson's work (1960, 1971), Silverstein referred to these metapragmatic effects as poetic, because they derive from the line-by-line structure of the interaction. In many cases, the implicit metapragmatic effects of speech result from the sequential flow of the conversation. Contrast Examples 2.5 and 2.6 following:

Example 2.5. Explicit metacommunication (repeat of Example 2.1)

(1)   A   Let's play Teenage Mutant Ninja Turtles.
(2)   B   OK!

Example 2.6. Reflexive metapragmatics, dependent on poetic structures. Katherine is playing with Rachel and Yung-soo.

(1)   Katherine   Pretend I was a doctor now, OK?
(2)   I'll get you a drink of water, Madames.

Example 2.5 metapragmatically regulates the play interaction that is to follow; these metapragmatic utterances are not themselves play enactment. These are explicit metacommunications that do not reflexively regulate themselves, but instead, propose a future path for the interaction. In contrast, Example 2.6 is a two-utterance sequence, in which utterance (1) explicitly metacommunicates that Katherine will be a doctor, and utterance (2) implicitly metacommunicates additional information. The second utterance reflexively regulates itself, metapragmatically commenting on its own meaning, rather than on subsequent utterances. The indexical entailments proposed are that (a) the other children are "Madames"; (b) they would like some water. This reflexive metapragmatic effect is dependent on the position of utterance (2) following utterance (1); otherwise, the resolution of the speaker's role would be ambiguous, and the meaning of the act of getting water would be ambiguous. Thus, the metapragmatic effect of utterance (2) is dependent on its position in the two-utterance sequence.

Like the conversation analysts, Silverstein suggested that conversation derives much of its coherence and structure from its poetic organization. Schegloff (1990) acknowledged that the interactional routines of conversation analysis are sometimes similar to these poetic structures. Silverstein applied these concepts to an analysis of poetic forms of indexicality in everyday adult conversation, discovering through microanalysis of transcripts that much of social interaction is played out at the multiutterance level of poetic indexicality (Silverstein, 1984). Silverstein's approach suggests that implicit metapragmatic effects are often found at the multi-utterance level. It may be difficult to identify implicit metapragmatic functions by analyzing isolated utterances. Most psychological studies of metacommunication code children's discourse at the utterance level, and do not examine sequence-level metapragmatics. This, in part, may explain why research has focused on explicit metacommunication: It is easier to operationalize at the utterance level.

A Model of Improvisation

In the following discussion, I refer to an idealized version of play interaction, in which the children are *absolute peers*; in other words, they have the same status, age, and interactional ability. In this case, each child would be expected to contribute equally to the emergent play drama. Of course, in the preschool classroom, many play groups contain children who are not equals. Often older or dominant children play with younger or relatively submissive children, and the following description must be read with these variants in mind. In spite of these asymmetric cases, most preschool play is between peers; in my classroom, which contained 3-, 4-, and 5-year-olds, children showed a clear preference for playmates who were the closest to them in age and play ability (see chapter 5).

In improvisations like children's sociodramatic play episodes, the interaction between participants is immediate and spontaneous. In the model shown in Fig. 2.1, each turn in the conversation is subject to a variety of interactional forces: (a) the speaker, who contributes something new to the flow of interaction through indexical entailment; (b) the other children participating in the play drama; (c) the constraints and expectations associated with the type of play drama being enacted, which are shared by the children prior to the play episode; (d) the independent, collectively created force operating on the turn which derives from the prior indexical presuppositions of the interaction; following Mead, I refer to this as the *emergent* (Mead, 1932).

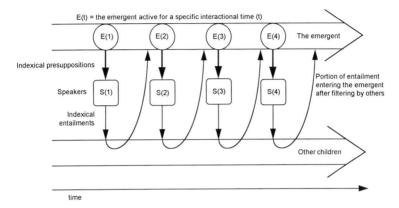

FIG. 2.1. A model of improvisation in children's play. Because no two-dimensional figure can adequately represent the complexity of real-time interaction, this figure should be viewed as one of many possible presentations of the theoretical model. Note in particular that the horizontal axis, time, represents the constantly changing nature of the emergent.

The Speaker

Improvisational creativity begins with a specific child's turn. When a child is speaking, whether in frame, out of frame, enacting a role, or voicing as a director, he or she has a range of possibilities available. The child may choose to enact the role that has already been assigned, in a relatively predictable way. If so, he or she is being *maximally coherent* with the indexical presuppositions operating on his or her turn. Alternatively, the child may choose to introduce novelty to the play situation by proposing a change to the play frame. This type of frame modification is metapragmatic because it regulates, or comments on, the framed structure of the play interaction. The proposal is entailing because it suggests a future direction for the play drama. The entailment is indexical because it is related to the ephemeral play frame active at that moment and cannot be interpreted apart from this emerging interactional context.

The Participants

The other children are equal participants in the collective improvisation of the play episode. No single child can unilaterally determine which direction the play will take. Consequently, when a child chooses to introduce a change to the play frame by indexically entailing that change, the participants have an opportunity to either accept or reject that innovation. This is not an "either/or" decision: the other children may partially accept the proposal, to varying degrees. They may slightly alter the proposal, or elaborate on it with a follow-on proposal.

The Type of Play

In preschool, children play repeatedly in the same locations, with the same toys, and often with the same playmates. After a few weeks in this context, the children develop expectations for how a given play episode will proceed, given a specific combination of location, toys, and other children. Generally these expectations are shared by all of the children, and form the basis for what has been termed *peer culture* (Corsaro, 1985). These expectations can be considered to be a special type of indexical presupposition, with a metapragmatic force on the entire play episode. Unlike the metapragmatic acts of concern here, these presuppositions are not internally generated or emergent from any single play episode.

Of course, play itself is an interactional genre, with rules, norms, and strategies of interaction distinct from other interactional genres familiar to the child, such as talking at dinner with parents, name-calling, or collaborating with a peer in building or painting. The genre of play is probably less constraining than any of the child's other discursive practices.

The Emergent

I have chosen to use Mead's term as a replacement for structuralizing terms such as *script* and *frame*, because it represents the contingent, moment-to-moment flow of interaction. In a play episode, the emergent may contain multiple topics, subtopics, and idiosyncratic interpretations of what is going on that are all in play and activated to varying degrees, the balance shifting with each child's action. The emergent is often heteroglossic, because each child may have a slightly different understanding of the play frame. In addition, the emergent contains all of the sociointeractional effects resulting from the flow of the play drama: relative role and status assignments of the children's play characters, invocations of prior play sessions, and voicings of recognized social roles and characters. The emergent is structured but ephemeral, changes with each child's turn, and emerges from the indexical presuppositions accumulated through the prior collective interaction. It is an intersubjective, social entity; it is not determined by any single child, and only partially constrained by the genre of play or of any given type of play. For play to continue as an intersubjective, shared activity, the children must work together in creating the emergent play drama. The requirements of intersubjectivity constrain each child to contribute turns that retain coherence with the emergent. Of course, what counts as coherence may vary with each play episode and play type, and the degree of constraint of an emergent can vary significantly; but there are constraints on how rapidly it can change, which in turn may be dependent on the type of play and the ecological context of the specific play episode. Through indexical processes that function metapragmatically, the emergent constrains a given turn on all levels mentioned above simultaneously: topic structure, relative role and status assignments, invocations of prior interactions, and voicings of recognized social roles and characters. At any given moment these different levels may be differentially affected.

One could equally have chosen to use Dewey's term, *experience*, although this term tends to place the focus on the individual, rather than the group. The term *entextualization* has been used by several linguistic anthropologists to describe similar processes (Bauman & Briggs, 1990; Silverstein, 1993). Yet this usage tends to focus on the denotational text of an interaction, making it less appropriate for describing processes of play frame negotiation.

The Process of Improvisation

Using Mead's notion of the emergent, we can characterize the process of improvisational creativity in children's play as follows (refer to Fig. 2.1). All children are constrained to operate within the genre of play and the type of the play episode. A given child's turn (collectively determined: see Ervin-Tripp, 1979; Sacks, Schegloff, & Jefferson, 1974) is more narrowly constrained by the emergent. The nature of this constraint is unique and specific to the play episode and the moment of interaction. In most play episodes, each child is expected to contribute something original to the evolving emergent, through acts of indexical entailment. In creating and proposing their entailments, children are subject to the constraints of the emergent. After the child's conversational turn, the other children evaluate its entailments, and the subsequent interaction determines to what extent the indexical entailment resulting from the turn affects the emergent. This evaluation is immediate and often not consciously goal-directed. A more skillful indexical entailment is more likely to enter the emergent, thus operating with more force on subsequent turns. As shown in Fig. 2.1, this is a continuous process: A child, constrained by the collectively created emergent, originates an utterance with some indexical entailment; the other children, through their responses in subsequent acts, collectively determine the extent to which this entailment enters the emergent; the new emergent then similarly constrains the subsequent speakers. Throughout this interactional process, the constraints of the play genre affect how much indexical entailment is considered acceptable, how speaker's turns are allocated, and how speakers form utterances that retain coherence with the emergent.

This model of improvisational linguistic interaction has many similarities with the contemporary variants of pragmatism discussed at the beginning of this chapter. Each participant contributes to the ongoing flow of interaction, while at the same time being constrained by the prior flow of the interaction. The model is consistent with studies of play metacommunication that found that children combine enactment and negotiation, or response and initiation, in each turn (Doyle & Connolly, 1989; Garvey & Kramer, 1989; McTear, 1985). Children's play conversation is dialogic, functioning on two levels simultaneously: maintaining an intersubjectively coherent play frame, while at the same time enacting roles within that frame.

In play, each utterance is an opportunity for children to propose a change to the play frame. Children can propose both interpretations of past events, and future expectations for the emergent. Children's proposals use a variety of metapragmatic strategies. However, children are limited in their creative options when proposing a change to the play; each proposal must maintain coherence with the prior play. The proposed entailment is successful to the degree to which it influences subsequent dialogue. The emergent play discourse leading up to the utterance results in indexical presuppositions that constrain the possible moves. On the one hand, children want to metacommunicate their new proposal as strongly as possible, and on the other hand, they know that the utterance must retain coherence with the operative indexical presuppositions, or else it will lose its effectiveness. Coherence must be met in order to fulfill the fundamental requirement of pretend play: The interaction must be maintained in such a manner that all children can continue to participate in an intersubjectively shared frame.

Given the existence of both implicit and explicit metapragmatic strategies, what contextual factors determine the child's selection? Why do children choose an explicit or implicit metapragmatic technique? As I noted previously, prior research has claimed that both children (Giffin, 1984) and adults (Goffman, 1974) display a strong bias toward implicit techniques. Giffin (1984) referred to this preference as the *illusion conservation rule*: Children collaborate in the attempt to avoid explicitly acknowledging that they are playing. The preference for implicitness suggests that implicit metapragmatics may be interactionally more effective in projecting play frame features than explicit metapragmatics. If so, children should tend to use more implicit statements as their competence increases.

Given the adult preference for implicit metapragmatics, children's use of explicit metapragmatics requires explanation. The previous discussion suggests that the primary constraint on a child's creativity is the requirement to maintain coherence with the set of indexical presuppositions established by the emergent. An effective implicit metapragmatic statement can only be formed within an appropriately developed discourse context. Thus, in addition to ecological factors such as age, friendship, and type of play, we would expect the balance of implicit and explicit metapragmatics to reflect the coherence of the discourse, the degree to which the evolving play frame is intersubjectively shared. In some emergent contexts, explicit metapragmatics may be more effective.

Figure 2.1 suggests that the emergent play frame has its own regimenting quality that increases and decreases in strength throughout the play session. As Goffman observed in the epigraph to this chapter, "conversation has a life of its own and makes demands on its own behalf" (1967, p. 113). When an emergent has evolved that is more stable and intersubjective, and that emergent is similar to a child's desired proposal, that child can use a greater degree of implicitness because the indexical entailments projected will match up with the indexical presuppositions of that emergent. When either condition weakens (a less stable intersubjective emergent, or an emergent that does not readily accommodate the child's desired proposal), metapragmatic statements must become accordingly more explicit because implicit metapragmatics will not be coherent with the intersubjective frame (Keenan & Schieffelin, 1976/1983). Giffin's (1984) work suggests that skilled children will use the most implicit statement possible. This provides us with an interesting empirical prediction: Among skilled children, the degree of implicitness of a statement is an index of the degree of constraint provided by the indexical presuppositions in play at that moment, as well as an index of the degree of compatibility between the speaker's intention and his or her perception of the emergent play frame. For example, if a child is accepting the proposed entailments, he or she should be more likely to be implicit; if a child is rejecting the proposed entailments, he or she should be more likely to be explicit. These hypotheses are among those examined in chapters 5 and 6.

Summary

This chapter has presented a theoretical model of children's play as improvisation, which integrates aspects of pragmatism, sociocultural psychology, and semiotics, and is based on three main concepts, *implicit metapragmatics*, *the emergent*, and *indexical entailment*. The motivation for developing this model was to theorize those play interactions that are particularly improvisational. When children's play is improvisational, structural models are difficult to apply. Many of the theories discussed in chapter 1 are structuralist, in that they propose static representations for the play drama, which are presumed to be shared by the children before, or shortly after, the drama begins. Of course, there are play episodes that seem highly scripted. Structuralist models of play are probably adequate to understand these episodes. However, there are also many play episodes that are not scripted, which wander from one theme to another, and which combine diverse themes in novel, creative ways. For play at its most improvisational, structuralist models are insufficient.

The improvisational model is also motivated by a desire to integrate the many recent studies of metacommunication in children's play. This review has emphasized several key points that emerge from prior research. First, children are capable of using both implicit and explicit metapragmatic strategies to propose changes to the play drama. Second, children propose changes using enacted, in-frame speech as well as directorial, out-of-frame speech. Third, implicit metapragmatic effects are often found, not in a single utterance, but within multiple-utterance sequences. Along with Giffin (1982, 1984), Goncu (1993a,

1993b), and others, I suggest that what develops in the preschool years are the processual characteristics of interaction. I have proposed the aforementioned model of improvisation to describe this interactional process. This model conceptualizes the constraints operating on the play episode that predate that episode as genre constraints, rather than as temporal structures of action sequences. The model allows us to conceptualize how children act strategically in each turn, and how they have the opportunity for innovation, while at the same time being constrained by the prior flow of the play drama. The constraints are not scripts, event schemata, or frames; rather, they are conceptualized as an emergent, a set of fluctuating indexical presuppositions, which constrain the creative possibilities available to the child at any given moment. When examined after the fact, the emergent may have the appearance of having been structured in a temporal event sequence, but this structure emerged from the contingency of play improvisation.

Research on peer relations suggests that the contribution of peer play to development may occur at the metapragmatic level of interaction, because the unique properties of peer play are its framed and improvisational nature. Thus, combining theoretical observations from developmental psychology, sociolinguistics, and semiotics may allow us to construct a more robust picture of how social pretend play contributes to social and conversational development. Developmental research needs a framework within which to conceptualize and operationalize both implicit and explicit metapragmatics.

At this point, we move into the empirical core of the book, which uses the model presented in this chapter to explore improvisation in children's play. Chapters 5 and 6 use this model to develop detailed operational definitions of implicit and in-frame metapragmatics. In these chapters, the unit of analysis is a multiple-utterance *interactional routine*, an intersubjective, collective event. The dependent variables in each of these studies are the *metapragmatic strategies* of each child's turn. I focus on two aspects of metapragmatic strategy: whether the turn is implicitly or explicitly metapragmatic, and whether the turn is spoken in frame and in a play character's voice, or out of frame and in a director's voice. I propose that these metapragmatic strategies are used by children to negotiate the flow of the play improvisation. This approach allows us to move beyond the focus on explicit metacommunication of prior developmental research. Thus, the studies presented in the following chapters are designed to elaborate and extend the psychological studies and theories previously reviewed. By reformulating metacommunication as metapragmatics, by expanding the concept to include implicit metapragmatics, and by focusing on the turn-by-turn sequences that are associated with different types of metapragmatic strategies, we can address many of the issues raised by these recent studies. By identifying relationships between social context and metapragmatics, we can clarify how the metapragmatic function allows children to experiment with using language to create social worlds.

3

Studying Pretend Play in the Preschool Classroom

We believe in play. Our classrooms are organized so that children learn to play and play to learn. ... We think that confidence and self-esteem, as well as cognitive development are best promoted in preschoolers along the natural pathways of play.
—Preschool Handbook

The classroom where I conducted this study is located in a pleasant suburban neighborhood. When the weather is nice, people walking down the sidewalk hear the familiar sounds of children playing in the yards behind the Victorian-era homes that house the preschool classrooms. From outside the fence, it sounds like nothing could be more simple and carefree: It is the play of children. Yet when one looks more closely, one realizes the complexity of play, and the meaning that it has for the children. This preschool is a big part of their social world, and here they will acquire social styles and skills that may still be recognizable in their adult personalities.

When I first began to visit the classroom, I was overwhelmed by the chaos. Twenty-four children, ages 3, 4, and 5, were all playing at once, and it seemed as if they were all talking at once, too. The noise level was surprising, and it made me uncertain about my plans to audiotape and transcribe their play talk. As the epigraph states, the administration of the school believes in play. The teachers strive to interfere as little as possible. Some parents take a while to adjust to this idea. Mrs. Winston, the head teacher, told me that every year, one or another parent would visit and express surprise at the unstructured nature of the activities. Shouldn't they be practicing some useful skill? Working at a computer? Of course, this always provides the teachers with the opportunity to explain the unique and irreplaceable value of play in young children's lives. These teachers are more convinced of the developmental value of play than any of the researchers I quoted in chapter 1.

To get into Mrs. Winston's first-floor classroom each morning, I turned from the sidewalk, went through two different gates, which I carefully closed to keep the children safe from the street, and walked through the backyard playground to the rear door. This is the same route the children take when they arrive with their caregivers each morning. As I entered the building, I walked through the room that has the children's "cubbies," each child's storage space labeled with a handwritten name tag. Then I entered the wide-open main floor of the house. Although the house has separate rooms, in classic Victorian fashion, on the main floor they are connected by wide openings, and it really feels like one big room. The teachers' station, with their papers on high shelves, is just inside the door, and during the play period, the three teachers stay here, watching but rarely intervening. There are three worktables surrounding the teachers' station; each of them seats one teacher and eight children, at the daily morning snack and at lunch. The morning snack is the break between the indoor play of the early morning, and the outdoor play of the late morning.

On the first day I had difficulty making sense of anything; the noise, the children frequently walking through in groups, groups of two or three children huddled together, whispering. As a single, young adult from a small family, I had no prior experience with children and was slightly intimidated. On the first day that I took field notes, I wrote the following:

> The children's play ebbs and flows in the room, almost like traffic or an ocean—it moves really quickly—kids come and go constantly, alone, or hand in hand, or a whole group may suddenly decide to move to a new room. Most of the dialogue today seems related to the spaceship made of blocks. The dialogue sounds staged already—spoken clearly and distinctly, almost unnatural:

> Child 1:   Let's go to the stairs!
>   Countdown—10, 9, 8, 7, 6, 5, 4, 3, 2, 1, BLASTOFF!
> Child 2:   We can't go to the stairs the sun is too hot
>   It will burn you
> Child 1:   That's why we have to go to the moon!
> Child 2:   The sun is coming toward us now!

On any given day, I would find three or four children sitting at a worktable, painting pictures. A few boys would be building with Lego™ blocks on the floor next to the table. Toward the front of the building, where the blocks were kept, two or three distinct groups of children would be building structures, playing with jungle animals, farm animals, or dinosaurs. Sometimes one of the children would ask a teacher to read a story from the library, the classroom's collection of children's books, and as many as four or five children would gather around. There were usually children playing with dinosaurs or animals in the sand table, a 2-foot-square tray about a foot deep, filled with sand. The old sunroom of the house, with its curve of large windows facing onto the street, was the doll corner, with a toy stove, toy kitchen utensils and pots, and play clothes. There seemed to be endless possibilities, an incredible variety of activities for a child to choose from on any given day.

After a few weeks in the classroom, patterns of play and peer culture began to emerge. I began to notice who liked to play together, what each child's favored activities were, what special games were unique to this group of children. I studied Mrs. Winston's preschool classroom for an entire 8-month academic year. The 24 children ranged in age from 39 months to 62 months. In the rest of this chapter, I go into more detail about the classroom. I also describe the methods that I developed to make sense out of this rich activity: how I identified a representative set of play locations and activities to focus on; how I was able to gather data that I could use to explore the improvisationality of play, and the specific performance strategies that children used.

I was introduced to Mrs. Winston several months before my first visit to the classroom. As the most senior of the three classroom teachers, her approval was critical. At our first meeting, I described my interest in children's play, and my desire to spend some time in her classroom. She was very enthusiastic about my project, and encouraged me to use her classroom for observation. Mrs. Winston then scheduled a meeting between me and the other two teachers, Mrs. Cobb and Mrs. Benson. Once again I explained my project, and I asked them their opinions about videocameras and audiotaping. They did not want me to use video cameras. They worried that the camera would be too intrusive (also see Gottman, 1983). I agreed to use a portable tape recorder and a microphone. I had already decided that audiotape, combined with simultaneous field notes, would be sufficient, because my focus would be on linguistic interaction.

Mrs. Winston also told me that I would need to get formal approval from the governing board of the school, and that I should notify the parents. Before beginning my visits to the classroom, I met with one of the assistant principals and discussed my project. She presented my proposal to the governing board, and the proposal was approved. At this time I also sent a letter to the parents describing my research goals and my proposal, with the following text:

> My research involves the observation of pre-school children in a natural setting. I am interested in children's group play during the ages of three to five, in particular, the ways they use language to initiate, maintain, and terminate a play interaction. My work involves only group (age and sex related) comparisons and not the comparison of individual children. Also, the research does not involve any type of testing of the children or attempts to structure their behavior for

observation. My goal is to record samples of play interaction which spontaneously occur in the nursery school setting.

I received acknowledgments and positive feedback from all of the parents. I felt that it was important to inform the parents, even though the literature given to parents by the school indicates that the preschool encourages and supports research by students at nearby colleges.

Naturalistic Observation

In my Introduction, I presented the metaphor of the book's title: Pretend play is a form of group improvisation. I discussed how I would translate this metaphor into a theoretically and empirically rigorous study, by focusing on two aspects of collective play: First, to examine how children structure and maintain their play interactions using metapragmatic strategies, and second, to explore how the use of these interactional strategies differs in different social contexts. I chose a classroom of children at the peak ages for social pretend play. Because many of the most important social dimensions of the preschool classroom are lost when dyads or triads are studied in isolation, I decided early on that I would need to conduct an intimate, lengthy study with a single classroom, rather than draw on a random sampling of dyads or triads for 30- or 60-minute observation. For example, I wanted to observe children self-selecting their play partners and activities, rather than pre-selecting the participants in a given play episode. I selected a methodology that is excellent for exploring these concerns: naturalistic observation of children during their everyday play. In our culture, children often play together in the organized institutional settings of a preschool or daycare center. Several researchers (Corsaro, 1985; Hartup, 1981) have suggested that the preschool environment can be conceived of as a peer culture, which can be approached using field entry strategies derived from anthropology.

However, I couldn't think of any reason that these ethnographic methods could not benefit from the analytic techniques of developmental psychology, including descriptive and analytic statistics. For complex reasons, there are very few ethnographic studies that have used quantitative measures. This has a lot to do with the ways in which social science disciplines tend to define themselves in terms of their methodologies. Ethnographic studies have focused on interpretive approaches drawn from anthropology—rich descriptions of context surrounding single examples. They rarely employ quantitative analysis. At the same time, psychological studies typically use experimental designs involving random sampling, with the oft-noted result that they are decontextualized, sociocultural context removed by design. In my analyses, I have attempted to combine the statistical methods of psychology with the rich understanding of this classroom, which I could only have acquired through an extended natural-istic study. Taking this approach entails a risk. Psychologists will correctly note that I have not controlled for unforeseeable interactions through random sampling or through experimental design. Anthropologists and qualitative sociologists may perceive the work as not being naturalistic enough because many of my analyses use the psychological paradigm of hypothesis testing and statistical evaluation. I have gotten reactions of both sorts when I have presented this material at seminars and conferences. Based on the data that I gathered during this extended naturalistic study, I present several types of analyses. To communicate the richness, that is, the social embeddedness of specific interactions, I borrowed the style and the techniques of conversation analysis and qualitative developmental psychology. To identify which metaprag-matic strategies and patterns are particularly important in play, I have presented statistical analyses of a large dataset of transcripts. By using this hybrid ap-proach, I hope to ameliorate several aspects of qualitative research that have made it a problematic method for psychologists. By retaining full transcripts, with accompanying field notes based on the entire 8-month school year, I hope to draw on the strengths of psychological coding methodologies, to focus closely on linguistic interaction.

Becoming a Part of the Classroom

When I tell parents of young children that I went into the classroom to observe play, they often ask, "How do you know they don't play differently when you're there with them?" I think this question is so common because children do play differently with their parents. Whenever a parent stayed in my classroom during the play period, the nature of the play changed dramatically. I did not want my presence to cause the children to play differently.

Corsaro (1985) outlined a field entry strategy that minimizes the influence of the researcher on the natural play setting. His study suggested that a long entry period is required to become a natural participant in the preschool environment. The first goal of this approach is to ensure that the children do not conceive of the researcher as a teacher or a parent, so that they won't suppress certain behaviors for fear of negative reactions. The second goal is to ease the subsequent introduction of the recording equipment. The third goal is to become intimately familiar with the children's local culture, so that analysis and interpretation can be guided by a sense of what the social context is for the children, what activities mean from the children's perspective.

Corsaro (1985) emphasized the importance of not acting like other adults. He observed that adults in preschool usually initiate contact with the children;

adults are active rather than reactive. When parents stay in the classroom, they often sit with a group and initiate a play activity. Teachers direct and monitor play, help in times of trouble, settle disputes, and enforce the rules of the classroom. Given these patterns, Corsaro determined that the best approach would be a reactive entry strategy: never to initiate activities with the children, but to respond when children approached him. Corsaro used this reactive field entry strategy to become a participant in the children's peer culture; he knew he had been successful when the children first included him in their play activity (1985). Corsaro was following the standard anthropological methodology called *participant observation,* with a unique twist: He was an adult participating in children's culture.

I chose to follow a similar strategy, but with one difference: I wanted to be accepted by the children, but ignored. My goal was to be the proverbial "fly on the wall." I did not want to be included in their play activities, but I did want to be nearby with the microphone, without it affecting the normal course of their play. I decided to pursue a reactive field entry approach, with the goal of becoming an accepted component of the children's environment, allowing me to observe and audiotape their play interaction at close range.

I decided to visit the classroom for 4 months before introducing recording equipment. During this time, I went to the classroom several times a week to sit and observe. Although I did not take any recording equipment, I did have a small notebook, which I occasionally used to make field entries. I hoped that during this time, the children would become accustomed to my presence; I wanted them to accept me as a natural part of their classroom environment. Unlike Corsaro (1985), I did not attempt to become a member of the peer culture; I decided in advance to avoid conversational interaction with the children. Because I knew I would have to take handwritten field notes to accompany my audiotapes, I wanted to avoid joining in play activities that would occupy my hands. I also believed that if I did not become a participant in play, the play would be more representative of peer interaction. On the few occasions during these 4 months when children approached me, I responded briefly, with neutral affect, and attempted to look disinterested (for example, by continuing to look intently at my field notes rather than making eye contact).

During the 4-month period before I introduced the microphone, I was addressed only three times. Whenever possible, I ignored the child; often this was enough for them to lose interest. When the child persisted, I would respond, but as briefly as possible, with minimum affect. This was relatively rare; more common were comments made in passing, like Jennifer's comment a month into my study. She said, as she walked past me, "Not you again!" But she continued walking, without attempting to engage me in conversation.

I believe that I acquired natural play interaction, and that my presence did not affect the play. I believe this for several reasons. First, there were very few exchanges between myself and the children during the 8-month period. These exchanges can be divided into the following types:

1. Questions about my presence included: (a) "Who are you?"; (b) "Are you a Dad?" (c) "Why do you come here?"
2. Questions, actions, or observations about my recording equipment included: (a) "What's that?" (pointing at the microphone) (b) touching the microphone; (c) speaking into the microphone; (d) asking permission to touch or speak into the microphone; (e) comments about the tape recorder (e.g., "Look at that cool radio").

There is more telling evidence that I was not perceived as an authority figure. During play, children are highly aware of what is and is not permitted in the classroom. When children were knowingly breaking a rule (e.g., "No pretend guns in school"), they would look into the next room to see if the teacher was watching, although ignoring the fact that I was looking at them from only a few feet away. On those occasions when authority was invoked or avoided, I was never the addressee. In most cases in which a child did something wrong, like throwing a toy at another child, someone would tell a teacher, or the children would scan the vicinity to see if a teacher had noticed. By the nature of my methodology, during many of these instances I was very close to the children. There were no incidents in which I was approached as an authority figure.

Initial Observations

In contrast to the improvisational spontaneity of the children's play, the school day has an invariant schedule. Children arrive soon after 8:30 a.m. By 9 a.m., most of the children have arrived, with a few stragglers arriving later. From arrival until 9:45 is indoor play time. This is unstructured play time; the children are allowed to choose their own partners and activities from among the toys and locations provided. During this period, the teachers usually have some worktable activity planned that the children can optionally engage in. These activities usually have a seasonal theme, and often result in gifts for the parents; for example, before Valentine's Day, the children made heart-shaped cards for their parents. Each child is encouraged to spend at least enough time at the worktables to engage in the project once. However, the teachers do not schedule, organize, or require this presence. For most of the indoor play time, the children group on the floor throughout the classroom (see Fig. 3.1), engaged in social pretend play.

At 9:45 the teachers announce, "Cleanup time!" and all toys have to be put back in their proper locations in bins or trays against the walls. This takes about 5 minutes. It's a frenetic period, as all of the children and the teachers work

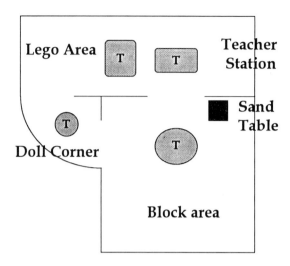

FIG. 3.1. Layout of the preschool classroom. The four tables of the classroom are labeled with "T." The wall at the right is the north wall; the classroom entrance is at the top of the figure, through the west wall.

together to put everything away as quickly as possible. Although they usually have to be gently persuaded to help, some of the children look forward to this group activity, sometimes asking the teachers 10 or 15 minutes too early, "Is it cleanup time?" After cleanup, the children separate into three groups of eight for a snack, one group for each teacher. Each group sits at one of the three work tables. If one of the children has a birthday, a special snack is prepared by his or her parent(s), and the children share the snack in a big circle on the floor in the block area, led by the teachers in singing "Happy Birthday."

After snack time, everyone goes outside for 45 minutes of outdoor play time. I was even more overwhelmed by this activity than by the indoor play, because of its chaotic, physical nature. The teachers stand in a group, observing the large back yard, to make sure no child gets hurt; but they rarely need to intervene. Outdoor time is characterized by physical, noisy activity, including running, chasing, and climbing on the various structures provided for the purpose. After the outdoor play period, some of the parents begin to arrive to pick up their children and take them home. Some parents opted to have their children stay for lunch, and some children stayed for a few hours after lunch as well.

Focusing on Play Discourse

I decided that I would focus on the indoor play time. During the outdoor time, the children were not as verbal, and their rapid movement made it hard to acquire audiotapes. Indoors, the children tended to stay in one play location for extended periods, and tended to engage in more verbal play interactions. The indoor behavior was exactly the sort of improvisational discourse that I wanted to focus on. Although the outdoor physical play was certainly no less improvisational, it was less verbal.

I wanted my audiotape dataset to be representative of the actual blend of play activities in the school. I particularly wanted to avoid any tendency to focus on particular children or activity types that I personally found more theoretically interesting, because this could have biased my findings. To insure that I taped the full range of play activities, I used the 4-month observation period to identify a set of five different play locations (refer to Fig. 3.1). I decided that I would sample the play in each location in proportion to the level of play activity found in each. I developed a 6-week schedule of taping locations before I began audiotaping, and I stayed in the day's assigned location regardless of the type or level of play, and regardless of which children were participating. This could occasionally be frustrating; on my fourth day in the doll corner I sat for 45 minutes alone with the microphone, although Mrs. Winston told me about wonderful play in the block area.

Children did not play by the teachers. At the worktables, they tended to focus on craft activities. Their play was concentrated in four main locations, each labeled in Fig. 3.1: the block area, the doll corner, the sandtable, and the Lego™ area.

The Block Area

This was the largest room, comprising almost half of the available play area of the classroom. It was large enough to accommodate up to three groups of children playing simultaneously, whereas the other locations rarely had more than one group. I decided I would spend the most time in this area.

There were many different sizes of blocks stored on shelves lining the walls of the block area. The smallest blocks were 2 inches on each side, and the largest blocks were almost a foot long. The small blocks were the most versatile play objects; they could be food, or guns on a spaceship, or missiles. The biggest blocks were usually used in construction.

Example 3.1. Sam and Eddy are playing with a giraffe, a lion, and an elephant. This example starts with one exchange, then skips about 25 turns before continuing.

(1) Sam   Come up and fight, giraffe!
(2) Eddy   Oh, but don't knock me over,
(3)   I have put animals in

| (4) | Sam | I'll be your friend, said the lion. |
| (5) | Eddy | OK. |

(lines 6 through 70 omitted)

(71)	Eddy	I ate up all the food, I ate up all the ate
(72)	Sam	I need some food!
(73)	Eddy	Well, we don't have anymore food!
(74)	Sam	Make some more food, and we'll eat it up!
(75)	Eddy	We should get some blocks for food!
		(Eddy goes to Artie, who is building a tower, to ask if they can use some of his blocks.)
(76)	Eddy	Can I have these?
(77)	Artie	I'm using those but you can play with those
(78)	Eddy	Well I don't need those.
(79)	Artie	You can't play with it, I'm using it.

Later in the play session, Eddy and Sam are joined by Bernie, and they use blocks to build a tower, an elevator for the tower, and a ladder, so that their animals can go up and down the tower.

The Doll Corner

This room had stereotypically female objects, including dolls, women's clothing, plastic high-heeled shoes, kitchen furniture and appliances, plates, and utensils. Because the play here was particularly verbal, I identified this location as the second most important. This was the only area not visible from the teacher's station, because it was a separate room.

There was often a group of three or more girls in the doll corner, with Kathy the most vocal child, making most of the play suggestions and frequently assigning roles to the other children.

Example 3.2. Kathy, Alicia, Yung-soo, Rachel in the doll corner. Kathy is trying to recruit Alicia to play with them. Alicia doesn't want to be assigned the role of baby.

(1)	Kathy	You won't be a baby.
(2)		You're our friends.
(3)		A sister.
(4)		A guinea pig.
(5)	Alicia	No, not a guinea pig.
(6)		I wanna be
(7)	Kathy	(2) Sister?
(8)	Alicia	Owp,

(9)		I wanna be a baby.
(10)	Kathy	A baby?
(11)		A lady.
(12)	Alicia	A lady,
(13)		a lady.
(14)	Kathy	Alright, you can be a lady.

(lines 15 through 23 omitted)

(24)		Which person are you gonna be?
(25)	Alicia	I'm gonna be the lady who's,
(26)		got the, um
(27)	Kathy	The mother?
(28)	Alicia	I'm gonna be the lady.
(29)	Kathy	Lady means neighbor.
(30)	Yung-soo	I wanna be a girl
(31)		I wanna be a sister.
(32)	Kathy	Right,
(33)		Yung-soo's the sister.
(34)		You're the neighbor.
(35)	Alicia	I'm not the neighbor!
(36)	Kathy	Well, if you say baby
(37)		If you say, lady, lady,
(38)		then you're a neighbor.
(39)	Yung-soo	Yeah.
(40)		If you say princess, then you're our
(41)		sister.

This doll corner play is classic role play, with the children enacting dramatic roles. The previous transcript is not unusual, in its focus on who gets to be which character. Sometimes it seems as if this role assignment is the primary purpose of the activity. For example, despite the clear importance of the role assignments, in many cases no enacting takes place after roles are assigned. After line 41, these children go on to play nurse, make some phone calls on the toy phone, and go to bed. When Eddy, a rare visitor, joins them about 15 minutes later he is immediately assigned a role:

Example 3.3. Later on the same day as Example 3.2. Eddy is attempting to join the group, which has been playing together since we left them at line (41).

(1)	Eddy	Who can I be?
(2)		Who can I be?
(3)	Kathy	You could be, the, King, or the princess
(4)		cause these are just visitors.

(5)	Eddy	I wanna be the King.
(6)	Kathy	Alright, you can be the King.
(7)	Eddy	Who are you?
(8)	Kathy	I'm a hopping, I'm a hopping Queen.
(9)		Yung-soo is the princess.

Note how play and reality overlap in this transcript. Eddy is rarely in the doll corner, and rarely joins Kathy in play. When Eddy asks who he can be, Kathy gives him two choices, both of them are "visitors." This play status is a reflection of the real (i.e., nonplay) fact that Eddy does not often come to the doll corner. Like most young boys, Eddy would choose to be the King rather than the princess.

The Sandtable

Many days, there was no play at all in the sandtable. However, any play that occurred here was highly verbal. There was only room for three children unless the table was pulled out from the wall, creating room for a fourth.

Example 3.4. Jennifer and Kathy are playing with toy animals in the sandtable. Kathy's animal is Cera, and Jennifer's is Littlefoot, characters from the movie *The Land Before Time*. In the following, they switch between "director" voice, and the voice of their toy character.

(1)	Jennifer	Pretend he fell down in the big underground
(2)		This was the underground (she indicates the floor under the sandtable)
(3)	Kathy	And the,
(4)		and the, and the
(5)	Jennifer	And that father said thanks to the longneck
(6)	Kathy	Thanks
(7)	Jennifer	You're welcome.
(8)	Kathy	And pretend pretend pretend the father said
(9)	Jennifer	Come on out!
(10)	Kathy	What did you do with me?
(11)	Jennifer	Well, he fell down in the big underground.

Sandtable play was some of the most improvisational, perhaps because there were more possible actions the children could enact with a small figure than they could enact as themselves in role play. In chapter 4, I discuss the importance of this type of play with figures, which I refer to as indirect performance style. Although common in the sandtable, this type of play occurred in all classroom locations; it was common in the Lego™ area as well.

The Lego™ Area

This was an open carpeted area, like the block area, but smaller and closer to the teacher's station. Of the free play areas, it was the one closest to the teacher's station. Perhaps because of a preference to be farther from the teachers, the children preferred the other areas, and the Lego™ area was often empty. Rather than blocks, there were large trays of Lego™ toys in this area, and the play was slightly more verbal than play with blocks.

Muhammed and John often played in the Lego™ area, sometimes joined by Sam and Eddy.

Example 3.5. Muhammed and John have been playing with legos and toy animals since the start of the play session. Karen is nearby, trying to join the play but is being ignored. In the following, they switch between "director" voice, and the voice of their toy character.

(1)	John	And mine can mash down trees.
(2)		Don't knock my thing down.
(3)	Muhammed	I won't.
(4)		I won't knock your things down
(5)		Here's my thing, right John?
(6)		Here's my thing, right John?
(7)	Karen	guys have jet packs on them
(8)	Muhammed	An emergency
(9)	John	My flying saucer comes up
(10)		He's a bad guy.
(11)		Pretend they were my guy's friend, and=
(12)	Muhammed	=but they were still good guys
(13)	John	Unhuh, and they, he,
(14)		And they din't know what's in it,
(15)		They were very curious
(16)		And so they opened it.
(17)		Now come on, let's play.
(18)		Don't open this OK, right, don't open this OK?

Among the boys, this kind of discussion about "good guys" and "bad guys" is common. This is typical of preschool-aged boys, as documented by Paley (1984, 1988). In contrast, I don't recall a single instance of girls assigning good and bad roles.

Miscellaneous Locations

The Stairs.   The stairs to the second floor had a landing about three steps up; above the landing was a gate preventing the children from going any higher.

When I sat here, I could hear the voices of the children in the second-floor classroom. This landing rarely supported continuous play activity, but often served as an intermediate location for a group that was moving around.

The Dollhouse.   The dollhouse was actually a bookshelf against a wall; vertical partitions created rooms on each shelf. Miniature furniture was in each room.

The Back Room.   This room was a small, carpeted area in between the coat room, with the children's cubby holes, and the rest of the classroom. There were two benches and several pillows in this room. This room adjoined the teacher's station.

Recording Preschool Conversation

In January, after I felt I had become an accepted part of the environment, I began to take the tape recorder into the classroom. I arrived early each morning to position my microphone before the children arrived. I planned to hang the microphone from the ceiling or tape it to a wall. Because I would always be focusing on a single group of children, I knew I could reduce some of the background noise by not using an omnidirectional microphone; instead, I chose a cardioid microphone, which records sound in a 180-degree zone in front of the microphone. I continued to sit some distance away with my field notebook. I began with test sessions on two different days. On the first, I hung the microphone from the ceiling in the doll corner, so that it was about 5 feet above the floor; on the second, I hung the microphone from the ceiling in the Lego™ block area, also about 5 feet above the floor. In both cases I sat in a chair against the wall, just as I had been doing for the first 4 months. I was reassured to observe that the children paid no attention to the equipment. I immediately transcribed these tapes, and convinced myself that I would be able to get acceptable audio quality. I then began to record the 45-minute indoor play period every day for 7 weeks, through February and March. I taped on 35 days, resulting in a total of 28 hours and 37 minutes of children's talk. During each session, I wrote continuously into my field notebook, noting bits of dialogue, physical movement, and nonverbal play activity. Each day resulted in an average of 10 handwritten pages, about one for every 5 minutes. These notes were extremely important, because much of the dialogue could not be interpreted without knowing what the children's gestures and body positions were.

I had decided to spend 1 week in the doll corner and then 2 weeks in the block area. In the block area there was no convenient way to reach the ceiling, so I used duct tape to attach the microphone to one of the radiator covers against the east and south walls. Resting on these, the microphone was about 3 feet from the floor. Unlike my test tapes from the doll corner and the Lego™ area, these tapes were very hard to transcribe; there was too much background noise. The doll corner is a small room, and usually only one play group is in it, but the block area is quite large and often had two or three independent groups playing only a few feet apart. I realized that leaving the microphone in a fixed location would not work, due to the combination of background noise and small movements of the children within the block area. I decided to risk a new approach: I would place the microphone on the floor next to a play group, and if the children shifted a few feet, I would relocate the microphone. This technique required that I sit on the floor near the children, rather than at the edge of the room. I was nervous the first time that I did this, worried that the children might avoid me, or try to play with me. To my surprise, even though I was only a few feet away, the children completely ignored me. Children would step over me and around me (to get more blocks), and would talk over me to other children. I was amazed at the degree to which I seemed invisible. Using this new technique, I typically had the microphone within a foot or two of the target group; sometimes the microphone was almost directly between a pair of children.

Holding and repositioning the microphone had several advantages over stationary placement. First, I was able to get extremely close to the children while they were playing, resulting in transcribable audiotaped data. Getting transcribable tapes is particularly difficult in a preschool classroom, because of the high level of background noise. Second, the block area and doll corner were large enough to accommodate multiple groups, and the groups often moved slightly within the play area. Holding the equipment allowed me to reposition the microphone when a group moved.

The children almost completely ignored the recording equipment. Several times they sat on the microphone or stepped on it while going to get more blocks, but they never noticed. The few utterances concerning the equipment took the form of a game in which the boys took turns speaking into the microphone. Interestingly, only one child seemed aware that this resulted in a permanent record; he was the only one to ask me if he could hear the tape. I told him he could listen later in the day, but he did not ask me again.

The Children of the Classroom

One of the advantages of the extended observational method is that it allowed me to develop a partial understanding of each child's personality, and of the social networks and connections among the children. Because I stayed in the same classroom for 8 months, I began to understand the history of these children's relationships: who their playmates had been earlier in the year, what play themes they had enacted with each other in the past, what their favorite play locations were.

In addition to my own observations, I gathered information about the class through questionnaires and interviews with the teachers, children, and parents. I did not use these for quantitative analysis, but this information helped flesh out my understanding of the classroom. For example, after I had completed audiotaping, I decided to attempt to interview some of the children about their friendships. There are obvious difficulties in interviewing a child of 3, 4, or 5, particularly when this involves interrupting the flow of play to monopolize a child for a few minutes. I primarily wanted to find out from the children if they had a "best friend," and who their friends were. Would their best friends be in this class, or would they be from the home neighborhood? My best success was when I presented this as a game to be played with my microphone. The game became one of "performing" a monologue about oneself. At one such session, I had five children around a table, passing around the microphone, and speaking all of the information I had requested, in the same formulaic prosody.

I frequently spoke with the three teachers in the afternoon after the children had gone home. I had told the teachers that I wanted to avoid speaking with them during the play, because I did not want the children to associate me with the teachers. Nonetheless, one of the teachers would often whisper a comment to me about one of the children, particularly when they were frustrated about a child's behavior. I also interviewed the head teacher at length about the children and their usual play partners.

I also felt I needed some basic information about the children's opportunities for peer play outside of the classroom. Did they have neighborhood friends? In particular, did they have any older siblings? I prepared a one-page questionnaire, which I asked the teachers to give to the children, to take home. Parents filled out the questionnaires at home, and mailed them back to me in a preaddressed, stamped envelope.

A summary of each child's representation in the data set is presented in Table 3.1. The mean age of the 24 children was 49.9 months, as of the first taping date. There were 12 boys and 12 girls. I've grouped the following descriptions of the 24 children into the most common play groupings. However, these were by no means uniform from day to day. Groups often formed that combined children that I have placed in separate sections.

Kathy's Play Group

Kathy (5 years, 2 months) was one of the most interesting children in the class. She always dominated her play group, usually selecting the location and assigning the play roles. In my 29-hour dataset, she speaks more utterances (2,532) and takes more conversational turns (976) than any other child, and

TABLE 3.1
Summary of Corpus by Child

Child	Age	Utterances Played	Utterances Spoken	Number of Turns	Sex
Artie	54	3,775	1,451	793	m
Alicia	40	60	25	23	f
Anne	41	0	0	0	f
Aretha	39	1,062	109	81	f
Bernie	41	2,352	525	361	m
Corinna	59	3,589	1,029	556	f
Eddy	43	3,956	1,135	703	m
Jennie	62	1,629	205	151	f
Jerry	38	228	21	18	m
Jan	52	767	74	56	f
John	62	3,669	1,370	750	m
Jennifer	62	4,646	1,566	791	f
Kathy	62	5,057	2,532	976	f
Karen	62	432	195	131	f
Karl	59	1,990	362	250	m
Kim	42	2,680	438	306	f
Matt	49	2,568	894	504	m
Mikey	41	182	48	35	m
Mark	44	617	117	77	m
Muhammed	48	4,493	1,089	767	m
Ned	51	1,085	256	150	m
Rachel	43	2,512	289	229	f
Sam	49	3,154	900	568	m
Yung-soo	55	3,406	357	266	f

has the highest number of utterances per turn (2.59). This play was almost always in the doll corner; a large percentage of my doll corner tapes are of the "Kathy" genre. It seems that she does deserve her own genre, because she so completely dominated the play session; she was a classic director of socio-dramatic play. She liked to dominate her play group; on a few occasions, when a child did not give in to her, she got frustrated and left the group. Almost always, there were three or more playing in her group. I also have several play episodes between Kathy and Jennifer, who is described later in another group.

Kathy usually played with Yung-soo (4 years, 7 months), Rachel (3 years, 7 months), and Karl (4 years, 11 months). Yung-soo was always playing with someone, although she tended to be one of the less verbal of whatever group she was in. She readily accepted most of Kathy's play proposals. As the youngest of the group, Rachel was the quietest, and I don't remember her ever saying much. Two thirds of the classroom play was either all-boys or all-girls; Karl's frequent presence in this group was the primary exception. I don't recall him playing with any of the other boys. Karl also frequently played with Jennifer.

Karl was one of the few children who approached me when I first started visiting. Early on he asked me "Whose father are you?" and told me a story about his father. Later, he took great interest in my four-color pen, and asked to write with it.

Jan (4 years, 4 months) was often found in the doll corner with Kathy's group. I don't have much of Jan on the tapes (only 56 turns total). She never seemed to instigate play, but rather went along with other girls, mostly Kathy. She was almost always in a group of girls. The few times I noticed her talking she seemed more spiteful and mean than the other girls. She often repeated the rejections of Kathy or Jennifer to other children, but in a more intense, "mean" way.

The Ninja Turtles

This group of three boys usually played together, and because they sometimes played at being Teenage Mutant Ninja Turtles, I refer to this group as the "ninja turtles." These boys were Eddy (3 years, 7 months), Sam (4 years, 1 month), and Bernie (3 years, 5 months). Partly because they were relatively young, their play was often physical. This play sometimes bothered the teachers because it frequently degenerated into activities that were forbidden indoors, like falling down, running, or wrestling. Nonetheless, I observed some fascinating pretend play improvisations among these boys.

Sam and Bernie had the strongest bond, and were perhaps "best friends": I sometimes heard them talking about visiting each other's houses in the afternoon or on the weekend. Sam seemed to need Bernie's friendship and would frequently ask "Do you love me?" of Bernie.

Bernie and Sam bonded very tightly, whereas Eddy seemed to have trouble really connecting in the trio. Even though they always played together, Eddy would frequently spin off into his own solo activity, and then return. I thought of him as a "free electron" because when he spun off he often entered other play groups briefly before returning to Bernie and Sam.

The teachers seemed to feel that Bernie was the one responsible for preventing constructive play. The teachers felt that Bernie caused the play to degenerate into silliness and physical roughhousing. I did observe that the play became less verbally interesting when Bernie arrived (he usually arrived last, after Eddy and Sam). Bernie would initiate a lot of singsong repetitive talk, which I sometimes found interesting, but less interactive than the older children's play. Bernie was sometimes pulled away by a teacher for instigating too much wrestling or running around.

The Block Builders

This set of six boys was usually found in the block area, building structures with the blocks or enacting a drama with plastic animals on a block structure. This was not a single cohesive group, because there were usually only two or three boys building together at a time. Roughly speaking, these six boys formed three pairs: Artie (4 years, 6 months) and Matt (4 years, 1 month); John (5 years, 2 months) and Muhammed (4 years); and Mark (3 years, 8 months) and Ned (4 years, 3 months).

Artie was one of the most verbal, and I thought he was the oldest of the children until I found out he was only 4½. However, he had problems playing with the other children, because he liked to have his way and was stubborn or possessive about the blocks or toys. The teachers thought of him as one of the brightest, but lacking in the social skills needed to get along with the other children. Most of the time, he was playing alone, in the front block area, building a large structure such as a tower or a spaceship, and often riding in the spaceship. Other boys, like Matt, frequently joined him, but they would usually not work together on the same structure; rather, they would each build their own competing structures side-by-side. Artie sometimes played with Jennifer, another of the more verbal children.

Matt (4 years, 1 month) started halfway through the year, in December, when one of the original children moved away. In addition to playing with Artie, he frequently joined Muhammed.

I liked Muhammed's (4 years) style of playing. He always seemed friendly and cheerful, and always preferred playing with another to playing alone. He was perhaps the most verbal of the boys, and could be creative in a single location for the entire hour. He took more notice of me than most of the children, asking me early on, "You come here every day! Why do you come here?" and asking about the microphone. He also seemed to remember me, to have a concept of who I was. The only other child who seemed to notice me was Karl. Muhammed usually played with John or Matt, but other partners were Artie, Mark, and Ned.

John (5 years, 2 months) was always intent on his playing, and played with Muhammed and Artie more than anyone; if not one of them, usually he'd play alone. He had a tendency to complain or whine when he couldn't have a toy or block he wanted, even if Muhammed had clear rights to it. John would say "I'm telling," quite readily. The teachers realized this and rarely took him seriously. He was frequently creative in play, suggesting an elaborate scenario; usually too elaborate for the others to pick up on. John didn't persist in proposing a scenario—he seemed to enjoy just creating them. There was interesting dialogue between him and Artie or Muhammed.

Mark (3 years, 8 months) was a fairly quiet boy, although he frequently would play with other boys. He usually didn't say much, perhaps because he was the youngest of the group. His play partners were usually Muhammed, John, Ned, or Artie.

Ned (4 years, 3 months) always played with other boys. He seemed to have trouble connecting with play groups, and often would play with objects (blocks or vehicles) alone. However, he seemed to want to play with other children; he would frequently stand near a group of playing boys, watching, clearly wanting to join them but seeming not to know how to introduce himself to them. He usually played with Mark, Muhammed, or John. Even when playing in a group, he would often drift off into his own solo activity.

The Girls at the Sand Table

These girls played at all of the classroom locations, and many other groups played at the sand table, but I felt that the sandtable play of these girls was the most representative of that activity. Of all these girls, Jennifer (5 years, 2 months) was the most verbal, and may even have been the most interesting player. She was always proposing new shifts or tensions in the play frame, and usually these shifts were designed to allow the other children to go along. Jennifer didn't seem to have a solid group of friends or even a best friend, though. She played with lots of different people: often with Corinna, less often with Artie, sometimes with Muhammed. Kim liked to play with her, but Jennifer saw this as a chore, and the teacher had to make her let Kim play. Jennie often joined them for a foursome around the sandbox: Jennie, Jennifer, Corinna, and Kim.

Corinna (4 years, 11 months) was quite verbal and accomplished at play, and her voice is on many of my best tapes. She usually played with Jennifer or Artie. Occasionally she would play in the doll corner with Kathy's group.

Jennie (5 years, 2 months) appears in my field notes as "little J" or "J2" to contrast her with Jennifer. Jennie was much less verbal and also physically quite a bit smaller, so I assumed she was a 3-year-old. I was later surprised to find out that they were both 5-year-olds. Jennie was quiet and only engaged in group play occasionally, usually with Jennifer but sometimes with other quiet children like Rachel or Alicia. Jennie often carried around a pair of horses, a "mommy" and "child," and she would create play drama between this family.

Kim (3 years, 6 months) liked to play with Jennifer, and sometimes insisted that she be allowed to join even when Jennifer resisted. She seemed younger than the other girls, usually very quiet, playing stereotypically girlish games, usually with dolls, or farm animals. She also played with Kathy's group.

Free-Floaters

The preceding groups were not rigidly consistent, but were rather the most typical of many possible ways of grouping these children. There were some children who could not be placed into any identifiable groups. These "free-floaters" were the youngest children, and of course younger children are usually less verbal and less socially integrated. In chapter 4, I present data demonstrating that the older children were significantly more verbal. The youngest children also spent more of their time at the worktables, nearer to the teachers, and less of their time on the floor engaged in play.

Mikey (3 years, 5 months) always played alone, but seemed to have plenty of energy for playing. He rarely talked, but when he did, it was usually hard to understand, to me and to the teachers. The teachers suggested this could be the result of his bilingual household.

Karen (5 years, 2 months) was unusual, in that she was verbal but never connected with any stable play groups. She did not create play dramas with other children; instead, she wandered around the classroom (sometimes in the plastic "ruby slippers" from the doll corner) carrying her favorite stuffed animal. Every now and then she would enter a room and say something loudly, and then leave.

Alicia (3 years, 4 months) was very quiet, and I don't recall her playing with anyone. Occasionally she would appear in the doorway of the doll corner, and look in as if interested, but she rarely joined in the play. I have only 25 utterances from Alicia.

Aretha (3 years, 3 months) seemed young, was rather shy, and usually did not engage in group play. She stayed at the worktables or near the teachers. More than once she approached me and covered my eyes with her hands, or sat on my lap, or kissed my cheek, but never said anything to me. Sometimes she would play with Kathy's group in the doll corner, but was not very verbal.

I do not recall Anne (3 years, 5 months) or Jerry (3 years, 2 months) being engaged in much play. They stayed near the worktables and the teachers. Anne is the only child of the 24 who does not appear anywhere in my transcripts.

Transcribing Play Discourse

As a student of language use in context, my object of interest is living, performed conversation. However, for rigorous analysis, only recordings of the performance are available; the performance itself is ephemeral and can never be observed again (Packer, 1995; Sawyer, 1996; Silverstein, 1993). Sociolinguists have often noted that transcripts can give a misleading impression of structure—having it on the page lends an aura of certainty to the flow of conversation, when in reality conversation has a moment-to-moment contingency that creates the necessity for improvisation. Although I focus on transcripts in this book, it is helpful to keep in mind that we are looking at only a trace of a socially situated performance. It is easier to do this when the discourse analysis is combined with a naturalistic research design, because the researcher participates in the social world of the speakers, and is thus better able to understand the creativity and uncertainty of interactions.

When transcribing, I used a separate text line for each utterance. For each utterance, I entered three columns of information. First, I typed in a one- or two-character code indicating the speaker. Then I typed the utterance. Utterances were delineated by pauses or an intake of breath. Thus, a child could have several utterances in a single conversational turn. In the third column, I wrote free-text comments about the nonverbal activities of the speaker or group. These comments included information about the child's tone of voice, such as when a high-pitched voice of a play character was being used. I also included nonverbal information, which I took from the field notes that I wrote during the play. Each day's transcript was between 15 and 20 pages.

The children's voices were sometimes difficult to understand, even though the microphone was usually only 1 or 2 feet away. Anyone who has ever been in a preschool classroom will understand the difficulties. First, with all of the play groups speaking at once, the level of background noise on the tapes is sometimes overwhelming. Second, some utterances are whispered, and these rarely make it onto the tape. Because of such unavoidable factors, transcription was a difficult, tedious process. In most cases, my field notes provided sufficient information to disambiguate utterances, but this still left a lot of hard-to-understand talk. I found myself frequently using the transcriber's rewind-and-replay foot switch, sometimes listening to a single utterance 20 or 30 times.

Field Notes

During taping, I always sat next to the microphone with my notebook and pen, noting physical movements and gestures that would help me later transcribe the tape. I received more comments from the children about my ever-present, four-color pen than about the recording equipment! Each day resulted in 7 to 10 pages of handwritten field notes. I always had my pen in hand, and would write furiously in an attempt to record as much as possible.

I used these field notes to fill in the rightmost column of each transcript. Although I incorporate nonverbal information in the transcripts, I have made no attempt to systematically identify and analyze every occurrence of nonverbal behavior or paralinguistic cues. I've included this information only to the extent necessary to capture the nature of the activity, or to help interpret the meaning of specific sequences of interaction.

I used the field notes for several purposes:

1. To associate voices on the tape with specific children.
2. To determine what objects the children were playing with, and what actions they were taking with them.
3. To note gross physical movements, for example, a child walking up to a group without saying anything, or temporary departures to get more toys.

4. To note potentially relevant activities in nearby play groups.

5. To note the addressee of an utterance, when ambiguous.

Here is a typical page from my field notes, indicating the types of information I recorded, and the somewhat cryptic shorthand I developed to increase the amount of information I could record.

Sandtable.   Kathy, Kim, and Yung-soo have been playing, and Sam wants to join their play. At minute 36, the group moves to the block area, and I follow (page 6 of 7 from notebook #4, minutes 33 to 39, 45 minutes total).

(33) S goes to get animals
Kf: It's gonna take 30 years
         Dig deep, see the yellow (the sandbox is yellow).
S brings animals back, sits in front of me—
Kf sends him to other side
next to Ki—She says no room
(34) Y leaves (gets a broom)
Kf: Y will be right back
(Y returns w/broom)
Kf: Get the brooms!
         We're not playing
S: I am!
Y→S: You play yourself
Kf to doll corner.
(36) They leave. I leave too—
Sit by south side, in chair—
Corinna, Muhammed, Artie, Sam
(38) C: We have to fight
         … every morning/Saturday

Notational System

In 1979, Ochs presented a classic theoretical and methodological discussion of different approaches to the transcription of children's talk. Corsaro (1985) used a transcription system based on this article. My system is a combination of Corsaro's page layout with Levinson's (1983) notations. I chose to use four columns: (a) the utterance number; (b) the speaker (and addressee, if there were more than three children playing, and the utterance was clearly directed to one of the other children); (c) the utterance; (d) text description of nonverbal and contextual information. Table 3.2 is a typical transcript segment.

TABLE 3.2
Sample Transcript

Line	Speaker	Utterance	Notes
4	mu*	That's these guys, right?	MU is handing A blocks
5	a**	Yeah, //no	
6	mu	//because they're SO strong	
7	a	They're so strong they could blow somebody's head off, right?	
8	mu	Yeah, and they could even	
9	mu	you=they could even=	
10	mu	they can even open their [dozies], right?	
11	a	[You can] tell everybody	
12	mu?	huh?	
13	a	I hope this is [day]	

* Muhammed
** Artie

The transcripts should be read from left to right and from the top down. Each line represents a separate utterance, rather than an utterance turn; there can be multiple utterances in a turn, like Muhammed's turn from line 8 to 10. If the addressee was clear from the context, for example, if there were only two children playing, only the speaker was identified. If the comment was addressed to the group at large, only the speaker was identified. If either speaker or addressee was unclear, I used a question mark. The transcription is not represented phonetically; instead, I used an orthography recommended by Ochs (1979) and used by some conversation analysts. This method involves typing out the utterances just as they sound, rather than in correct English spelling. For example, I used terms like *gonna, gimme,* and so on, to capture the flavor of actual talk, rather than transcribing such utterances as *going to* or *give me.* I also attempted to capture nonsense sounds and invented words in the same manner, by spelling them out so that "reading them as they look" would recreate the same utterance. Figure 3.2 itemizes specific notational conventions (see Corsaro, 1985; Levinson, 1983; Schenkein, 1978).

Interactional Events as Units of Analysis

In chapter 2, I reviewed several recent trends in psychological research, usually associated with Vygotskian and sociocultural psychology. These researchers have argued that a focus on the individual child makes it difficult to capture

CAPITALS	Relatively high amplitude
?	Marks terminal pitch rise and questions: "Let's go, OK?"
!	Marks exclamatory utterance
=	Marks both self- and other-interruptions
//	Marks overlapping speech
/	Marks an utterance boundary (if on the same line)
nX	Repeat of prior utterance, n times
[]	Surrounds uncertain passages of transcript
(0)	Pauses and silences, in number of seconds
-	Abrupt break, stop, or brief (subsecond) pause

FIG. 3.2. Transcript conventions.

social and contextual factors. If the unit of analysis is the child, then the best one can do is to consider the social environment as a variable that affects individual behavior in some way. Much of ecological psychology (Bronfenbrenner, 1979), interactional psychology (Magnusson & Endler, 1977), and social psychology takes this approach: Operationalize certain aspects of the social context as independent variables, and operationalize certain measures of individual behavior as the dependent variables.

But if the psychologist doesn't focus on the individual, how can psychological study proceed? The response of the socioculturalists, inspired by Vygotsky's writings as well as the American pragmatists, is that the psychologist must focus on events in context as the units of analysis (see especially Rogoff, 1982). The event includes all of the participating individuals, all of their individual behaviors during the event, and their interactions during the event. When the focus is the event-in-context, the event also includes, by definition, the sociocultural context of the participants. To study an event, it helps to have some understanding of the history leading up to that event, and the later consequences of the event, but these factors not part of the event itself.

This focus on the event is grounded in the psychological tradition, because what is primarily of interest is individual behavior. But the shift in focus from the individual to the event is critical. It allows the analyst to integrate context, interaction, and individual behaviors and competences, rather than drawing boundaries between individual and context.

This focus on the event allows the analyst to combine a situated, naturalistic approach with statistical analyses, to demonstrate the generalizability of specific examples to the entire corpus, and to measure statistical significance, or deviation from expectations. Yet an unavoidable problem with event data is that the units of analysis are not technically independent, because they have not been randomly sampled. Thus, if statistical methods are to be applied to event data, the results must be interpreted with an awareness of the dependencies among the units of analysis. This awareness is required of all psychologists; such problems are shared by most psychological research. For example, statisticians agree that one of the typical psychological methods, in which the subjects are drawn from the undergraduates at a university, violates the assumptions of random sampling. Yet such studies have taught us a great deal about human psychology. With any psychological use of statistics, the important thing is to always understand the nature of the dependencies among units of analysis, and how might it affect the results.

The degree to which dependencies will affect the results varies with the level of analysis. In observational studies like this one, there are three levels of analysis at which statistical analyses could be conducted:

1. *The event.* The main source of dependence at the event level is that the same children participate in multiple events. Thus, if the true source of variation is due to an individual-level characteristic, and certain individuals are over-represented in the sample of events, results may appear significant at the event level that actually result from individual-level properties.

2. *The group or dyad.* The dyad level of analysis has different dependencies than the event level, because the same dyad may participate in multiple events; if all dyads are not equally represented in the sample of events, a source of variation at the event level may actually be due to dyad-level properties. The dyad level has different dependencies than the child level, because most children participate in more than one dyad.

3. *The individual.* This is the traditional unit of analysis of psychology. In my study, even these units are not independent, because the children were not randomly sampled; they are all members of the same preschool classroom. This is a common form of dependency in psychology experiments; for example, subjects may all be students of the same university course.

The analyses in chapters 4, 5, 6, and 7 were conducted at the event level. In chapter 4, the event is the play group episode, a continuous interaction among a stable group of children that could last anywhere from 30 seconds to 30 minutes. In chapters 5 and 6, the event is the interactional routine, one child's proposal and another child's response. In chapter 7, the event is the extended improvisational sequence, when interactional routines are chained together to collectively, creatively construct an emergent play performance.

Some of the most interesting results of these chapters emerge from the event level of analysis, when the variables of interest were properties of the event only, and not of the group or the child. For example, if one wants to analyze the relationship between the metapragmatic strategies of two utterances in a sequence, that sequence, as an event, is the only appropriate unit of analysis. There are other hypotheses that could be evaluated at the group or child level. The dependencies at all three levels are difficult to determine, due to the nonexperimental nature of naturalistic data; I chose the event level as the most appropriate way to address the theoretical questions of the study.

4

Performance Style and Performances

The theory of play as performance is a theory which says that play is not ever simply solitary action, but always a performance before real or imagined others. The player may be both director and player on his own stage.
—Brian Sutton-Smith (1979, p. 298)

Children's play improvisations take place within a complex, organic environment: the social world of the preschool classroom. If we consider pretend play to be an improvisational performance, then the classroom is the stage setting and the theater for that performance. In a very real sense, children are also the audience for the performance. Children in this age range could be considered to form an entire subculture of theater. This performance metaphor guides the development of several of the concepts in this chapter.

Improvisational performers are taught early in their training that it is important to define the basic facts of a performance first: the location, the dramatic roles, the relationship between the characters. Most important is the location, the physical space within which the actors find themselves. One of the critical skills of an improv actor is the ability to mime, to interact with an invisible physical environment, to hold and manipulate invisible objects. Before actors begin a scene, they often decide who will perform in that scene, and roughly how long the scene will last. These are the most basic parameters that affect the resulting performance. These parameters are one focus of this chapter: the participants in a play episode, and the length and definition of that episode.

Improvisational actors are quite good at maintaining the boundaries between the staged performance and the off-stage reality. They have to maintain the distinction between the stage and the audience, an invisble boundary that they call the "fourth wall"; they also must maintain a distinction between their staged roles and relationships, and the relationships they have with each other off-stage. In contrast, children blend the boundary between play and social reality all the time; their nonplay relationships sometimes have a big effect on their play. A variety of research has demonstrated that social context has a significant effect on play. Because play has been demonstrated to vary in so many ways from one social context to another, any analysis of play metapragmatics must take social context into account.

Social context is a complicated and theoretically elusive notion. Definitions can be very specific, like the operationalized variables of psychologists. For example, some developmentalists have studied ecological variables like age, gender, play group size, or classroom location. Definitions can also be sometimes broad and all-encompassing. Some researchers speak of a peer culture of the preschool classroom, suggesting that the social network and relationship histories of the children in a classroom form a cohesive culture, distinct from the adult culture in which the classroom is embedded. Corsaro is best known for applying this concept to the study of preschool children. He suggested that children embellish the patterns, routines, and rituals of adult culture to create their own distinct cultural patterns and rituals (Corsaro, 1985).

Because my study of this classroom was an extended observational study, I learned a lot about the peer culture of this group. Many of the transcript analyses that follow draw on my own experiences in the classroom. It's difficult to fully understand any single interaction between children without also being familiar with prior play episodes among the same group, without knowing about the types of play that tend to occur in the same location, without knowing how this unique group of children tends to play with the toys present in the classroom. Most ethnographers would argue that this sort of deep understanding is difficult to capture using purely quantitative methods.

Nonetheless, at the same time, I wanted to quantify wherever possible the relationships between social context and play metapragmatics. I decided to focus on several aspects of social context, including age, gender, group size, and friendship. These social context variables were doubly interesting to me because much of the research into children's play has focused on one or another of these variables.

In my classroom, I noticed an interactional context factor that seemed to have a strong influence on the play, one that has appeared in the literature in different guises. The way the children performed their dramatic roles seemed to guide the entire episode. This "performance style" determined the overall feel of the play episode. I also noticed that the performance style seemed closely associated with other aspects of the social context, like age and gender. Later in this chapter, present some statistical analyses that explore these observations.

At the end of chapter 3, I introduced the notion of using *events in context* as the units of analysis. Many researchers have separated children's play sessions into extended events, play episodes that seem to be a single, unified performance. In my classroom, although the play was constantly in flux, the play discourse could be grouped into units of relatively stable, cohesive play. I refer to these units as *group episodes*. I begin this chapter by specifying how I defined a group episode, and how I used this concept in the rest of the analyses. After this definition, I describe what I mean by performance style and present several examples to illustrate the concept.

After presenting these two concepts, which were the highest-level categories used in my analyses, I describe how I defined and operationalized the social context variables that I thought might influence play metapragmatics: age, group size, gender, and friendship. I then present a series of quantitative findings that show remarkably strong relationships between many of these constructs.

The Group Episode

A group episode is a continuous sequence of play turns among a group of children who have acknowledged each other and agreed to play together. The group episode can be thought of as a single performance, a single scene in an improvised play. In a classroom of 24 children, there are many such scenes being performed simultaneously, so the entire morning play session would make an unorthodox performance, were it ever to be staged. To conduct any useful analyses of children's play, one has to focus closely on specific groups of children, performing one small scene in the ongoing classroom drama.

The group episode, as an event, is the unit of analysis in this chapter. I defined a group episode to be:

> Two or more children, engaged in social play, from the time that they start playing together (with a shared focus, or play frame) through the time that they stop playing together as a group. If a child enters or leaves the group, the group composition changes, and a new group episode begins.

I defined the *play group* to be the group of children playing together in a group episode. When the play group composition changes, this ends one group episode and begins another.

This definition is based on Goffman's (1963) notion of *face engagement* or *encounter*, as elaborated by Cook-Gumperz and Corsaro (1977). In an application of this concept to children's play, Cook-Gumperz and Corsaro's unit of analysis was the *interactive episode*:

[Interactive episodes are] those sequences of behavior which begin with the *acknowledged presence* of two or more interactants in an ecological area and the *overt attempt(s)* to arrive at a shared meaning of ongoing or emerging activity. Episodes end with physical movement of interactants from the area which results in the *termination* of the *originally initiated activity*. (1977, pp. 416–417)

The beginning of the episode is identified as the first attempt to arrive at *shared meaning*, collective social play in a shared play frame. Defining the termination of the episode is more problematic. Corsaro reasoned that the end of an episode occurred when the children left the area and activity (1985). Corsaro concluded that the episode should be defined primarily in terms of the activity, and that this activity may continue with different children, even if the original children leave. Because the social context is different for each grouping of children, I have chosen to use a slightly different definition: Whenever the group composition changes, the group episode terminates, and a new episode begins.

Conversational Turns

As I noted in chapter 3, each line of the transcript is a single *utterance*. Each utterance was a connected phrase; when a child stopped for a breath, or paused more than one second, I began the next utterance. A *conversational turn* is the set of utterances spoken in sequence by a single child, up to the point where another child speaks. Thus a turn's length could range from a single word—for example—answering "Yes" to a question, up to many utterances.

Example 4.1. Muhammed and Artie are playing on the stairs with blocks.
(1)	Muhammed	Yeah
(2)		Come on
(3)		We got the ninja rope!
(4)		Come on!
(5)		Get down [the ninja rope]
(6)		Quick! Quick! Quick!
(7)	Artie	I'll make it [bigger]

Muhammed's six utterances, from 1 to 6, are a single conversational turn. Turns were also considered to be delimited by pauses of 5 seconds or more in a child's talk, even if no other child spoke during that time.

The turn is the basic coding unit used in chapters 5 and 6.

Performance Style

I noticed that the way that the children enacted their play roles had a major influence on how the play improvisation proceeded. I refer to this as the children's performance style. To help interpret my observations, I drew on

Goffman's dramaturgical approach, Bakhtin's notion of voicing, and my own metaphor of play as improvisational performance.

The term *performance style* refers to the way that children perform their play roles. I've identified three different performance styles: *direct*, *indirect*, and *collective*. Like Piaget's and Parten's taxonomies of play, I've defined these play categories to be properties of the play group, not of individual children. Only at the group episode level, across children and multiple utterances, can a performance style be defined.

Direct Performance Style

Direct style refers to play activity in which the child himself acts out a play role that is different from the roles of his interlocutors. In this case, the child's body becomes the play character. This is the style of traditional theater: Each actor plays a character. The following episode is such an example, in which the children enact socially recognized family roles (note that this example appears in the Introduction, as do the two subsequent examples.):

> Example 4.2. Karl, Kathy, Corinna, Yung-soo, and Jan are pretending that they are going on a camping trip. They are loading up the "car" and "bus" (both are large baskets big enough for the children to sit inside) and getting ready to leave.
>
> (1) Jan   Who gonna drive the car
> (2)   who gonna drives the bus
> (3)   I'm already driving the car
> (4) Corinna   Let's get in the car, Yung-soo
> (5)   Let's get in the car, Yung-soo
> (6) Kathy   Well, there's two people in this one.
> (7)   That's not a really big car.
> (8)   This is (indicating "bus")
> (9) Corinna   And then someone will sit right there.
> (10) Karl   Yung-soo
> (11) Kathy   Now sit down!
> (12) Jan   Wait! I forgot my backpack.
> (13) Karl   Oh shucks I forgot I have to drive!

This is an example of Parten's highest level, cooperative play. Most developmental research has focused on this role-playing type of play. In the taxonomy of McLoyd, Warren, and Thomas (1984b), this example would have been coded as *domestic role enactment*. Although most of the direct style that I observed had a domestic theme, some of the direct style play fit into McLoyd et al.'s *occupational role enactment* category. Although in theory, children could engage in *fantasy role enactment* in the direct style mode, I did not observe any such group episodes. Fantasy play was always one of the following two styles.

Indirect Performance Style

Indirect style refers to play activity in which the child enacts the play role through the medium of a toy figure such as a zoo animal or a dinosaur. Usually, each child manipulates one toy, but sometimes a toy is held in each hand, allowing a single child to speak for two characters. When the children speak as the toy character's voice, they typically wiggle the corresponding toy. This is sometimes referred to as *replica play*. This performance style can be compared to theater, which uses puppets or marionettes. This type of play was common at the sand table:

Example 4.3. Jennifer and Muhammed are playing with toy animals at the sand table. Jennifer has a little duck, and Muhammed has a dinosaur.

(1)	Jennifer	Oh big dinosaur	(high-pitched voicing, as duck)
(2)		I cannot	
(3)		(screams)	
(4)	Muhammed	No, you can get on me	(in deep, gruff voice)
(5)		I just won't care	
(6)		(Jennifer puts her duck on the dinosaur's back.)	
(7)	Jennifer	He said, he said	
(8)		You bad dinosaur	(in deep voice)
(9)		Quickly, she hided in the sand (pushing the duck into the sand)	
(10)		so the dinosaur	
(11)	Muhammed	No, pretend he killed her	
(12)		Ow!	
(13)		He's already killed	

Cook-Gumperz and Corsaro (1977; also Corsaro, 1986) referred to this type of play as *spontaneous fantasy* (Cook-Gumperz & Corsaro, 1977). Fein, Moorin, and Enslein (1982) referred to it as *external agent play*, and identified it as the most advanced of 11 developmental levels. In light of these recent observations about indirect style, it is interesting that most of the developmental taxonomies reviewed in chapter 1 do not code this as a distinct category. It's unclear how the Parten- and Piagetian-derived taxonomies would code this type of play.

The *fantasy role play* of McLoyd et al. (1984b) is quite similar, in practice, to indirect style, because most indirect style has what they would call a fantasy theme, rather than a domestic or occupational theme. They found that fantasy role play demonstrated more play interaction and more metacommunication than any other type of role play. These studies seem to suggest that the indirect style is the most complex form of pretend.

Collective Performance Style

Collective style is a subtype of direct style, and is perhaps the most difficult one to define. *Collective style* is a type of play in which a group of children collectively perform a single play role. In this case, there are no relationships between specific children, and there is no negotiation about role relationships. Instead, each child speaks for the group, "voicing" as the role being collectively enacted. Unlike direct and indirect style, which could in principle be coded at an individual behavioral level, collective style can be operationalized only at the group level. A single child can be observed in direct or indirect play, even if that play is solitary; but the distinction between direct and collective style can only be made at the group episode level.

This performance style was common among children who were building block structures in the block area:

Example 4.4. Artie, Eddy, and Muhammed are in the block area. Each of them builds his own rocket using wooden blocks. They are about 5 feet from each other, and each boy's gaze is focused on his own construction as he speaks. They don't look at each other, except for occasional glances.

(1)	Eddy	I am making a rocket like …
(2)	Artie	That's not even a rocket, that's a small rocket
(3)		Mine is bigger than yours
(4)	Eddy	Mine is even bigger, mine smaller than yours
(5)	Artie	You can't even sit on it
(6)	Eddy	I am this …
(7)		make a rocket …
(8)		looks like a rocket, but it's not a real rocket
(9)	Artie	That not a real rocket at all
(10)		(laughs)
(11)	Muhammed	Mine shoots poison in their eyes
(12)	Eddy	Mine shoots poison all the poison in their eyes
(13)	Muhammed	Mine shoots billions and billions of poison in their eyes
(14)		… kind of poison
(15)	Artie	Doesn't this look like a dumb rocket?
(16)	Eddy	(laughs as his own rocket falls down)
(17)	Artie	I eat lots of food
(18)	Muhammed	I don't need lots of food
(19)	Artie	Yes we do, I have been in space for 9 years

The existence of this type of play discourse is particularly fascinating. Because it is not a straightforward enactment via a body or toy object, it seems to indicate a form of group awareness. In theater, collective style has an analogy in the chorus, a collective or impersonal voice that comments on the dramatic action. Although there are no relationships between individual roles to be negotiated, the participation as one voice in a polyphonic play character may require a distinct sort of sociolinguistic skill. The difference between collective and direct style is reminiscent of Mead's distinction between the *generalized other* and the *particular other* (Mead, 1934). In collective style, each performer is interacting with a single generalized other, and in direct style, each performer is interacting with specific, particular others.

These three performance styles also recall the discussion of Bakhtin in chapter 2. In Bakhtin's terminology, each of these styles could be referred to as a way of *voicing* a character. In the same way that a novelist writing dialogue has to "voice" as the fictional character, a child performing a dramatic pretend role voices as that play character. Like the novelist, this provides the child with opportunities for double-voicing, or *dialogism*; the child can blend an out-of-play voice with the play character's voice, and use this as a strategy for metapragmatic negotiation (the topic of capters 6 and 7). We might expect the nature of the child's voicing and double-voicing to be different in different performance styles, because the mechanics of voicing are so different. A child speaking through a plastic tiger is voicing as the tiger, but there is a sharp visual and corporeal distinction between that tiger and the child himself, which is obvious to all of the play participants. When a child voices "as herself," enacting a play role directly, the distinction is not as clear visually (although it may be just as clear to the other children).

The boundary between speaker's voice and the performed voice of the play character is perhaps the most blurred in collective style, where there is a single voice for the group. This form of discourse emphasizes the musical connotations of the Russian word for voice: Many compositions have a single motif or theme, which is played by all of the instruments in the orchestra. In collective performance style, there is only one voice flowing through the episode, but several children are each voicing as that same play character.

Although this might not have been the case, it turns out that all children in a given play group perform their characters in the same performance style. For example, I never saw one child speak as "the mother," in direct style, to address a toy animal, manipulated by another child to perform the "baby" role. Toy animals were only addressed by other toy animals; the play group used one performance style exclusively. I also noticed that the performance style did not change within a group episode. Children never switched from one style to another during a group episode. Thus, I have defined performance style to be a property of the group episode.

Note that these styles, while overlapping with many prior play categorization schemes, are different in a fundamental way: They are not defined in terms of the structure of the play interaction (Parten), nor in terms of cognitive developmental level (Piaget). Instead, they are defined in performance terms, a definition based on interactional process, rather than play frame or cognitive structure.

Social Context Variables

Because so much research has demonstrated that social context affects play, I wanted to incorporate such measures into my analyses. I defined all of these variables at the group episode level. Because, by definition, the play group and social context stay constant during a single group episode, the values of these variables do not change during a group episode.

Age

Age was often mentioned by the children. The children all knew their age, and they knew the ages of their play partners. In my classroom, this awareness was reinforced throughout the school year by the frequent birthday parties, perhaps the only ritual that I observed in this multicultural classroom. On those days when a birthday party was scheduled, many of the children talked about their age. Developmental psychologists generally assume that age, whether developmental or biological age, is a predictor of pretend play skills. The theories reviewed in chapter 1 emphasize the age of the child as the independent variable. Other studies have examined the effects of relative age on the speech of children. Some studies have shown that by the age of 4, children can modify their speech according to the age of the addressee, suggesting the beginnings of intersubjective ability (Dunn & Dale, 1984; Masur, 1978; Shatz & Gelman, 1973). For example, 4-year-olds use longer and more complex utterances with other 4-year-olds than with 2-year-olds (Masur, 1978). In a similar study, Sachs and Devin (1975) found that 3- to 5-year-olds' speech to babies differed from speech to peers and adults along a variety of grammatical dimensions. Brownell (1990) demonstrated that even in dyads of 18- and 24-month-olds, toddlers adjust the complexity of their social behavior to the age of their partner. These studies suggest that a child's speech and play behaviors are related to the age of the other children in the group. Because my classroom combines children of different ages, the relative age of the children must be considered.

For all analyses, I measured age in months, as of the start date of the 6-week audiotaping period. But note that age as a property of the group can be measured in (at least) two different ways:

1. *Mean age of the play group.* A rough measure of developmental level of the group, for those cases when a measure of an individual is inappropriate. Derived by taking the mean of all children in the play group at a given utterance.

2. *Relative age of the speaker and addressee.* This is a rough measure of the status differential between the children. Different behaviors may be observed with older and younger partners.

Gender Composition

There has been a significant amount of research on gender and children's speech, although the impact of these results on our study of play improvisations is unclear. It is widely assumed that women's speech is more indirect and polite, whereas men's speech is more direct. This common-sense cultural belief has been examined by many researchers (Brown & Levinson, 1978; Gilligan, 1982; Goodwin & Goodwin, 1987; Lakoff, 1975; Lever, 1978; Piaget, 1960). For example, Lever (1978), in a study of sex differences in the play of fifth graders, found that boys' play was more explicit than girls' play. They were more explicit in stating their goals, and specified play rules more explicitly.

Most research on gender and language has examined grade-school children or adults, rather than preschool children. Sachs (1987) has been the only comparative study of indirectness during the preschool period. This study compared pairs of girls and boys, between 24 and 64 months of age, playing with "doctor" toys. There was no sex difference in the amount of pretend play. However, boys assigned themselves the doctor, or dominant, role 79% of the time; girls only 33%. In proposing new role assignments, boys and girls used both questions, like "Will you be the patient?", and imperatives, like "You're the patient." There was a strong gender difference in usage: 72% of the boys' proposals were imperatives, whereas only 20% of the girls' proposals were imperatives.

In contrast to these findings, Goodwin and Goodwin (1987), in an analysis of arguments among boys and girls, did not find that girls were more indirect, or that they avoided conflict more than boys. Instead, they found that girls were not only just as skilled in argumentation as boys, but also that they had arguments that were both more extended and more complex than the boys' arguments. Their observations of boys and girls arguing suggested that girls are perhaps even more direct than boys. They concluded that the only way to examine these issues was through a closer focus on transcripts of play conversation in context. Once again, we are led to a close focus on metacommunication and its relationship to social context.

In addition to these studies of indirectness of speech, several other studies have examined differences in role enactment between boys and girls. McLoyd et al. (1984b), in a study of four different types of role enactment, found that only boys engaged in fantasy role enactment, enactment of a character that the child would never encounter or enact in later life: creatures from outer space, Superman, or other superheroes. Twenty-eight percent of the boys' play was of this type. The girls never engaged in fantasy role enactment; in contrast, 90% of the girls' play was domestic role enactment. Sanders and Harper (1976) also found that boys engaged in more fantasy play than girls. Some studies have found that boys produced a larger variety of fantasy themes (Marshall, 1961; Singer, 1973).

The previously mentioned findings suggest that gender is related to two aspects of play: the type of role enactment, and the indirectness of interaction. Indirectness is often undertheorized in these studies: For example, questions are considered indirect, whereas imperatives are direct. Yet it's not hard to construct examples of imperatives that seem relatively indirect, and questions that seem relatively direct. In spite of the lack of pragmatic theoretical backing, "indirectness" seems to be similar to implicit and within-frame metapragmatics. Using these metapragmatic measures provides an alternative to syntactic measures such as the question-imperative distinction. A study of metapragmatics during play may help clarify these contradictory findings.

To study the effects of gender on performance style and on metapragmatic usage, I defined a set of *gender mixes* to reflect the make-up of the group. I chose to use the following five, based on the typical groupings within my classroom: (a) all boys; (b) mixed, mostly boys; (c) mixed, balanced; (d) mixed, mostly girls; and (e) all girls.

This can be thought of as a progression from "boy-ness" to "girl-ness" of the play group. Category (c) includes those groups with at least two boys and two girls, because these groups were not dominated by either gender.

Group Size

Group size is the number of children in the play group.

Friendship

Friendship is different from the preceding variables, because it is collectively determined by the children. As such, friendships rely heavily on communicative interaction for their establishment and maintenance (Corsaro, 1985; Rawlins, 1991). Many studies have demonstrated that social pretend play is a fundamental component of friendship during the preschool period, and that coordinated play is both a marker of social competence, and is the primary task of friendships (e.g., Gottman, 1983; Howes, 1992). Corsaro (1985) argued that children develop friendships as a way to maximize the probability of successful entry into a play group and to protect their play space from other children. Friendship is a strategic tool to be manipulated to satisfy the goals of always having someone to play with. There is some evidence that friendship increases with age, and that the number of strong friendships increases with age (Green, 1933).

There are several different ways of defining preschool friendships. Because friendship is a property of dyads and groups, it cannot be defined at an individual level, and thus is particularly appropriate for event-level analysis. In most studies of peer relations and friendships among preschool children (Challman, 1932; Green, 1933; Marshall & McCandless, 1957; Parten, 1932) friendship has been operationalized as frequency of contact, or propinquity. In developmental studies of the child's conceptions of friendship, preschool-age children are found to define a friend as someone they play with frequently (Damon, 1977; Selman, 1976; Youniss, 1975). This classic definition of friendship is still the most commonly used. For example, Howes (1987a) defined friends to be children who were within 3 feet of each other during at least 30% of their total play time, and who displayed positive affect during this time. Many studies confirm that friends play more and talk more (Doyle, Connolly, & Rivest, 1980; Garvey & Hogan, 1973; Gottman & Parkhurst, 1980; Mueller, 1972; Schwarz, 1972).

Other ways to measure friendship include teacher nominations (the researcher asks the teacher to name the friends of each child) and peer nominations (the researcher asks the children to name their friends). Several studies have correlated propinquity measures of friendship with these other measures (Hays, 1989; Howes, 1987a; Marshall & McCandless, 1957; Nezlek, 1993). Marshall and McCandless (1957) found that both teacher and peer identifications of best friends correlated at .001 with amount of time the children played together. Howes correlated her propinquity measure of friendship with both teacher and peer nominations; there was bilateral friendship nomination for 72% of the behaviorally identified friends, and unilateral friendship nomination for an additional 18%, for a total of 90% overlap. This measure agreed with teacher nominations for 85% of the dyads. An additional benefit of the behavioral measure was its superior reliability to sociometric nominations. These results confirm the validity of using measures of time together as an index of friendship.

Several different propinquity measures of friendship have been proposed. Challman (1932) developed a *friendship index* based on amount of time each pair was observed playing together. Green (1933) used the friendship index and a *quarrelsome index* for the percent of time a pair was arguing. To study the role of friendship in play metapragmatics, I calculated a 100-point friendship index for each pair of children. The friendship index is derived from the total number of utterances played together in the 29-hour corpus. I normalized this number to a 100-point scale by adding the number of utterances the pair played together, and dividing this total by the average of the total number of utterances played for the two children. Thus, this can be thought of as the percentage of the total play time of these two children during which they played together. To determine the friendship index of a play group of three or more children, I calculated the mean average of the pairwise dyadic scores.

For some of the figures presented in chapters 5 and 6, I've converted this 100-point measure into 10 ranks of 10 points each; rank 1 represents friendship scores 0 to 9, rank 2, scores 10 to 19, and so forth. For analyses that focus only on friends, I've dichotomized the index at level 20. A friendship index of 20 means that this pair spent 20% of their averaged play time with each other. Thus, friends are those children who spent at least one fifth of their time together. The selection of this threshold value was guided by my own observation, interviews with teachers, and prior research.

As with prior studies (Gottman & Parkhurst, 1980; Howes, 1983, 1987a, 1987b), I found that friendships in my classroom displayed a high degree of stability throughout the academic year. In particular, friendships did not change during the 6-week audiotaping period. Thus, I have calculated a single value on the friendship index for each pair of children, which I used for all analyses.

Quantifying Play Talk: Characteristics of the Corpus

For each group episode, I calculated the group size, the friendship index, the performance style, the gender composition, and the mean age. The following list itemizes some general descriptive statistics:

1. The total number of utterances was 18,212.
2. The average number of utterances in a group episode was 94, with a range from 6 to 635.
3. There were 192 group episodes, for an average episode length of 9 minutes (192 episodes divided by a total of 29 hours).
4. The average friendship strength for play groups was 32.4; the strongest dyadic friendship was 78.9.
5. The average age of the children was 49.9 months; the mean age of all play groups was 52.4.
6. The average group size was 3.1 children, with groups ranging in size from 2 to 7.
7. The number of utterances for each gender mix was: all boys, 8,280; mostly boys, 1,133; evenly mixed, 2,059; mostly girls, 2,930; all girls, 3,810. Note that 12,090/18,212 utterances, or 66% of all play, was in a homogenous-sex play group.
8. 61% of the group episodes were all-boy or all-girl groups (118/192).

I performed a few basic linguistic measures for each child, to compare my classroom with prior studies of this age range. As with prior studies, age was correlated with several verbal measures. Older children were more verbal than younger children. The total number of utterances per child was related to age, $r(24) = .52, p < .01$. There was also a significant relationship between age and MLU (mean length of utterance), $r(24) = .50, p < .01$. There was a stronger correlation between the total number of utterances and MLU, $r(24) = .61$, $p < .01$. Corresponding to these utterance level measures, there were also significant correlations between age and number of turns, $r(24) = .47, p < .01$, and between age and number of utterances per turn, $r(24) = .56, p < .01$. As expected, on all of these measures older children talked more than younger children.

Relationships Among Social Context Variables

Because the social environment of the preschool classroom is a complex, organic entity, influenced and maintained by 24 children, I didn't expect my variables to be independent. I wanted to find out what the relationships were among the social context variables. For example, did group size increase with age? Did friendship increase with age? Before analyzing the relationships with performance style (the following section) and with metapragmatic usage (chapters 5, 6, and 7), I wanted to understand these relationships.

Gender was matched across age, with one exception. Of the five 5-year-olds, four were girls. Of the five children between 4 and 4;6 years, four were boys. This could have an effect on those statistical measures that relied on gender, because gender might be conflated with age. In particular, we should be cautious about findings that seem to demonstrate that girls are more developmentally advanced than boys, because in this classroom, the oldest children are girls.

The mean age of the group was negatively correlated with the friendship strength of the group, $r(192) = -.30, p < .01$. Groups with a lower mean age had a higher group friendship index. Younger children played more with stronger friends, and older children played more with children they were not as friendly with. Because friendship was based on percentage of total time played together, one possible interpretation of this result is that younger children concentrated their play with a few close playmates, whereas older children distributed their play sessions among a larger set of playmates.

There was a relationship between gender composition of the group and the size of the group. All-boy groups were smaller than groups of other gender mixes,

$r(192) = -.37, p < .01$. When groups with an even number of boys and girls were excluded, mostly-girl groups were found to be larger than mostly boy groups, $r(192) = .19, p < .01$. These two results suggest that girls played in larger groups than boys.

Performance Style and the Play Group

I was particularly interested in the relationships between the age, gender, group size, and friendship of the play group, and the performance style of the play episode. Of the 192 episodes, 58 were in direct style, 63 in indirect, and 61 in collective. There were 10 episodes which were coded as not enacted. Thus, 182 of 192 episodes (95%) were enacted pretend play. This is high compared to other studies of this age range, perhaps because play is the expected activity during the indoor play period.

Structural theories of development imply that children at different ages will engage in different performance styles. For example, direct style seems to correspond to the most advanced play stage of Parten's scheme. If these theories are correct, we should see correlations between performance style and mean age of the play group. The incidence of collective style, a more parallel verbal interaction, should decline as children get older, and either direct style (in structuralist models) or indirect style (in Fein et al.'s 1982 model) should increase with age.

The following analyses measure the relationship between the mean age of all of the children in the play group, and the performance style of the group episode. There was a negative correlation between play group age and collective style, $r(192) = -.25, p < .01$. There was a positive relationship between play group age and indirect style, $r(192) = .32, p < .01$. There was no relationship between play group age and direct style. Figure 4.1 displays the relationships for play group age and performance style.

These results support some prior findings, while apparently contradicting others. Among the youngest children, more than half of the play episodes were collective style, and among the oldest children, the majority were indirect style. Because the incidence of direct style did not change with age, these two curves account for almost all of the developmental change in performance style. Most staged models, by neglecting indirect style, fail to account for the most significant trend in these data. Only Fein et al. (1982) and Corsaro (Cook-Gumperz & Corsaro, 1977; Corsaro, 1986) incorporated this type of play into their taxonomies, as a distinct, advanced level of play. These data confirm both studies' claims that indirect style is the most advanced form of play.

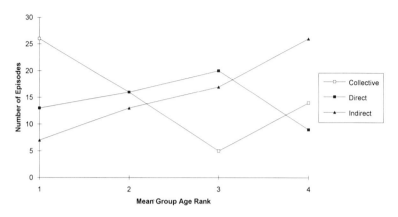

FIG. 4.1. Number of episodes in each style, by mean group age rank.

Of the three performance styles, only indirect style play episodes were related to the average friendship of the group. The friendship of the group was negatively correlated with the incidence of indirect style, $r(192) = -.22$, $p < .01$. Play episodes that were indirect style tended to be performed by groups that had less strong friendships. If children were stronger friends, they were more likely to engage in direct or collective style, although the correlations between friendship and either direct or collective style were not significant. Perhaps indirect style can support play among lesser friends, or friends prefer direct and collective styles.

Perhaps the most interesting findings were the relationships between gender and performance style. Collective style was associated with groups containing only boys: $r(192) = .57$, $p < .01$. Forty-nine of the 61 collective style episodes (80%) were all-boy episodes; 49 of the 76 all-boy episodes (64%) were collective style.

When groups with an even number of boys and girls were excluded, direct style was associated with groups that were mostly girls, whereas groups that were mostly boys tended not to engage in direct style: $r(192) = .46$, $p < .01$. Thirty-eight of the 47 direct-style episodes (80%) were performed by mostly girl play groups.

Group size was related to performance style: group size was associated with direct style, $r(192) = .37$, $p < .01$; group size was negatively correlated with collective style, $r(192) = -.29$, $p < .01$; there was no relationship between group size and indirect style. It may be that direct style can support a larger play group size. However, recall that girls played in larger groups than boys. This suggests that the group-size/direct correlation might really be one of gender: Girls use more direct style, and their groups are larger, so it's perhaps not really a group-size phenomenon.

There are two strong relationships to be explained. First, collective style was found primarily in all-boy groups; even the presence of one girl (the mostly boys category) seemed to shift the play to indirect. Second, direct style was associated with groups dominated by girls: Groups with mostly girls or all girls spent more time in direct style than groups that were mostly boys or all boys. Several studies have shown that boys engage in more fantasy play, and girls in more domestic play (Marshall, 1961; McLoyd et al., 1984b; Sanders & Harper, 1976; Singer, 1973). Although my data do not allow conclusive results to be drawn, because I have not coded for the role-playing categories used in the preceding studies, my field observations suggest that the type of role enacted (domestic, occupational, fantasy) is related to the performance style. Direct style in my classroom was almost exclusively domestic, whereas collective and indirect styles were predominantly fantasy play. Some collective style involved occupational roles (e.g., building a house, racing cars), and some indirect style involves domestic roles (e.g., families of horses). These data suggest that prior findings that boys engage in more fantasy play may only apply to the direct style/collective style distinction; boys and girls both engaged in equal amounts of indirect style. Like Corsaro's studies (Cook-Gumperz & Corsaro, 1977; Corsaro, 1986), indirect style was the most likely to involve fantasy themes in my preschool. The fact that it is also the only gender-neutral mode calls into question those studies that found correlations between fantasy play and gender.

These gender differences by performance style echo Lever's (1978) observation about fifth graders' gender differences: "In Meadian terms, it may be that boys develop the ability to take the role of the *generalized other* while girls develop empathy skills to take the role of the *particular other*" (p. 481). The distinction between collective style and direct style is consistent with Mead's (1934) terminology. The boys' enactment of a collective group identity could contribute to the development of a generalized other, whereas direct style seems to better contribute to the development of relationship skills. There are suggestive parallels with the differences in moral development proposed by Gilligan (1982): She observed that boys develop a moral approach based on appeals to abstract, general rules, whereas girls are more relationship-oriented (see particularly Gilligan, 1982).

Summary

This chapter began by comparing the preschool classroom to a theater, and comparing play episodes to improvisational performances. The performance metaphor has guided the development of several of the concepts in this chapter. The group episode can be thought of as a single improvised performance, or perhaps as one scene in an improvised play. The performance style of a play group is also a dramatic concept, because it is defined in terms of how the children perform their dramatic roles.

In Mrs. Winston's preschool classroom, 95% of social interaction during the indoor play period was enacted pretend play. Recall that my method of gathering audiotapes, described in chapter 3, did not favor play interaction over nonplay interaction, although I did choose the part of the day most conducive to such play, the indoor play period. This play was much more verbal and fantasylike than interactions during snacktime, while collaborating on tasks at the work-tables, or during the outdoor play period. During the indoor play period, children choose and direct their own activities, and they overwhelmingly choose to engage in sociodramatic play.

Peer play has been shown to provide unique developmental benefits during the preschool years. Because so much of the peer interaction in my classroom was pretend play, the effect of peer relations on social development may be mediated, in part, through play. Studies of peer relations during these years should include analyses of pretend play. This finding reinforces one of the implications of the research discussed in chapter 1, that peer relations contribute to development through the unique properties of pretend play interaction. Play is a framed performative activity, and it requires the use of metapragmatic strategies to achieve intersubjectivity.

Now we are ready to move on to detailed analyses of specific play interactions. This chapter has set the stage for the following chapters by describing the fundamental influences of social context and performance style. All of the factors covered in this chapter have been shown to have various degrees of influence on pretend play. Now that we have identified these influences, we can proceed with the analyses of metapragmatics, using these findings to help interpret the results. The following three chapters focus on specific interactional strategies used by children during play, and how these strategies are related to social and interactional context.

5

Joining the Performance:
The Metapragmatics of Play Entry

Children who find themselves alone consistently attempt to gain entry into one of the ongoing peer episodes. As a result, children develop a broad and complex set of access strategies, some of which are directly related to friendship.
—William Corsaro (1985, pp. 122–123)

Imagine yourself at the age of 3, 4, or 5, starting the new year at a new preschool. If you don't want to be limited to playing alone and doing crafts at the worktables, you have to acquire some social skills. Almost all of the 24 children in my classroom spent the majority of the morning play time engaged in play with one or more partners. Even when a group of children decided to stop playing and spend a few minutes on the day's craft activity, they usually went to the worktable together, and turned the doing of the craft into a kind of play. The importance and predominance of social play that I observed has been noted in every study of this age group. In my 6 weeks of audiotaped preschool discourse, only 5% of the total utterances were not play, and even this 5% was almost always social. The first and most fundamental skill that children learn is how to get another child to play with you. Once children learn how to accomplish this *play entry*, even if they are still beginners at play, they can enter a play frame, which will then allow them to learn more sophisticated metapragmatic skills.

During an improv theater performance, the actors who are not actively participating in the current scene stand or sit at the back or sides of the stage.

They do not want to interfere with the ongoing performance; but, at the same time, they have to be close enough to the action to detect when it would be appropriate to enter the performance as a new character. During a long-form improv performance, which typically lasts 30 minutes, successive scenes are delineated by actors simply entering and leaving the stage. There is no stage direction; no director stands in the wings and tells the actors when it's time to enter for the next scene. Like everything else about improvisational theater, these entrances and exits are collectively, spontaneously determined.

When an actor decides to enter the center of the stage and join the performance, he or she will walk on and speak a line of dialogue, or begin miming an action. The actors who are already on stage must then adjust their performances, and redirect the emerging plot to incorporate this new character. At no point does any actor step out of character to discuss the change, or to direct the performance. Everything is done in character. As described in the Introduction, the "no denial" rule applies: The new actor must be incorporated into the ongoing improvisation. The option to reject the new actor and continue as before is not available.

Contrast this with the situation in the preschool classroom. Although adults might take play entry for granted, it's a difficult task for children. There is always the possibility that your request might be rejected. Yet to engage in play, you must overcome the fear of rejection and make the attempt. Here's an example of what can happen when a child is rejected:

Example 5.1. Muhammed and John have been playing with Legos™ in the Lego™ area since 9:05. At 9:15, Bernie attempts to join them.

(1)	Bernie	Can I play with you?
(2)		Can I play with you?
(3)		Can I play with you?
(4)	Muhammed	No!
(5)	Bernie	You need some animals?
(6)	Muhammed	No!
(7)		Then I won't be your friend again. Right, John?
(8)	John	Right
(9)	Bernie	Those are animals, so can I play with you?
		(Bernie offers toy animals "in trade" for being allowed entry, but to no avail.)
(10)		(Bernie is ignored.)

A few seconds after this, Bernie is saved by the timely arrival of Sam, a frequent playmate. Bernie and Sam walk through the east doorway into the doll corner and begin playing. Sam was one of Bernie's usual playmates; their friendship index was 78.9. Because Bernie arrived before Sam, he had to seek out different playmates. Muhammed and John had been playing happily for 10 minutes, and they were not interested in having Bernie join them. Muhammed and John were frequent playmates; their friendship score was 34.2. Perhaps they were aware that Bernie's play was a different style from theirs: He often turned the play activity into what the teachers referred to as silly behavior, making funny noises, wrestling, and engaging in loud speech play.

There have been many psychological studies of peer group entry that have demonstrated how difficult it is for children, and how fundamental a skill it is for social development (Corsaro, 1981, 1985; Garvey, 1984; Putallaz & Wasserman, 1990; Zarbatany, Van Brunschot, Meadows, & Pepper, in press). Corsaro focused on the access strategies children used to gain play entry, observing that whenever children found themselves alone they consistently attempted to gain entry into a play group. The potential for rejection is quite high: Corsaro (1981) found that among acquainted 3- and 4-year-olds, 53.9% of initial entry attempts were rejected. This high percentage of rejection, among a classroom of children who, like mine, knew each other, suggests how hard it is to accomplish play entry successfully. Paley wrote an entire book, *You Can't Say You Can't Play* (1992), about the year when she instituted a new classroom rule, that play entry attempts must always be accepted. She documents how difficult it was to get the children to accept this new rule.

As adults, our attempts to enter conversation are often easy and natural, and don't require much thought. In unusual situations, we may have to think about how to approach a person or a group. For example, at an academic conference, when a prominent speaker completes a talk, interested members of the audience may approach the speaker with a specific entry strategy in mind. Several researchers have studied conversational access among adults. Goffman (1971) observed that among adults, almost every interaction is initiated by an *access ritual*. Goffman and others (Goffman, 1963, 1971, 1974; Schegloff, 1968; Schiffrin, 1977) have demonstrated the complexity of adult access rituals, and their importance for the production and maintenance of everyday interaction. Schegloff (1968) coined the term *opening* to refer to the access rituals that initiate conversations. The opening became an exemplar of the type of *conversational routine* that is associated with conversation analysis. Schegloff's classic paper presented an analysis of the exchange of conversational turns that proceeds at the beginning of a phone call, the opening of the phone conversation. That paper also introduced the idea of a special kind of two-turn sequence, the *pair part*, through an exploration of the *summons–answer sequence*. Schegloff observed that pair-parts have a property he termed *conditional relevance*: Given the first part of the exchange, the second part is expectable. Using this terminology, play entry is a pair-part access ritual, because the access attempt leads to an expected response, either positive or negative.

At a microinteractional level, children's play entry is analogous to these adult rituals. Children's play entry strategies are developmental precursors to adult access rituals, and they may serve to organize the children's peer culture in the same way that adult access rituals help to construct their social world (Corsaro, 1979a). Social pretense may be an important context for the acquisition of these essential adult social skills.

In chapter 2, I discussed how the strategy of a speaker's turn can be characterized along two metapragmatic dimensions: the *explicitness* of the turn, and the *frame* that the child voices from. On the first dimension, play entry attempts can be either explicit (about play entry) or implicit; on the second dimension, they can be either in the play frame or outside the play frame. This frame dimension is closely related to the performance role of the child. When speaking as the play character, a child is in frame; at times, a child speaks out-of-character but still in the pretend frame. Because prior to play entry, there is not yet an intersubjectively shared play frame, in-frame entry attempts are extremely rare (see Example 5.4, following).

Because openings are pair-part sequences, responses to play entry attempts are also of interest. Like the entry attempt, responses can be explicit or implicit, in-frame or out-of-frame. Because the conversational position of a turn within the ongoing flow of interaction has been suggested to influence the speaker's strategy, I predicted that the strategy of the response would be related to the strategy of the play entry attempt. I was also interested in exploring other effects on strategy selection. Do children use different strategies when they are accepting than when they are rejecting? Are certain response strategies associated with certain entry strategies? How does strategy vary with age, gender, and friendship?

Play Entry in Mrs. Winston's Classroom

My analysis of play entry focused on three things that earlier studies have neglected: (a) the relationship between the strategy of the attempt and the response, (b) the relationship between the responder's goal (to accept the new child, or to reject the child) and the type of interactional sequence observed, and (c) the effect of the strength of friendship on these interactional patterns.

In Example 5.1, Bernie's attempt to join Muhammed and John was rejected. Mark's entry attempt in Example 5.2 occurred later on the same day. Unlike Bernie's experience, Mark's attempt was successful.

Example 5.2. Muhammed and John have been playing in the Lego™ area since John arrived at 9:05. They continue building spaceships with Legos™ until cleanup time at 9:44. At 9:40, Mark enters play, and after this entry, the three play together until cleanup.

(1) Mark   Can I play with you?
(2) John   yes, yes

Both Example 5.1 and Example 5.2 involve verbal exchanges of the type well-documented by Corsaro (1985). His study demonstrated how children use the explicit invocation of friendship as a strategy for achieving play entry. However, he did not present examples like those mentioned before, with friendship being used by a pair of responders to exclude a third child. In contrast to stage entrances in improvisational theater, which are implicit and in frame, the aforementioned exchanges are explicit and out of frame. The child attempting play entry explicitly mentions play entry, and he speaks outside of the established play frame of the children he is attempting to join. In some cases, children are implicit about play entry, while still speaking out of frame:

Example 5.3. Implicit, out of frame entry attempt. Yung-soo approaches the trio Kathy, Rachel, and Jennifer, who have been playing on toy telephones.

(1)   Yung-soo   OK, I'm here!   (She walks in.)
(2)   Kathy   Oh, hello, Yung-soo!
(3)   You were calling us!

Note that the both the entry attempt and the response are implicit: neither mention play entry, like Examples 5.1 and 5.2. Although implicit, both children speak out of frame: Yung-soo and Kathy are not yet speaking in character, not yet sharing an intersubjective play world. Play entry and acceptance are usually done out of frame, before a joint frame is established. However, there are cases of play entry that are implicit and in frame:

Example 5.4. Implicit, in frame entry attempt. Kathy had been playing earlier with Jennifer and Rachel, had recently left the room.

(1)   Kathy   I'm home!   (Enters room.)
(2)   Rachel   Here's your baby.   (Hands her a baby doll).

Like the improv example, utterance (1) serves two functions: It is an attempt at play entry, and it also entails a play frame activity, the play character returning home. In Example 5.4, the positive response is also in frame, and also implicit. In-frame entry attempts are usually *continuations*, returns to play after a recent exit from the same play group, and the in-frame entrance is often performed consistently with the dramatic frame in effect when the returning child left the group. A few minutes before Example 5.4, Kathy left with the following exchange:

Example 5.5. Kathy leaving Rachel and Jennifer. She has been talking on the phone, and hangs up at (2):

(1)   Kathy   Allright, I'm a lawyer, I'll help you.
(2)   Bye bye.   (Hangs up.)
(3)   Gotta get my coat!

(7)	Jennifer	Where are you going?
(8)	Kathy	I'm going to somebody's house that=
(9)		It's it's very dangerous.

| (13) | Jennifer | What about your baby? |
| (14) | | She's naked! |

(18)	Kathy	You guys dress her,
(19)		And, and put her in,
(20)		This nice bed, cause that's my bed.
(21)	Jennifer	OK.
(22)	Rachel	Allright!
(23)		(Kathy leaves.)

Kathy's return in Example 5.4 projects an elaborate play frame onto Rachel and Jennifer: They are at home, and Kathy is returning home. Rachel's response accepts both Kathy's play entry, and the projected entailments, while simultaneously projecting its own entailment: Rachel is holding Kathy's baby. This entailment is consistent with the emergent play drama when Kathy left at the end of Example 5.5, while continuing to elaborate the improvisation.

Sometimes play entry is not verbal at all. The following is an example of a successful nonverbal play entry. Note that this entry established the dyad Muhammed and John, who were later approached in the aforementioned Examples 5.1 and 5.2.

Example 5.6. Muhammed has been playing alone with Lego™ blocks since 8:55. At 9:05, John arrives and walks over to Muhammed. John does not speak before the following:

| (1) | Muhammed | (upon seeing John) Hi Johnnie ... Hi John! |
| (2) | | (John sits down and begins to play with the Legos™.) |

Example 5.6, a nonverbal entry attempt, can be distinguished from entry sequences that I refer to as *recruitments*. In a recruitment, a child or group that is already playing in a location sees a nearby solitary child, and calls to that child, asking her to join the play. Example 5.7 is a typical recruitment:

Example 5.7. Muhammed and John are playing together in the block area. They notice Jennifer near the shelves along the north wall, alone, tying her shoelaces.

(1)	Muhammed	You can play with me, right?
(2)	John	You can play with us
(3)	Jennifer	OK I don't have anyone to play with.

| (10) | | Do I need to get some animals? |

Recent Research on Play Entry

Researchers have studied play entry, the influence of friendship on play, and the use of metacommunication during play. Although some studies have combined two of these three, none of these studies have considered all of these notions together. Some developmental research has analyzed the structure of play entry sequences through a focus on transcripts of naturally occurring, self-selected play groups (Corsaro, 1979a, 1985; Goncu, 1987). However, these studies did not consider the influence of social context. A separate tradition of developmental research has explored the relationship between play entry success and popularity (Dodge & Schlundt, 1983; Putallaz & Gottman, 1981; Putallaz & Wasserman, 1990) and success and friendship (Howes, 1981; Phinney & Rotherham, 1981). However, these studies examined only play entry strategies, and did not examine the relationship between entry and response strategies. After reviewing these studies, I outline the implications for the metapragmatic model, and describe how the perspective of play interaction as improvisational performance allows us to explore how social context is related to the use of different entry and response strategies.

It's surprising that so few studies have examined the relationship between metacommunication or metapragmatics and the social context of play. This is particularly surprising because so much of the research and theory on adult pragmatics and metapragmatics emphasizes the importance of social and cultural context (cf. chapters 1 and 2). Nonetheless, some studies of play have indirectly suggested that implicit metapragmatics are more successful than explicit in accomplishing play entry. In one of the earliest studies of play entry, Phillips, Shenker, and Revitz (1951) observed that the most successful entry strategy for children is to first determine the frame of reference of the playing children, and then to demonstrate that they share this frame of reference. More recent studies like that of Putallaz and Wasserman (1990) also found that children are more successful when they begin by attempting to share the frame of reference of the already playing group. Nonverbal and implicit strategies are more successful, because they tend to be those that share the frame of reference of the playing children. Only after the child has successfully joined the group can they risk more direct, more explicit strategies, in an attempt to influence the group's emerging play frame (Putallaz & Wasserman, 1990).

Goncu and Kessel (1984, 1988) identified play entry as one of the interactional sequences in which metacommunication plays a significant role. Goncu (1987) observed that direct entry attempts tended to fail, often being rejected explicitly, whereas indirect entry attempts were more often successful. Both Goncu (in press) and Corsaro (1979a) noted that this parallels adult group entry in large unstructured social settings, like parties; they hypothesized that children's play entry socializes children into the etiquette of the adult social world.

Corsaro (1979a) compared the preschool classroom to Goffman's (1961) *multi-focused party*, at which the participants feel a need to circulate from one group to another. When people at a cocktail party find themselves alone, they also try to gain access to one of the ongoing conversations.

Similarly, Corsaro (1979a, 1985) found that children preferred indirect, nonverbal strategies, even though the direct verbal strategies were as successful. Two of the most successful strategies were direct: *request for access* (48% success) and *questioning participants* about their activity (52% success). Two equally successful strategies were indirect: *greetings* (58% success) and *reference to affiliation* (50% success). These four strategies, among the most successful, were also the most similar to adult entry attempts. Nonverbal attempts were the largest single category used (34%) even though they were successful only 16% of the time. Corsaro found that overall, 65% of entry attempts failed (1979a). Yet children did not show a preference for the strategies that worked better. Also, the older children did not use the more successful strategies any more than the younger children. He concluded that the older children were learning to sequence entry attempts, using the nonverbal ones first.

Several recent studies explored how the popularity of a child affects the type and the success of the entry attempt (Dodge & Schlundt, 1983; Putallaz & Gottman, 1981). Putallaz and Gottman (1981), studying acquainted second- and third-graders, found that unpopular children were less likely to be accepted into the group, and more likely to be ignored, than popular children. However, even popular children were rejected or ignored 26% of the time. Both popular and unpopular children used all eight of the strategies identified by the researchers. Because all children were capable of using all eight strategies, competence with a strategy was not a guarantee of popularity. Among popular children, they found that the use of the eight types correlated with the effectiveness of the type, whereas there was no such correlation for unpopular children. The unpopular children were more likely to try to exert control and divert the group's attention to themselves, rather than trying to integrate themselves with the ongoing conversation of the group; they were more likely to introduce new conversational topics abruptly and to direct the conversation to themselves by making self-statements, stating their feelings and opinions, and disagreeing with the hosts more than the popular children. Although not directly focusing on language, these studies indirectly suggest that implicit metapragmatics will be more successful at gaining play entry.

In addition to these studies of the effect of popularity, several studies have related play entry success and the degree of friendship between the entering and the already playing child. In a study of 35- to 49-month-olds, Howes (1981) actually defined friendship in terms of successful play entry attempts. In a naturalistic study of play entry in preschool, Phinney and Rotherham (1981) also found that invitations to friends were more successful than invitations to acquaintances, and that this relationship was particularly pronounced for nonverbal entries and for invitations to play.

Although not directly examining friendship, Dodge and Schlundt (1983) examined both popularity and increasing familiarity, by bringing together unacquainted children for eight successive play sessions. In the second of two studies, they examined naturally occurring entry attempts. Like Corsaro (1979a), they found that certain sequences of strategies were more successful than others. They found that the strategy selected changed over the eight sessions. As children became more acquainted, they used more high-risk strategies (Dodge & Schlundt, 1983), which are more likely to be explicit than implicit. Like the other studies just cited, children were more successful when they tried to join the existing play frame.

The previously mentioned studies suggest that any analyses of the differential success of strategies between children should take their friendship into account. At the same time, these studies on popularity and friendship do not directly address which strategies will be more successful during play entry, although they suggest that implicit and in-frame strategies are more successful.

The Play Entry Sequence as the Unit of Analysis

No single study has addressed the relationships between play entry sequences and social context. Studies of the conversational structure of play entry sequences have not measured the influence of social context, and studies of play entry and social context (e.g., popularity and friendship) have not examined conversational structure. However, taken together, the studies previously reviewed have implications for studies of metapragmatics in improvisational play. To examine potential relationships between the metapragmatics of play entry sequences and social context, all play entry attempts in the transcribed corpus were identified and coded. The coding scheme was based on the theoretical framework of metapragmatic strategies presented in chapter 2. This framework proposes two dimensions of metapragmatic strategy: explicitness and frame. Because the model hypothesizes that conversational sequences influence the selection of a strategy, both the play entry and the response were considered to be part of the play entry sequence.

A *play entry sequence* was defined to be a pair of successive turns: first, the attempt by a child (the "guest") to join a single child or a group of children in play, and second, the response of the playing child (the "host"). If the guest was rejected and attempted entry again, each attempt-response pair was coded as a distinct play entry sequence. Entry attempts were coded as a *success* or a *failure*, based on whether the guest was accepted in the response, and actually began playing with the host child/children.

If the guest had been playing with this same play group earlier in the day, and this entry was a return to that play group, the entry attempt was coded as a *continuation*. If the host called out to a single child to invite them to join their play, this was coded as a *recruitment*; in this case, the first part of the entry sequence was spoken by the host, rather than the guest.

For each entry sequence, the strategies of the guest and of the host were coded. Strategy was defined as a combination of two metapragmatic variables: the explicitness and the frame of the utterance. For both the guest and the host, explicitness was coded as either *explicit* or *implicit*, and frame was coded as *in frame (IF)* or *out of frame (OF)*.

These two variables resulted in five possible strategies: NONVERBAL, IMPL-OF, IMPL-IF, EXPL-OF, and EXPL-IF:

1. **NONVERBAL**. GUEST: The guest walks up to the existing group without saying anything. HOST: The host(s) accepts the guest into play through physical action, without saying anything. Or, the host(s) ignores the entering child (avoidance of visual gaze, no verbal acknowledgment of the entry attempt).

2. **EXPL-OF** (Explicit, out-of-frame). GUEST: The guest explicitly mentions group entry; and so forth, "Can I play with you?" HOST: The host explicitly mentions play; and so forth, "Come play with us!" (success) or "You can't play with us!" (failure). Note that all explicit utterances, in this context, are *out of frame*, are not enacted as a play character.

3. **IMPL-OF** (Implicit, out-of-frame). The GUEST's or HOST's utterance does not explicitly mention play entry, and the utterance is not spoken in the play frame. Such out-of-frame statements include "Hi Josh!" and "I'm here!" In neither case is play entry explicitly mentioned, and neither utterance is enacted in the play frame.

4. **IMPL-IF** (Implicit, in-frame). The GUEST's or HOST's utterance does not explicitly mention play entry, and the utterance is spoken in the play character's voice. For example, "Hi, Mom, I'm home!"

Note that the fifth possible strategy, **EXPL-IF** (Explicit/In–frame), does not appear in the list. I did not observe this strategy, and in fact, it is difficult to even think of what such an attempt would look like.

In an exploratory analysis of play entry sequences, I did not find any significant relationships with the in-frame/out-of-frame variable. This may be because these children are not yet skilled in using an in-frame entry strategy effectively. Unlike improvisational theater, the children usually do not stand nearby and observe the group before attempting entry; their entry attempt is usually made before they have any knowledge about the current play drama. It seemed that only strong friends could use the implicit and in-frame strategy successfully. I decided to focus the analyses on the explicitness dimension.

I engaged a graduate student assistant to calculate the reliability of the coding scheme. The coder was a graduate student in developmental psychology, experienced at observational coding, but unfamiliar with prior research in this area, and was not aware of the hypotheses of this study. Before training, 20% of the transcript dates were randomly selected to be used for the formal measure of reliability. The coder was then trained on a different 20% of the transcript dates. Out of the 20% of transcripts jointly coded (almost 4,000 utterances), the researcher's and the coder's agreement on what counted as a play entry sequence was 85%. Discrepancies were discarded, and reliability of coding variables was measured only on this 85%. Percentage agreement measures were: *recruitment or not*, 93.9%; *success or failure*, 96%; *continuation or not*, 93.9%. Strategy reliability was measured for guests and hosts combined. With frame no longer being considered, there were three possible strategies: NONVERBAL, IMPLICIT, and EXPLICIT. Intercoder reliability was high: Percentage overlap was 86%, and Cohen's kappa was .75.

Play Entry, Metapragmatics, and Social Context

In this section, I evaluate the statistical significance of the relationships between play entry, metapragmatics, and social context. These analyses demonstrate that many of these relationships are statistically significant. At the same time, one of the reasons that I did an extended observational study was to be able to identify relationships and patterns that may not have shown up in statistical analyses. Thus, I am interested not only in the findings of significance, but in those hypotheses that were inspired by my classroom observations, but that were not statistically significant. I discuss both positive and negative findings in the following.

A total of 221 entry sequences were coded. Of these, five occurred when the play group had briefly moved away from the microphone, so that the strategy could not be determined, although the guest was successful in all of these cases. Unless otherwise noted, the following analyses include 221 entry attempts for measures of success, and 216 sequences for measures of strategy. Fifty were continuations and 23 were recruitments, leaving 150 standard entry sequences. Fifty-five percent of all entry attempts were successful. Seventy-eight percent of continuations were successful, and 57% of recruitments were successful. For the 196 entry attempts that were not recruitments, 54% were successful. For the 150 entry attempts that were neither recruitments nor continuations, 47% were successful.

These success rates are consistent and with prior research, and with my expectations. I expected that continuations would be successful more often than other attempts; in fact, I was a little surprised that they failed 22% of the time.

Recruitments are slightly more successful, but I was also surprised that there was not a more dramatic difference (57% for recruitments, 54% for nonrecruitments), because I expected that a solitary child would be easy to recruit.

Implicit Metapragmatics and Development

Because past research has neglected implicit strategies, the first question must be to what extent children make use of these strategies. If we find that children do use implicit strategies, how often do they use them, as opposed to explicit strategies? I hypothesized that children would use more implicit strategies than explicit, both with entry attempts and responses, and that the use of implicit strategies would increase with age. For all analyses of strategy, I excluded entry attempts and responses that were nonverbal.

My hypothesis was confirmed. Sixth-two percent of the verbal play entry attempts were implicit, 54% of the responses were implicit, and in 47% of the sequences, both attempt and response were implicit (see Table 5.1). Implicit strategies are common in preschool play entry sequences.

I hypothesized that implicit play entry strategies would be more successful than explicit, because these were more similar to the indirect strategies of prior studies, and these prior studies found that indirect strategies were more successful. When I excluded nonverbal entry attempts, and compared the success rates for explicit and implicit entry attempts ($N = 155$), the relationship between entry strategy and success was not significant (Table 5.1).

There was no difference in the success of the verbal play entry strategies. However, the implicitness of the response was related to the success of play entry; $r(127) = .43, p < .01$ (nonverbal entry attempts and response excluded).

TABLE 5.1
Strategies Used by Entering Child, and Success Rates, by Age Rank

Age[a]	Strategies Used		Success Rate	
	Implicit	Explicit	Implicit	Explicit
36–41	8	7	.38	.43
42–47	19	14	.63	.43
48–53	13	13	.62	.54
54–59	27	14	.67	.50
60+	30	10	.33	.60

[a] In 5-month ranks. The oldest child was 62 months old. From the youngest rank to the oldest, the ranks contained 6, 4, 5, 4, and 5 children.

When a host was accepting the guest into the group, the acceptance was more likely to be implicit.

I was surprised that implicitness was not more successful. If I had not done the statistical analysis, I would have been sure that implicit strategies worked better, based on my extended experience in the classroom. This is an example of why quantitative analysis is important: In retrospect, I think that my observational conclusions were influenced by my own theoretical framework. Of course, as with any study, the predictions that are not significant can be just as interesting as those that are. Why wasn't implicitness more successful? Some of the following analyses provide a partial explanation: Implicitness only works in the appropriate social and interactional context.

It seems intuitive that older children should be considered more desirable play partners because they generally have higher status in the classroom. If so, older children should be approached more, and when older children are attempting entry, they should be more successful. Younger children should be approached less, and should be less successful when they attempt entry. I expected that older children would be more desirable play partners, and that age, and relative age (guest age minus host age) would be positively correlated with success. Older children should be more successful overall, and the extent of the age difference should influence the degree of success. If this were the case, then I would have to take age into account before drawing any other conclusions about statistical relationships.

I was surprised to find no significant relationships between success and either speaker age, addressee age, or relative age. Prior research confirms our intuitions that popular children, who it seems would be older, are more successful at entry than unpopular children. Nonetheless, success of entry did not increase with age, and did not increase with relative age. I found an interesting result that could help explain this. There was a strong preference to attempt entry with a same-age peer (Fig. 5.1).

This result is surprising, in light of those studies that found relationships between sociometric status, or popularity, and play entry success, although these studies have all used same-age children. Perhaps we would see a similar inverted-U curve for sociometric status; that is, children might choose play partners of the same status, rather than preferring partners of a higher status.

Because adults are almost always implicit when they attempt to join an ongoing conversation, I hypothesized that older children would be more implicit than younger children. Both strategy selection and acceptance rates are presented by age rank in Table 5.1. The hypothesis was supported: Age was correlated with the implicitness of play entry (when contrasted with explicit + nonverbal), $r(219) = .20, p < .01$, and the implicitness of entry response, $r(219) = .21, p < .01$. I also hypothesized that implicit strategies would be more successful than explicit ones. This hypothesis was not supported: The relationship between the success of an attempt and the strategy used was not significant.

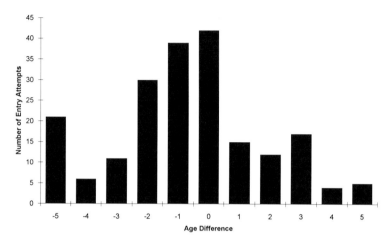

FIG. 5.1. Number of entry attempts for each age difference. The horizontal axis is scaled in ranks of 4 months each. Rank 0 means the guest was either the same age as the host, 1 or 2 months older, or 1 or 2 months younger. Rank 1 means the guest was 3, 4, 5, or 6 months older than the host; Rank -1 means the guest was 3, 4, 5, or 6 months younger than the host.

The Interactional Context of the Play Entry Sequence

In chapter 2, I suggested that each turn in a conversation creates an indexical entailment, a force that acts to influence the subsequent turn. The entailment proposes a change to the structure of the play frame, and the responding child has to decide whether to adopt that proposal into the play frame. The entailment also has an effect on the strategy used in the subsequent turn. A request to join a play group is a metapragmatic act, because it is a proposal regarding the participant structure of the play performance. The entailment being proposed is that the speaker be allowed to join the group.

This model leads to many specific predictions. For example, the use of a strategy in a turn entails the continued use of that strategy, in addition to the specific frame change being proposed. I predicted that implicit entry attempts would receive implicit responses, and explicit entry attempts would receive explicit responses. Another claim I made in chapter 2 was that it would be interactionally more difficult to reject an entailment than to accept an entailment. Because implicitness is easier to use when a child is adopting an entailment, a rejection of the entailment should require a child to be more explicit. In a play entry sequence, I predicted that if a child wanted to reject an implicit attempt, they would respond with a more explicit strategy, and if they wanted to accept an explicit attempt, they would respond with a more implicit response.

The first prediction is that the response strategy will tend to match the entry strategy, whether the response is rejecting or accepting the entry attempt. The use of an implicit strategy should evoke an implicit response, and the use of an explicit strategy should evoke an explicit response. For this analysis, nonverbal entry attempts and nonverbal responses were excluded. The correlation between entry and response strategy was significant, $r(127) = .56, p < .01$. The hypothesis was supported (see Table 5.2).

The second prediction applies to those cases where the response strategy differs from the entry strategy. I predicted that these cases would be influenced by the goal of the responding child, whether to reject or accept the entry attempt. Rejecting an implicit entry attempt should be more explicit than accepting the attempt, and accepting an explicit attempt should be more implicit than rejecting the attempt. There were 28 cases in which the response strategy differed from the entry strategy (see Table 5.2). The correlation was quite high, $r(28) = .92, p < .01$.

Although the numbers are relatively small because three quarters of the responses were the same strategy as the attempt, the results are a striking support of the prediction: Only one of the rejecting responses was more implicit than the attempt, and when the response was more explicit than the attempt, it was always a rejection. When the response strategy differed from the entry strategy, all but 1 of the 28 cases followed the predicted pattern.

Social Context

I analyzed the broad and amorphous notion of "social context" by focusing on specific variables that were significant to the children. These include age, gender, group size, and friendship, as defined in chapter 4. I predicted that there would be relationships between these components of social context and the metapragmatic structure of the play entry sequence.

More than any other aspect of social context, I expected that the strength of the friendship between two children would influence the entry sequence. As in prior studies, I expected to find the friendship index of a dyad to be positively correlated with the success rate of entry of either child to the other. I also wanted to clarify the implications of some of these prior studies by examining whether friendship was associated with a greater use of implicit strategies, in both entry and response. For this analysis, all entry attempts were included (see Table 5.3).

TABLE 5.2
Distribution of Types of Entry Sequences

	Implicit Response		Explicit Response	
Strategy of Entry	Accept	Reject	Accept	Reject
Implicit	41	19	0	19
Explicit	8	1	16	23
Total	0	49	16	42

The correlation between success and the friendship index was significant, $r(221) = .42, p < .01$. This result confirms and extends prior research: The success of entry attempts increased as the strength of the friendship increased. Between the strongest friends, those with a friendship index over 70, entry attempts were 94% successful.

Based on my observations in the classroom, I had a strong feeling that friends would be more implicit and less explicit with both entries and responses. This prediction was consistent with some of the research previously reviewed. I was surprised to find that the correlation between friendship and implicitness of entry attempt was not significant (nonverbal entry attempts excluded, $n = 155$). However, there was a small but significant relationship between friendship and implicitness of response, $r(172) = .24, p < .01$ (nonverbal responses excluded).

In the prior section, we found that the strongest interactional context effect, with a correlation of .92, were the explicit-shift rejections and implicit-shift acceptances. When children accept an implicit entry attempt, they were never explicit; when they reject an explicit entry attempt, on only one occasion were they implicit. The other finding was that the response strategy was the same as the entry strategy in 78% of the sequences. Because of the significance of these findings, I wondered whether these relationships would vary with friendship. I measured the average friendship strength, across all entry sequences in which the attempt and response were both verbal, for the four possible strategy combinations, for both successful and failing entry attempts.

Table 5.4 shows that implicit acceptances were associated with stronger friendships. This is consistent with the previously mentioned finding that friends respond more implicitly. Because we also found that friends are more

TABLE 5.3
Friendship, Success Rate, and Metacommunicative Strategy

Friendship Rank[a]	Success Rate	Entry Strategy	
		Explicit	Implicit
1	.24	19	36
2	.50	12	7
3	.79	5	7
4	.64	11	17
5	.75	4	9
6	.71	4	14
7, 8	.94	3	7

[a] The 100-point Friendship Index was ranked into ten 10-point ranks, Rank 1 containing entry sequences between friends with a friendship index between 0 and 10, Rank 2 between 11 and 20, etc. Rank 7 contained only two entry sequences, so these were collapsed with Rank 8. The highest friendship index was 78.9, in Rank 8.

TABLE 5.4
Average Friendship of Entry Sequences

| | Accepting Response | | Rejecting Response | |
Entry Strategy	Implicit	Explicit	Implicit	Explicit
Implicit	36.2	—	14.3	28.4
Explicit	38.6	28.4	—	15.3

successful, we would expect acceptances to have higher friendships than rejections. This was the case. The numbers for rejections show an interesting pattern. When rejecting an attempt, implicit responses are not associated with greater friendship. In other words, implicitness is associated with friendship only in successful responses. Another interesting finding is that the explicit-shift rejection is associated with the highest average friendship. This is consistent with the concepts of indexical presupposition and entailment presented in chapter 2. Because friendship establishes a presupposition that entry attempts will be accepted, rejecting a friend's entry attempt should be more difficult. In chapter 2, I suggested that implicit strategies are associated with turns that maintain coherence with the indexical entailments of a proposal. The entailing force of a friend attempting entry is relatively strong; thus, denying that entailment requires a more explicit response.

I also expected different entry sequences for approaches to a single child or to a group of children. I hypothesized that a single child would be more likely to accept another child's entry attempt, regardless of other factors like age or friendship, simply to have a play partner. Likewise, if two or more children were already playing together, they might be more likely to reject another child, regardless of age or friendship. Because this seemed like a strong possibility, I wanted to measure this effect to see whether it might conflate any of the other findings. I was surprised to find that this was not the case: The relationship between group size and success was not significant, $r(221) = .07$ (n.s.). I also predicted that children would be more implicit when approaching a single child, because implicit strategies only work in an appropriate discourse context. If approaching larger groups is more difficult, children should switch to an explicit strategy to more strongly project their entry attempt. This hypothesis was not supported: The relationship between group size and entry strategy was not significant. The size of the group being approached has no effect on the likelihood of acceptance, nor on the entry strategy used.

Gender

Because of the many studies suggesting that girls in this age range are more indirect than boys, I predicted that girls would be more implicit and nonverbal in both entry attempts and responses. Recent research has suggested that this difference in speech style begins to emerge during the preschool years (see chapter 4). Although not the same construct, indirectness is closely related to the notion of implicitness used in this study. The relationship between the use of a nonverbal play entry strategy and gender was not significant, nor was that between the use of a nonverbal response and gender. When nonverbal entry attempts and responses were excluded, the play entry attempts of boys were found to be significantly more explicit than girls, $r(127) = .20, p < .05$. The relationship between explicitness of response and gender was not significant; $r(127) = .14$ (n.s.) The correlation for entry strategy results from the fact that boys used more than twice as many explicit strategies as girls (34 to 14 attempts), whereas boys and girls used the implicit strategy in comparable amounts (40 to 39 attempts). Although the numbers for responses were similar, (boys were explicit 40 times to girls' 18 times, boys were implicit 38 times to girls' 31 times), this relationship was not significant. Because the correlations were not high, these results should be viewed as only partial confirmation of this hypothesis. Nonetheless, these results are consistent with prior studies that have found that girls are more likely to be indirect than boys.

Summary

Our improvisational metaphor has led us to some interesting findings related to play entry. The metapragmatic model presented in chapter 2 is supported by many of the findings presented in this chapter, particularly its emphasis on implicit metapragmatics, indexical entailment, and conversational sequence. Children used both implicit and explicit strategies in attempting play entry, and in response to play entry attempts. The use of a particular strategy was associated with the strategy used just before. Thus, future research on metapragmatics during play should be extended to focus on implicit, as well as explicit, strategies, and to take into account the conversational context of an utterance. I also hypothesized that social context would have an effect on the strategies that children used. This hypothesis was partially supported by the relationships identified between strategy and friendship, age, and gender.

My dataset demonstrated a similar play entry success rate to those found in prior studies. For example, Corsaro (1981) found that even among acquainted 3- and 4-year-olds, 53.9% of entry attempts were rejected; in my data, when continuations and recruitments are excluded, play entries were rejected 53% of the time. However, I did observe higher success rates in these two excluded categories: Recruitments were successful 57% of the time, and continuations were successful 78% of the time. These higher success rates aren't surprising: Returning to a group should be easier than entering a group for the first time;

and asking a solitary child to join a group should be accepted more often than the play entry attempt of a solitary child to a group.

Several of the results support a prediction that I made in chapter 2, that interactional sequences influence the strategy selected. For example, the response was likely to be the same strategy as the entry attempt. The entry attempt seems to establish an indexical entailment that the response will use the same strategy. One of the indexical entailments resulting from the use of a strategy would be the projection "we are now talking in this way," whether implicit or explicit. The strong relationship between strategy shifts and acceptance or rejection (correlation = .92) indicates that rejecting indexical entailments required a more explicit response, whereas accepting indexical entailments allowed a more implicit response. This suggests that studies of metapragmatics must incorporate such sequence-level influences. Analysis only at the utterance level is insufficient.

There was some evidence that friendship influenced the selection of a strategy. Friends were more successful at entry, and friends were more implicit with responses. These findings are particularly interesting because none of the literature on peer relations has suggested such a result. In the only prior study of friendship and conversation, Corsaro (1979a, 1985) argued that friendship was used as a way of gaining access and protecting interactive space, and that children maintained friendships to assure themselves of play partners. In other words, friendship is only found in its explicit invocation; Corsaro concluded that friendship would not influence play interaction beyond these explicit invocations. The differences in my data could result from the large contingent of 5-year-olds in my classroom, whereas Corsaro's classrooms were age segregated into either 3- or 4-year-old classrooms. These results suggest that future studies of play entry and of metapragmatics must recognize the influence of friendship.

I predicted that younger children would prefer older children as play partners. Prior research has shown that popular children are more successful at entry than unpopular children, and we might expect older children to receive higher sociometric rankings. Yet there was no statistical support for this prediction. Success of entry did not increase with age, and did not increase with relative age (guest minus host's age). What I found instead was that children tended to approach same-age classmates.

There was partial support for research on gender and conversational interaction that has argued that girls are more indirect than boys. The play entry attempts of girls were more implicit than those of boys; however, there was no difference in the response strategies used by boys and girls. There was not a significant relationship between the use of nonverbal strategies, perhaps the most indirect, and gender. In future studies, the concept of *indirectness* should be more carefully elaborated; this could result in a better understanding of exactly how girls and boys are being socialized to use language differently.

It was interesting to find that implicit entry attempts were not more success-ful, but that children become more implicit with age, both with entry attempts and responses. Although the older children were more implicit, these were relatively weak correlations: .20 for entry attempts, and .21 for responses. Why would children gradually become more implicit if that strategy was not any more successful? One possible interpretation is that implicitness is an index of social maturity, and thus results in increased social status in the classroom. Another possible interpretation of these results is that the older children, rather than simply learning to be implicit, learned how to be implicit in appropriate contexts.

In other words, perhaps children expand their understanding of which contexts implicitness will work in. If it is true that implicitness requires a certain interactional context to be successful, then we might expect children to broaden their understanding of how to use implicitness appropriately with age. Future work should extend this study to kindergarten-age children, because at some point in development, implicitness must rise with age (because adults are almost exclusively implicit); the theoretical framework of chapter 2 suggested that children will become progressively more implicit with age until they achieve the adult norm of being almost exclusively implicit.

Another general finding was that implicitness tended to be used in situations where there was less conflict, greater expectation of success. Responses to friends were more implicit, and responses were more implicit when they were used to accept an entry attempt than when they were rejecting an entry attempt. Children seemed to use explicit strategies when they were doing something difficult or unexpected. This hypothesis was suggested by the concepts of indexical presupposition and entailment pre-sented in chapter 2: When an interactional turn is more coherent with the indexical presuppositions operative, that turn is more easily constructed in an implicit fashion.

There was some evidence of a developmental progression. Older children were more implicit than younger children. It's interesting that there were no corresponding relationships between age and friendship (as reported in chapter 4, older play groups had weaker friendship indices), or age and success. Even though older children were more implicit, they did not become more successful. Perhaps implicitness is an index of age, of maturity, independent of its success. If so, older children might be more implicit partially to reflexively index their social status as older children, and this goal may be more important than the immediate goal of play entry.

In summary, the metaphor of play as improvisation seems to be a useful way of conceptualizing play interaction. The strategies used in play entry sequences have several relationships with the social context of the classroom. The positive correlation between the metapragmatic patterns observed during play entry with the strength of the dyad's friendship demonstrates that these linguistic practices are indicative of such social relationships. It is possible that in addition to being indexical of social relationships, such exchanges play a constitutive role in creating and maintaining the relationship.

6

The Improvisational Exchange: Using Metapragmatic Strategies to Negotiate the Play Frame

Two boys have blocks, which are now "pepper shakers" which shake "poison pepper." When Jennifer's dinosaur becomes a little too threatening, they chant "Pepper, Pepper," and shake at the dinosaur. Jennifer doesn't want her dinosaur to die; she says "Pretend he just sneezes from the pepper, he doesn't die." The boys agree.

—Sawyer (field notes)

In chapter 5, I analyzed metapragmatics during play by looking at play entry sequences, the conversational exchanges used by children to negotiate play entry. My focus on two-turn sequences is similar to that of conversation analysis, which has many specialized terms for the study of conversational sequences, including *adjacency pairs, conditional relevance,* and *pair-parts.* In chapter 5, I combined this conversation-analytic approach with tools from developmental psychology: coding manuals, reliability measures, and statistical analyses. This combination of contextual conversation analysis with coding and statistical analysis is often found in sociocultural psychology. For example, Barbara Rogoff, a proponent of this approach, argues that psychologists should study *contextual events* to better understand how collective action is mediated by language, and how it influences individual behavior (Rogoff, 1982).

In this chapter, I continue to explore metapragmatics in play by focusing on the interactional sequences that children use to collectively improvise social play. These two-turn *improvisational exchanges* are the building blocks of inter-subjectivity, because they are used to collectively create a shared play frame. Improvisational exchanges have a two-turn structure, like the play entry sequences of chapter 5. The first turn is a proposal for a change to the play frame, and the second turn is the response to the proposal. This response may reject or accept the proposal. In many cases, the responding child elaborates on the proposal, or suggests a counter-proposal. The proposal is indexically entailing (see chapter 2) because it proposes that the ensuing play proceed in a certain way. The exchange is metapragmatic because the referent of the proposal is the play frame itself, the pragmatic structure of the interaction.

Several recent studies of children's pretend play have called for a more detailed focus on metacommunication in these proposals (Black & Hazen, 1990; Garvey & Kramer, 1989; Goncu, 1993a; McLoyd et al., 1984b). Although Bateson pointed out the importance of both implicit and explicit metacommunication, most studies of play have been restricted to explicit metacommunication alone. In chapters 2 and 5, I elaborated the metacommunication concept by proposing that the metapragmatic strategy of a child's turn can vary in two ways, from implicit to explicit, and also from in frame to out of frame. Researchers have focused on explicit, out-of-frame proposals like those in Example 6.1:

Example 6.1. Explicit, out-of-frame proposals. Indirect performance style. Jennifer and Muhammed are playing with a duck and a dinosaur in the sand table.

(1)	Jennifer	Pretend her name was Cera, OK?	(referring to the duck)
(2)		OK?	
(3)		Cera!	(enacting as the duck)
(4)	Muhammed	Pretend he was Redhead, OK?	(referring to his dinosaur)
(5)	Jennifer	Redhead!	(enacting as the duck)

Utterances (1) and (4) are both examples of explicit metacommunication. The children explicitly acknowledge the fact that they are pretending. These utterances are out of frame as well, because the children speak as themselves, rather than as their play roles. Both of these utterances indexically entail a role assignment to a toy figure. These role assignments are properties of the play frame. In contrast, utterances (3) and (5) are enacted, and in frame, although neither proposes a new aspect of play. Rather than proposing new indexical entailments, these "enactments" are fully consistent with the indexical presuppositions of the play emergent. Muhammed's turn (4) is both an acceptance of Jennifer's proposal, and an extension of her proposal: He implicitly accepts Jennifer's role assignment of Cera, and extends the play by proposing a role assignment for his own toy figure. Jennifer accepts Muhammed's extension at (5), and her acceptance is both implicit and in frame.

Most studies of explicit metacommunication are based on the assumption that children's play discourse can be separated into two types. The utterances of interest are called *metacommunicative, negotiatory*, or *out of frame*, in contrast to utterances which are *enacted* and *in frame*. This dichotomy assumes that indexical entailments result only from explicit, out-of-frame metapragmatics, and that enacted utterances are completely consistent with the play frame, and are not used to negotiate changes to the frame. The research on adult sociolinguistics discussed in chapters 1 and 2 shows that this is not the case in adult conversation; among adults, the collective negotiation of the structure of an interaction is done implicitly and in frame. One of the unanswered questions of pretend play studies is how a child's enacted talk can have metapragmatic effects.

Chapter 5 explored different strategies that children use when negotiating play group entry. After play entry is accomplished and the children start playing, the two-turn improvisational exchange is the building block of play improvisation. One child proposes a variation, extension, or a completely new feature of the play, and the play partner responds, either accepting the proposal, rejecting it, or accepting it and then extending it with a subsequent proposal. As children use these exchanges to collectively construct an improvised play reality, they experiment with and learn about intersubjectivity. In chapter 5, I showed that the metapragmatics of play entry were related to the social context, and in this chapter, I explore whether the metapragmatic structure of improvisational exchanges is related to the social context of play. If so, children's play interaction can be viewed as functioning on two levels: working to maintain an intersubjectively coherent play frame, while simultaneously working to collectively create a shared peer culture.

Examples of Improvisational Exchanges

Because of my interest in the collective aspects of play improvisations, I focus on the *improvisational exchange*, a conversational sequence between two children. In an improvisational exchange, one child proposes a change to the play frame, and the other child responds to this proposal. The response may propose an entailment of its own. These exchanges are metapragmatic and regulatory, because they are negotiations about how the play improvisation is to proceed. I have not analyzed proposals that were not responded to, because they lack a minimum level of uptake, of intersubjectivity. Like play entry sequences, proposed entailments are the first half of an *adjacency pair*, and as such display properties of *conditional relevance:* The proposal implicitly requires a response from the interlocutor, and that response can be interpreted as being associated with the proposal (Schegloff, 1968). Yet the lack of a response is not as marked as Schegloff noted it is among adults, because children's proposals are frequently ignored.

Responses can be affirmative or negative: The proposed change to the play frame can be either accepted or rejected. Even in the case of rejection, a certain level of intersubjectivity is nonetheless present because a rejection requires interactional uptake. In addition to the basic responses of *accept* and *reject*, I explored two additional response types, those in which the responder chooses to *extend* or *modify* the proposal. An *extension* is an acceptance combined with another proposal, which builds on the original proposal. A *modification* is a rejection but a rejection by way of proposing an alternative to the proposal. Note that both extensions and modifications require an increase in intersubjectivity: An extension indicates more intersubjectivity than an acceptance, and a modification more than a rejection.

Most researchers have defined metacommunication to be explicit, out-of-frame proposals like utterances (1) and (4) of Example 6.1. Example 6.2 contains both a proposal and a response that are implicit and in frame:

Example 6.2. Indirect performance style. Jennifer is enacting a big horse; Jennie is enacting as a zebra. They are playing on a block structure on the floor. They have already established that Jennifer's horse is the mother of Jennie's zebra.

(1)	Jennie	Momma! Help!	(Her toy zebra is on top of the blocks)
(2)		I can't get down!	(High-pitched voice)
(3)		Help!	
(4)		It's too scary!	
(5)	Jennifer	I'm not gonna get you down	(Angry voice.)

Jennie's sequence (1–4) maintains coherence with the prior frame by addressing Jennifer's horse as "Momma," and by using a high-pitched prosody associated with young children, consistent with her established role assignment as the baby. At the same time, by enacting a scared baby zebra, stuck on top of a wall, she is indexically entailing this new situation, and she is implicitly proposing the act of "rescue" for Jennifer. The proposal has two entailments: first, it proposes the baby zebra's emergency situation by enacting it; second, it proposes a rescue action for Jennifer. Jennifer accepts the first proposal (that Jennie is on the wall), but rejects the proposal for her character (that she rescue Jennie). Note that her response is also in frame, although it seems more explicit than Jennie's proposal.

In Example 6.2, Jennie is doubly implicit: Not only is she implicit about the fact that they are pretending, in contrast to the use of the verb *pretend* in Example 6.1, but she is implicit about the content of her proposal. She could have spoken in character, not using the verb *pretend*, and yet been more explicit about the proposal; for example: "Help! I'm stuck on the wall! Come rescue me!" This version does not explicitly acknowledge pretend play, but explicitly denotes the entailed situation and action, "rescue." Children can be more or less explicit about a proposed change to the play, without being explicit about the fact that it is play.

Example 6.3. Corinna, Jennifer, and Kathy are playing in the dollhouse.

(1)   Corinna   I've got an idea.
(2)   Here's a bed   (Hands a block to Jennifer.)
(3)   Jennifer   Here's a bed, but we don't=
(4)   Corinna   =Here's a pillow

Corinna, although not explicitly mentioning play, is explicit about her proposal: The block will be a bed. An explicit mention of play would be, "Let's pretend this is a bed." Note that she also speaks out of frame to make this projection. Jennifer accepts the proposal by repetition, and attempts to elaborate with proposal of her own, but is interrupted by Corinna.

Many researchers' definitions of metacommunication would exclude even the relatively explicit proposals of Example 6.3, because play is not denoted in the utterances, and the children are not clearly speaking out of character. These are examples of how the two metapragmatic dimensions, frame and explicitness, occur in different combinations. In the aforementioned three examples, explicitness seems to coincide with speaking out of frame, and implicitness seems to coincide with speaking in frame. In fact, much research on pretend play has made the assumption that these were coincident dimensions. Based on this prior research, we would expect a strong correlation between these two dimensions. Nonetheless, if they represent different dimensions of metapragmatic strategy, we would expect to find examples of children being explicit while in frame, and implicit while out of frame. I observed many such interactional strategies.

Example 6.4. Explicit, in-frame metapragmatics. Eddy, John, and Sam are playing with animals in the sand table.

(1)   Eddy   And sometimes they would put us in jail.
(2)   John   No they wouldn't

Eddy, speaking in character and in frame, explicitly proposes an event that sometimes happens to their animal characters (although note, he does not explicitly mention play). John's rejection is in frame, if ambiguously in character, and equally explicit.

We also find cases of children speaking implicitly, but out of frame. In Example 6.5, the children do not explicitly mention "pretend" or "play." Yet, it's not entirely accurate to say that they are implicit, either. Fully implicit proposals, like Jennie's in Example 6.2, are rare among children, perhaps because they require a higher degree of intersubjectivity than children this age can manage. Nonetheless, there seem to be degrees of explicitness, even when the proposal is denotationally present in the utterance.

Example 6.5. Implicit, out-of-frame metapragmatics. Jennifer and Kathy are playing with animals in the sand table. Kathy's animal is "Cera," Jennifer's animal is "Littlefoot."

(1)	Jennifer	Littlefoot in the big valley
(2)		And there's
(3)		Know what else?
(4)		um Littlefoot goes to the great beast
(5)	Kathy	OK.

Jennifer speaks using a narrator's, or director's voice, rather than the character's voice. She is implicit about play: She does not explicitly mention play or pretending. At the same time, by using present tense descriptions of states of affairs and of events, Jennifer is relatively implicit about her proposed entailments, more so than Eddy in Example 6.4. She makes no explicit projections onto Kathy. This dialogic voice, which could be called *narratological* or *directorial,* is common in indirect performance style.

When children are more implicit, it is sometimes more difficult for the other children to identify exactly what has been proposed. Implicitness is more ambiguous, and thus more difficult to analyze, than explicitness. In spite of this difficulty, I wanted somehow to explore this intuition that degrees of explicitness were meaningful for the children, that there were different metapragmatic strategies that could be used to propose the same thing. The metapragmatic model of improvisation suggests a terminology and a framework for analyzing these degrees of explicitness. Using the framework of chapter 2, in the following analyses I elaborate the notion of explicitness in terms of the degree of *entailing force* of a proposal. A strongly entailing proposal tends to be more explicit, in the terminology of prior play research, and a weakly entailing proposal tends to be more implicit. The metapragmatic model suggests that these different proposal strategies have different influences on the emergence of the play improvisation.

After summarizing the results that have emerged from prior research on children's metacommunication during play, I define four different levels of explicitness. I also propose four levels of frame, the degree to which the speaker is in the play frame, outside the play frame, or is blending both frames in a dialogic fashion. These two dimensions result in a set of 16 possible metapragmatic strategies that I use to explore how implicit and in-frame talk can be used to negotiate the emerging play frame.

Metapragmatics and Pretend Play

Most of the relevant research in developmental psychology has used Bateson's concept of *metacommunication* rather than Silverstein's notion of *metapragmatics*. In chapter 2, I summarized Bateson's influence on developmental research. These researchers have combined the metacommunication concept with Goffman's conception of play as a framed activity. I argued in chapter 2 that negotiatory discourse about the play frame is more accurately termed *metapragmatic*. It's not really metacommunicative, because the referent is not any other utterance; rather, the referent is the interactional context, the relationships between the speakers, and these aspects of interaction are pragmatic, not denotational. In most cases, developmental studies that use the terminology of metacommunication are actually studies of the metapragmatics of interaction.

Past Studies of Metacommunication During Play

Several recent studies have examined how children coconstruct play using both in-frame and out-of-frame utterances. Giffin (1982, 1984) was one of the first to analyze how metacommunication could be implicit as well as explicit. To do this, she equated implicitness with being in frame, and proposed a continuum of seven different metapragmatic strategies, from fully in frame to fully out of frame. Her definitions of these seven strategies include both descriptions of explicitness and descriptions of the frame spoken from. Using this framework, Giffin argued that children become progressively more implicit during the preschool years. However, the results are difficult to interpret because she did not provide any evidence of intercoder reliability, correlations with other aspects of the play, or measures of construct validity.

Auwarter (1986) also found that children become more in frame with age. He used a two-dimensional coding scheme to analyze transcripts of children's hand-puppet play. This type of play is a genre of indirect performance style, because the children voice as the puppets. Each of Auwarter's two dimensions had three possible values, resulting in nine strategies. The first dimension, *scope of validity*, indicated the frame within which the proposal had to be interpreted. The frame was identified as either (a) everyday reality, (b) the preparatory "backstage" reality of the puppet theater, or (c) the fictional "staged" reality of the play. The second dimension, *speaker identity*, indicated the role that the child voiced. Speaker identity was coded as either (a) the child's true personal identity, (b) an impartial narrator, or directorial identity, or (c) the role identity of the fictional character. These two dimensions are an expansion of the in-frame/out-of-frame continuum. Auwarter found that children became increasingly in frame with age: The most out-of-character, out-of-frame category constituted over 70% of the 3-year-olds' utterances, and dropped under 30%

by age 5. The most in-character, in-frame category constituted under 20% of the 3-year-olds' utterances, and increased to about 40% by age 6, and almost 90% by age 8. The oldest children, ages 7 through 10, engaged almost exclusively in in-frame, in-character metacommunication. These results confirm Giffin's claim that children become increasingly in-frame with age.

Giffin and Auwarter both found that older children are more in frame and more implicit than younger children. In an apparent contrast, other studies have found that older preschool children use more explicit metacommunication than younger children. For example, Fein, Moorin, and Enslein (1982) proposed a five-level developmental progression of play skill. The third level was in-frame play enactment (which they assumed was not metapragmatic), and the fourth level was out-of-frame, explicit metacommunication. In contrast to Giffin, they argued that explicit metacommunication is more advanced than enactment. They identified indirect performance style as the fifth, most advanced level. McLoyd, Thomas, and Warren (1984a) also found that explicitness increased with age. However, this study used a time-segment observational coding methodology rather than analyzing discourse, and examined only explicit metacommunication. Triads in two age categories were randomly selected, 3½ years and 5 years. Through a sequential analysis methodology, they examined the transitions between solitary, dyadic, and triadic play. They found that explicit metacommunication was more frequent among the 5-year-olds, and that it facilitated maintenance, but not initiation, of interactive states. This study suggests that explicit metacommunication is most frequent among older triads. However, because McLoyd et al. did not code for implicit metacommunication, we can't know what percentage of all metacommunications was explicit. It could be that both explicit and implicit metacommunication increased with age, and implicit metacommunications increased at a higher rate.

In another relevant study, Sachs, Goldman, and Chaille (1984) found that the percentage of out-of-frame, or planning utterances, did not change with age. For dyads of 2, 3;6, and 5, about half of play utterances were out of frame, and half were enacted. Like Fein et al. (1982), they did not examine whether the enacted utterances had indexically entailing effects. However, in their conclusion, they observed that the most implicit strategies, *role characteristics*, were used by the most advanced 5-year-olds. Such statements have an indexically entailing effect similar to those of Example 6.2. For example, the utterance "I have a sore throat," spoken to a child who is enacting the "doctor" role, implicitly projects the act of "treatment" onto the addressed child, much the same as an explicit equivalent like "Put a thermometer in my mouth."

Social Context

None of the previously mentioned studies looked for potential relationships between metapragmatics and social context. A few recent studies have examined how metacommunication varies with social context. Studies have focused on gender, sociometric status, and role enactment. For example, McLoyd et al. (1984b) examined metacommunication in 3½- and 5-year-olds, with a focus on the differences in play within four types of role enactment: domestic, occupational, fantastic, and peripheral. They found that only boys engaged in fantastic role enactment. Role enactment in girls was almost exclusively domestic (84% and 95% for the two age groups). Among boys, metacommunication was more frequent in fantasy play than other types of play. As in other studies, only explicit metacommunication was considered. They interpreted these results as suggesting that fantastic play is a more mature form of pretense, because it incorporates more explicit metacommunication. Their analysis noted that fantastic play is less scripted, and suggested that improvisational play is more advanced. Of the three performance styles defined in chapter 4, indirect and collective styles contain more fantasy role enactment than direct style. Thus, their result indirectly suggests that we might find the least explicit metacommunication in direct style.

Doyle and Connolly (1989) analyzed the relationship between metacommunication and social competence. They defined two types of play interaction: *negotiation*, or "out-of-play negotiations with play partners about roles, object properties, and actions" (p. 289); and *enactment* of pretend play episodes. They hypothesized that negotiation and enactment were mutually exclusive, thus implying that indexical presupposition and entailment are never blended in single utterances. Although they acknowledged the existence of implicit metacommunication, note that this scheme assumes that all negotiation is denotationally explicitly and out of frame, and that implicit and in-frame turns cannot be metapragmatic. They found that enactment was related to social competence, and that negotiation skills were invariably practiced during such enactment. They concluded that the developmental benefits of play come from both negotiation and enactment together. They suggested that the most important development during preschool may be the ability to shift easily between negotiation and enactment, rather than skill at either negotiation or enactment. In contrast to Giffin's claim that children become more implicit with age, or other claims that they become more explicit, it could be that older children may use a broader range of metapragmatic strategies, in more appropriate combinations, than younger children.

The Metapragmatics of Improvisational Exchanges

In chapter 2, I proposed a model of improvisation, suggesting that children use metapragmatic strategies to collectively create the play drama. I proposed two dimensions on which interactional turns vary in indexical metapragmatic effects. Like chapter 5's analysis of play entry, the following coding scheme is based on these two dimensions. In chapter 5, each of the two dimensions, explicitness and frame, had two possible values, and the analyses focused on the explicitness dimension. In this chapter's analysis, I've extended both dimensions to contain four possible values. This results in a 2-dimensional 16-cell table that incorporates a broad range of interactional possibilities; both negotiation and enactment, both indexical presupposition and indexical entailment.

I defined an *improvisational exchange* to be two successive interactional turns. In the first, the *proposal*, one child proposes a new element to the play. For example, this could be a new role assignment for a child or toy figure, a new activity for the play, or a new event to be dealt with. In the second turn, the *response*, the play partner responds to the proposal, perhaps elaborating or proposing a counter-proposal. The variables that I coded included *speaker*, *responder*, *proposal strategy* (16 possible values), *response strategy* (16 possible values), and *response type*. I only coded exchanges having to do with the play frame definition. Nonplay discussions were not coded as exchanges. This would exclude, for example, discussions about whose birthday it is today, or what the weather is like outside.

By definition, the improvisational exchange is negotiatory. In the first turn, a child proposes a new indexical entailment for potential addition to the play emergent. This proposal may be in frame or out of frame, enacted or not enacted. By restricting the analysis to proposals with an identifiable response, we know that the proposal was interpreted to be a proposal by the other children, even in those cases where the child was speaking in character or implicitly. I coded the response type as *acceptance, extension, modification*, or *rejection*. In an *acceptance*, the proposal was accepted without modification; in an *extension*, the proposal was accepted, and then extended or elaborated on in the same turn; in a *modification*, the proposal was rejected, but by correcting it or suggesting an alternative; in a *rejection*, the proposal was denied, without an alternative being suggested. If a modification or an extension was also responded to, it was coded as a subsequent improvisational exchange.

Frame

I expanded the frame dimension to include four possible values. This was necessary because *in-frame* has been used in two ways in the literature: (a) to indicate that the child is speaking in character, as the play role, and (b) to indicate that the child's speech presupposes play transformations (see previously mentioned reviews of Auwarter, 1986, and Kane & Furth, 1993). For example, a child may speak out of character and still be referencing play objects and events that only make sense within the play frame. To handle intermediate cases like this, I added two intermediate codes to the two that were used for play entry. Levels 1 and 2 are in character, and Levels 3 and 4 are out of character.

Frame Level 4: Out of Character, Out of Frame.   Out of character, not enacted, and not using any references to play frame transformations. Includes announcements of what is being done: "We're building a rocket."

Frame Level 3: Out of Character, Blended Frame.   Spoken as the child's real self (not enacted), but with some references to in-frame play transformations. Directorial and narrative statements are Level 3. If it was unclear whether the child was in character or not, Level 1 was used. The in-frame play transformations can be of roles, objects, or events. Turns are Level 3 if they include personal pronouns that refer to in-frame characters: "Pretend he killed her." "He" and "her" resolve to established play transformations.

Frame Level 2: In Character, Blended Frame.   Spoken as a play character (enacted), but with some references to out-of-frame, nonplay objects, events, or people. Includes primarily speaking as a play character, but using another child's real name (e.g., "Jennifer, is this our baby?" when Jennifer is the child's name, but only in pretend does she have a baby).

Frame Level 1: In Frame.   Completely in frame. Enacted, referencing only play frame transformations. For example, Jennifer voices as a toy dinosaur, speaking to smaller dinosaurs: "Alright, time to go to sleep, children!" Reflexive role assignments like "I'm the Mom" or "We're sneaking guys" are coded as Level 1.

Explicitness

I reformulated the notion of explicit metacommunication, using the metapragmatic model, as the strength, or directness, of the indexical entailment of a turn. In most cases, this is similar to the notion of explicit metacommunication. However, instead of being defined in terms of the denotational content of the turn, entailing force is defined in terms of the strength of the entailment being projected onto the play partner, and how much freedom or constraint it leaves for the partner. It would be difficult to operationalize denotational implicitness, because by definition, the child is not saying what she is proposing. Such an analysis would depend on unreliable attributions of intention to the children. This difficulty is ameliorated by focusing only on proposals that are responded to, as part of a two-turn improvisational exchange. Note that all proposals, because they are entailments that are responded to, project with some degree of force onto the other children.

This extension was also designed to explore conflicting definitions of meta-communication used in past research. Many researchers, including Giffin (1984) and McLoyd et al. (1984a, 1984b), defined explicitness as the presence of a "play" verb, like "Let's pretend" or "Let's say you're … ." But even when children are implicit about the fact that they are playing, they can be explicit about their proposed entailment (see Table 6.1). The proposal can be explicit even if "play" is not explicit. Other studies have used this broader definition of explicit metacommunication (e.g., Doyle & Connolly, 1989).

Explicitness Level 4: Mentioning the Play Frame. Unlike Levels 1, 2, and 3, the child explicitly references or acknowledges the play frame, the fact that they are pretending. This includes all statements that begin "Let's pretend," "Let's say," "Say that I was," and so forth. Also Level 4 are role assignment requests and statements like "I wanna be the Mom" or "I will be …" (in contrast to "I'm the Mom," which is Level 1). In these cases the verb "to be" is considered a synonym for "to play."

Explicitness Level 3: Performatives. Like Levels 1 and 2, these are implicit about play. Unlike Level 2, they are not continuative. Level 3 entailments are phrased such that the entailed state of affairs was not the case, will not be the case, until after the turn. For example, saying "We're gonna bury him" is Level 3, although "We're burying him" is Level 2. Second-person statements are often Level 3, because they result in a strong entailing force on the responder. Level 3 is as explicit as the child can be without mentioning or acknowledging the play frame. Level 3 includes explicit prompting and commands, where the action being projected is encoded in the verb, as in "Say so-and-so" or "Move him like this"; these can be past, future, or conditional tense. Level 3 includes explicit role assignments to other children, like "You are a princess," toy figure role assignments directed at the other child, like "Here are the good guys" or "This is a road." Discussion about another child's ownership of play objects is Level 3: "Your bed's gonna be over here." Most future tense descriptions of events are Level 3: "The earthquake will be right here." The use of a modal auxiliary "was" or "were" is also coded as Level 3: "This guy was in the tunnel now."

If the proposal clearly addresses the responder, either by naming the responder or as indicated on the transcript, it cannot be Level 1: It must be at least a Level 2 or 3. If continuative, it is level 2; if a noncontinuative projection of a future state of affairs, it is Level 3.

Explicitness Level 2: Continuative Entailments. Like Level 1, these are implicit about play. Unlike Level 1, they make a projection onto the responder. Level 2 statements are usually phrased in a continuative aspect,

TABLE 6.1
Coding Chart for Explicitness

Level	Summary	Role Assignment	Action	Event
1	1st person; role-enacting	I'm mommy.	I'm burying him.	I'm falling into the hole!
2	"We"; continuative; warning, announcement	Hi Mom.	We're burying him.	Look out! Earthquake!
3	"You"; future; command	You're the mommy.	Let's bury that guy.	Next, there was an earthquake.
4	"pretend," "play"	Let's say you're the mom.	Pretend we buried him.	Let's pretend there was…

Level	Traits	Object Transformation	Object Properties	
1	I'm sick.	I'm eating this food.	My guys are orange.	
2	Does baby feel sick?	We need more food.	Orange guys!	
3	You're sick now.	Here's some food.	They're orange.	
4	Let's play you're sick.	Let's pretend this is food.	Pretend they were orange.	

indicating that the projected state of affairs is currently the case, and will continue to be the case. For example, warnings and announcements will be Level 2, if the event is happening now; if the event is going to happen in the future, code Level 3 instead. They are often first-person plural (whereas second-person is usually Level 3). Third person ("it," "he") turns can be Level 2, if they refer to a play object that all children are playing with. A canonical example is the statement "We're burying him now." Another example of a continuative aspect entailment is the *implicit performative nomination*, such as "Hello Princess!" to assign the role of "princess" to the addressee.

Proposals that were phrased as questions were coded Level 2.

Explicitness Level 1: Hints.   The least projecting type, and thus the most implicit. The child does not mention play explicitly, and does not directly project an entailment onto the responder. Instead, the child proposes something about himself or about her objects, with unclear implications for the play partners. These are almost always first-person. This gives the responder maximum freedom of response. These are usually past or present tense. These can be completely implicit about the action, involving some sound effect, which suggests the action. Responses that simply enact the proposal is often Level 1, when not extending its own proposal.

Improvisational Exchanges, Metapragmatics, and Social Context

In the following, I test the statistical significance of some of the potential relationships between metapragmatics and social context. These analyses demonstrate that many of these relationships are statistically significant. At the same time, one of the reasons that I did an extended observational study was to be able to identify relationships and patterns that may not have shown up in statistical analyses. Thus, I am interested not only in the findings of significance, but also in those patterns that were not statistically significant, even though I had observed them in the classroom. I discuss both positive and negative findings in the following.

Thirty percent of the transcript dates were selected for coding. The dates selected had a proportional representation of play locations. A total of 324 proposal routines were identified and coded (see Table 6.2). The total success rate for all 324 proposals (response type of acceptance or extension) was 74%. On the explicitness dimension, 63% of the proposals were the intermediate Levels 2 and 3; only 23% of the proposals were the most explicit type, Level 4. On the frame dimension, 45% of the proposals were Level 1, in frame and in character; only 18% were Level 4, out of frame and out of character.

TABLE 6.2
Number of Proposals in Each of the 16 Possible Metapragmatic Strategies

	1	2	3	4
	(Most In-Frame)			*(Most Out-of-Frame)*
1 (Most explicit)	38	1	5	0
2	71	19	9	3
3	38	24	29	13
4 (Most implicit)	0	0	33	41

Implicit Metapragmatics and Development

Because past research has neglected implicit metapragmatic strategies, my first goal was to find out to what extent children make use of implicit strategies. If we find that children do use implicit strategies, how often do they use them, relative to explicit strategies? Because adults are almost exclusively implicit, I predicted that children would use more implicit strategies than explicit, both with proposals and responses, and that the use of implicit strategies would increase with age.

Because I have proposed two metapragmatic dimensions, in place of the single dimension from *negotiation/metacommunication* to *enactment* used in most previous studies, I also wanted to evaluate the independence of these two dimensions. To the extent that a one-dimensional taxonomy of metapragmatics is accurate, my two dimensions should be correlated. That is, more implicit strategies should be combined with more in-frame strategies.

I addressed both of the previously mentioned predictions with the summary numbers in Table 6.2. A large percentage of the strategies used were the more implicit and more in-frame strategies. Only 41 of the 324 were the most explicit, most out-of frame strategies that have usually been defined to be metacommunicative. As with play entry, these numbers indicate the importance of including both implicit and explicit metapragmatics in studies of pretend play.

The two metapragmatic dimensions were strongly correlated. For proposals, $r(324) = .68, p < .01$; for responses, $r(324) = .68, p < .01$. Stated another way, these correlations mean that explicitness predicts 46% of the variance (R^2) in the frame. These are high correlations, which partially justify combining the two dimensions. At the same time, half of the variance in these dimensions is not explained by the correlation. These findings confirm that there is a basis for using a single metapragmatic dimension, but also suggest that there may be some benefit to distinguishing the dimensions. In the other analyses following, I explore whether these two dimensions are differently related to social and interactional context. If they are, future studies will need to incorporate both dimensions; if their relationships are parallel in many cases, then perhaps a single dimension is sufficient for most analyses.

Note from Table 6.2 that the explicitness level was generally a little higher than the frame level because the distribution is skewed to the lower left. It was more common to be explicit while in frame than it was to be implicit while out of frame. These are cases in which children make an explicit proposal while voicing as their play character. This finding suggests that an in-frame proposal may be less strongly entailing than one out of frame, and this reduction in entailing force on one dimension requires an increase on the other. Then why shouldn't an out-of-frame proposal allow for a more implicit proposal? Perhaps it's just too difficult to construct an implicit utterance when outside the play frame. Implicitness seems to presume an equivalent degree of frame, whereas explicitness does not require being out of frame.

I predicted that implicit proposals would be more successful because the improvisational model claims that implicitness requires a higher degree of coherence with the play frame. If a child is more consistent with the play frame, the proposal should be more likely to be accepted. A proposal was successful when the response was either an acceptance or an extension. The correlation between explicitness and success was not significant. However, I noticed that while the three most implicit levels (1, 2, and 3) succeeded at approximately the same rate, each about 75%, the most explicit strategy was the least successful, about 65%. I examined the correlation for Level 4 versus Levels 1, 2, and 3 combined. This contrast was mildly significant: $r(324) = .13, p < .05$. Recall that Level 4 is the only level at which the play itself is explicitly denoted.

For the same reasons, I predicted that in-frame proposals would be more successful than out-of-frame proposals. This correlation was not significant. Thus, there is very little evidence that success is related to the strategy of the proposal. This finding parallels that of chapter 5, that there was no relationship between implicitness and success of the entry attempt. Although I was surprised by these results, this suggests the inadequacy of a competency model, which posits implicitness being more effective and more developmentally advanced. The use of one or another strategy by a child is not simply an attempt to be more successful.

Because of prior research showing that older children use more affirming responses than younger children (Goncu, 1993a, 1993b), I thought that older children would receive more affirmative responses (acceptance and extension), and give more affirmative responses. I also thought that an increasing percentage of the negative responses would be modifications rather than straight rejections. These predictions were not supported by the analyses. The age of the speaker was not related to the response type. And in fact, responder age was negatively correlated with affirmative responses, $r(324) = -.19, p < .01$. Older children were more likely to reject a proposal. However, the age difference (speaker age minus responder age) was correlated with affirmative responses,

$r(324) = .17, p < .01$. A child was more likely to accept the proposal of an older child.

Prior research presents conflicting suggestions on how strategy use would change with age. Will older children become more implicit or more explicit? Or will they begin to use a more balanced repertoire of strategies? Some research suggests that implicitness would increase, others that explicitness would increase, and others, that the blend of strategies used would increase. I found small, but significant, correlations showing that older children were more explicit and more out of frame. Older children's proposals were more explicit, $r(324) = .13, p < .05$, and more out of frame, $r(324) = .21, p < .01$. Older children's responses were not more or less explicit than younger children's, $r(324) = .09$ (n.s.), but were more in frame, $r(324) = .19, p < .01$. The correlation with frame is higher, and more significant, than the correlation with explicitness, for both proposals and responses. Note that although older children's proposals were more out of frame, their responses were more in frame. This result suggests the importance of studying metapragmatic strategy within discourse context, because age alone cannot explain these changes in strategy usage.

Looking at Figs. 6.1 and 6.2, we see that the older children used more of Level 4, the most explicit strategy, and less of the in-character strategies, Levels 1 and 2. These figures also show that, with age, children use a more even blend of strategies. The oldest children used the most even blend of the four explicitness levels and of the four frame levels. It's also interesting to observe that all strategies are found at all age ranks; even the youngest children are capable of using all four explicitness levels and all four frame levels. If we do identify differences in metapragmatic usage, we must look for explanations other than age.

Interactional Context and Metapragmatic Strategy

In chapter 2, I proposed an improvisational model that claimed that a child's selection of a strategy would be influenced by the preceding flow of the play improvisation. Each turn in an improvisational performance creates an indexical entailment, a force that acts to influence the subsequent turn. This influence should be found at both the denotational and the metapragmatic levels. This general hypothesis leads to many specific predictions. For example, I predicted that implicit proposals would receive implicit responses, and explicit proposals would receive explicit responses. At the metapragmatic level of interaction, the use of a particular strategy entails the continued use of that style or strategy.

For this analysis, nonverbal initiations and responses were excluded. The correlation between proposal explicitness and response explicitness was high, $r(324) = .69, p < .01$. The correlation between proposal frame and response frame was also high, $r(324) = .77, p < .01$. These are high correlations, and explain a large portion of the variance in response strategy.

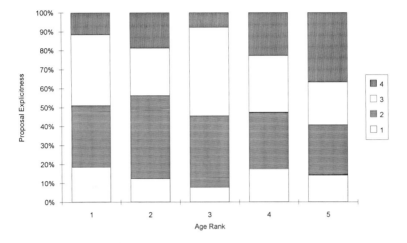

FIG. 6.1. Age of speaker and proposal explicitness.

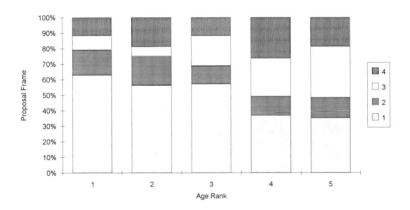

FIG. 6.2. Age of speaker and proposal frame.

The model also makes predictions about those exchanges in which the strategies of the proposal and response are different. Proposals project an entailing force onto the responder. Because of the interactional force created by a proposal, rejecting a proposal should require a more explicit response, and accepting a proposal should allow a more implicit response. For the same reasons, rejecting an in-frame proposal should require a more out-of-frame response, and accepting an out-of-frame proposal should allow a more in-frame response.

To evaluate these hypotheses, I examined the improvisational exchanges in which the response and proposal strategy were different. When all four types of response were included, as shown in Table 6.3, the correlation between the direction of the explicitness strategy shift and the response was significant, $r(100) = .39$, $p < .01$. Because the main effect seemed to be the contrast between acceptances and rejections, I then excluded extensions and modifications. When acceptances were contrasted with rejections, the correlation was high, $r(51) = .76$, $p < .01$.

Strategy shifts along the frame dimension show a similar pattern. When all four types of response were included, the correlation was significant, $r(51) = .39$, $p < .01$. When extensions and modifications were excluded, and acceptances were contrasted directly with rejections, the correlation was high, $r(36) = .66$, $p < .01$.

When the response differed from the proposal strategy, acceptances were almost always more implicit and more in frame, and rejections were almost always more explicit and more out of frame. The lower correlation when extensions and modifications were included were also consistent with the hypothesis: Because extensions are responses that project their own indexical entailments, we would expect these to be more explicit than the acceptances.

Together, the previous findings demonstrate that the majority of the variance in response strategy is predicted by a combination of the proposal strategy and the goal of the responder. These findings are so strong that it may seem unlikely that we would find other significant factors relating to metapragmatic usage. Because so much of the variance in response strategy is explained by these sequence-level effects, small correlations between response strategy and social context take on an increased importance.

Social Context and the Improvisational Exchange

In chapter 4, I described and defined those aspects of social context that were most important to the children. These include age, gender, group size, and friendship. I predicted that there would be relationships between these components of social context and the metapragmatic structure of the improvisational exchange. Of all these variables, I expected friendship to have the strongest relationship with metapragmatics, because it is an aspect of social context that

TABLE 6.3
Response Type and Relation of Response Strategy and Proposal Strategy

Response Shift	Response Type			
	Acceptance	Extension	Modification	Rejection
More explicit	30	20	4	3
More implicit	1	14	4	17
More in frame	18	13	5	3
More out of frame	3	9	5	12

is created and maintained by the children. Because entry success increased with friendship, I also predicted that proposal success would increase with friendship. This was the case: The correlation between friendship and success was significant, $r(324) = .25, p < .01$.

Among friends, I predicted that a stronger friendship would result in more implicit and more in-frame proposals and responses. When I looked at this relationship for all exchanges, including those between friends and nonfriends, the correlation was not significant. However, an exploratory graph of the data showed that although there was no pattern for nonfriends, among friends, implicitness increased as friendship strength increased. I considered children to be *friends* if their friendship index was greater than 20 on the 100-point scale. 275 of the 324 exchanges were between friends. As friendship increased in strength, proposals became more implicit, $r(275) = .22, p < .01$. There was a slightly lower, but still significant, correlation for friendship and implicitness of response, $r(275) = .14, p < .05$.

When I looked more closely at the different degrees of implicitness, there were parallel trends for both proposals and responses. There was almost no effect of friendship on the use of Level 1, the most implicit strategy. The most salient effect of friendship was a decrease in Level 4, and an increase in Level 3 explicitness. This shows the source of the statistical significance: Closer friends used less of the most explicit strategy (Level 4), and more of Level 3. However, I didn't find the increase that I predicted in the other implicit strategies, Levels 1 and 2.

I also predicted that better friends would use more in-frame proposals and responses. As with implicitness, when I included both friends and nonfriends, the correlation was not significant. Although there was no pattern for nonfriends, among friends, better friends were more in frame. As friendship strength increased, proposals became more in frame, $r(275) = .37, p < .01$, and responses became more in frame, $r(275) = .32, p < .01$. When I looked more closely at the specific frame strategies that increased with friendship, I noticed that the better friends used more of the in-character strategies, Levels 1 and 2 of the frame dimension, whereas the out-of-character strategies, Levels 3 and 4, declined as friendship strength increased. The trends were almost identical for both proposals and responses.

Overall, the correlations between strategy and friendship are not very strong. When all exchanges are included, among both friends and nonfriends, there are no significant relationships. Although there are significant correlations with friendship strength when nonfriends are excluded, the high N is partially responsible for the significance level of the rather low correlations.

Because of research and theory suggesting that girls are more indirect than boys, I predicted that girls would tend to be more implicit and more in frame than boys. For example, Sheldon (1992) argued that girls use the play frame more frequently to resolve conflicts, in a double-voicing strategy that entails a

TABLE 6.4
Usage of Explicitness Strategies Among Boys and Girls

Gender	Explicitness			
	1	2	3	4
Boys	24	57	74	18
Girls	20	45	30	56

new proposal while accepting the past proposal (our extensions). This is similar
to McTear's R(I) concept, as applied by Hazen and Black (1989, p. 868; see
discussion in chapter 1).

I analyzed proposal strategies first. Table 6.4 shows that boys and girls used
roughly equal amounts of the most implicit Levels, 1 and 2, so I compared the
usage of Levels 3 and 4. The contrast was significant, $r(178) = .46, p < .01$
(proposal Levels 1 and 2 excluded). Boys used more of Level 3, and girls used
more of Level 4, the most explicit level, in which play or pretend were denoted
in the turn. This seems to imply that girls were more direct, because I defined
explicitness in terms of the directness and strength of the indexical entailment.

I then examined frame of proposal and gender. Table 6.5 shows that the
primary contrast is that boys used more of frame Level 1, whereas girls used
more of Levels 2, 3, and 4. The contrast between Level 1 usage and all other
levels was significant, $r(324) = .23, p < .01$. Boys used the most in-frame
strategy almost twice as often as girls.

After conducting these measures of proposal strategy, I performed the same
analyses for the explicitness and the frame of the response. The results were similar.
For explicitness of response and gender, $r(169) = .29, p < .01$ (response Levels 1
and 2 excluded). For frame of response and gender, $r(319) = .14, p < .05$.

These findings contradict my prediction that girls would be more implicit
and more in frame. Boys were more implicit, and more in-frame. Girls used more
of Level 4 explicitness than any other strategy, more than three times as often
as boys. In contrast, boys used more of Level 3. Both boys and girls used more
of Level 1 frame than any other level; but boys used Level 1 almost twice as
much as girls, and girls used Levels 2, 3, and 4 more than boys.

Summary

These findings provide general support for the theoretical framework presented
in chapter 2, and replicate and extend the patterns I found in play entry. These
analyses of improvisational exchanges demonstrate that most of children's play
negotiation is implicit and within frame, and that these metapragmatic strategies have indexically entailing effects on playmates. In fact, implicit and

TABLE 6.5
Usage of Frame Strategies Among Boys and Girls

Gender	Frame			
	1	2	3	4
Boys	97	19	32	25
Girls	50	25	44	32

in-frame strategies are more successful than the explicit, out-of-frame strategies emphasized in prior studies of metacommunication. These results extend prior studies that distinguished between enactment and negotiation.

The strongest findings were that interactional context had a strong influence on the responder's selection of a metapragmatic strategy. Response strategy was correlated with proposal strategy. In those cases for which the response strategy was different from the proposal strategy, an acceptance tended to be more implicit than the proposal, and more in frame than the proposal. In contrast, rejections tended to be more explicit and more out of frame than the proposal. It may be that all strategies, both explicit and implicit, work only in appropriate contexts of use. Younger children may err on the side of implicitness, perhaps observing that it is more successful in general. As children get older, they may get better at choosing the appropriate metapragmatic strategy, which might be implicit or explicit, in frame or out of frame, depending on the play frame, and on the indexical entailments of the prior turn. In future research, the notions of indexical presupposition and entailment need further elaboration and operationalization, so that relationships between interactional context and metapragmatic strategy can be clarified and elaborated.

As with chapter 5's analysis of play entry, we found that the selection and success of a metapragmatic strategy varies with friendship, age, and gender. This is evidence that social context is both indexed and constituted by the metapragmatic level of interaction. Children use different discursive practices within different relationship contexts.

Most of the social context variables that were related to play entry strategies were also related to the metapragmatics of the improvisational exchange. As with play entry, the success rate of proposals increased with the strength of the friendship. Accepting a partner's proposal is indicative of friendship, and is also a constitutive practice: Responding positively increases the desire to play with each other, and increases the likelihood of future play with that partner.

Unlike with play entry, I found relationships between friendship and metapragmatic strategy. As friendship strength increased, the metapragmatic strategy changed, for both proposals and responses. Better friends were more implicit and more in frame. Because so much of the variance in strategy is predicted by the strategy of the prior turn, and the response type, these small but significant correlations take on greater importance. These results suggest that in future studies of metapragmatics, social context, including friendship in particular, must be considered.

Many prior studies suggested that gender would be related to metapragmatic usage. These studies suggest that girls will be more implicit and more in-frame than boys. Although I did find this relationship in opening routines, this was not the case with improvisational exchanges. In contrast, I found that boys were more in-frame, and more implicit. With both proposals and responses, girls are more explicit than boys, and are out of frame more frequently than boys. This suggests that in future research on gender and speech styles, the notion of *indirectness* needs further elaboration and clarification.

I also found that the most explicit proposals, Level 4, were the least successful. Recall that in chapter 5, implicit openings were not significantly more successful than explicit openings. Nonetheless, this result is particularly interesting, given the exclusive focus in prior research on explicit, out-of-frame metapragmatics. I also expected older children to be more implicit and more in frame. This was not the case; older children were less in frame, and less implicit. Although older children's proposals were not more successful, the age difference between the speaker and responder was correlated with success.

Our study of the improvisation exchange demonstrates that play improvisations are fundamentally collective social creations, and that the strategies used to negotiate the flow of the improvisation are affected by social context and by peer relationships. Supporting the improvisational model of chapter 2, we found that the strategy a child uses is strongly related to the strategy used by the other children just before. These effects are found at the metapragmatic, negotiatory level of interaction. I have interpreted these interactional effects using a concept introduced in chapter 2, *indexical entailment*, a force that a proposal projects onto the other children. To be effective, children must select a strategy that maintains coherence with the play frame, while simultaneously incorporating their interactional goals, whether to reject or accept a play transformation. These findings suggest that studies of play improvisations cannot be limited to single utterances, nor to individual children. Metapragmatics must be studied by focusing on collective social processes.

7

The Performance of Play: Children's Group Improvisations

A scene is almost never about what the players think it's going to be about. Once underway, the actors follow the scene along, but they shouldn't try to control it. The scene is the result of the relationship between the characters, and the relationship grows from those explored moments.
— Charna Halpern, Del Close, and Kim Johnson (1994, pp. 73–79)

The emergent when it appears is always found to follow from the past, but before it appears, it does not, by definition, follow from the past.
— George Herbert Mead (1932, p. 2)

When I first visited Mrs. Winston's classroom, it seemed like pure chaos. After a few weeks, however, I became more comfortable with the children. Rather than 24 undifferentiated youngsters, I began to see faces, personalities, and quirks. I began to notice individual preferences for toys, play activities, and other children. The chaos did not diminish, but I began to enjoy the ebb and flow of play activity, the way it started out slowly, gradually rising in intensity to a peak, quieting and later intensifying. I was reminded of a passage from Gadamer's writings: "We find talk about the play of light, the play of the waves.... In each case what is intended is the to-and-fro movement which is not tied to any goal which would bring it to an end" (Gadamer, 1975, p. 93; recall the epigraph to the Introduction). Occasionally, after an intense peak of noisy activity, a sudden silence would be fraught with the tension of knowing that it would shortly be broken again.

Because of my own experiences as a performing musician, I kept thinking of musical metaphors. I thought of the Javanese Gamelan orchestra, in which approximately 20 xylophone-like instruments each play a different cyclic pattern. The cycles peak at different times, and the combination of many different overlapping cycles results in an ebb and flow of musical peaks and valleys. Another metaphor that came to mind was free jazz, which aficionados call the ultimate form of improvisation. In free jazz, performances are not based on known songs; unlike mainstream jazz, the musicians do not start with a melody and chord structure. Instead, the musicians wait for inspiration before playing whatever comes to mind, in whatever key; or they may wait for another musician to play first, and then use that as inspiration. The interaction between the musicians in a free jazz performance results in an ebb and flow, which is similar to Gadamer's play.

These musical metaphors helped me to embrace the chaos, the apparent cacophony of children's voices, and guided my analyses of the messy, complex nature of classroom play. In the last two chapters, I've analyzed pretend play by focusing closely on specific interactional sequences. In this chapter I build on these analyses of two-turn improvisational exchanges, and begin to examine the broader patterns of preschool play. When play becomes more sophisticated, the proposals, elaborations, and counter-proposals begin to follow one another, and the children begin to create extended coherent sequences that take on the characteristics of improvisational performances.

These musical metaphors suggest that children's play can be thought of as having multiple voices, motifs, or themes, simultaneously active and performed in parallel. I noticed play motifs running through play episodes, through each day's play session, and through the entire year. These motifs provide a pool of shared play themes that each play group can draw on and use to create their emergent play frame. These shared play themes reminded me of the "peer culture" of Corsaro's classroom (1985); they are created by and for the children, and are unique to each classroom.

In an improvisational theater performance, different motifs and themes are constantly suggested by the performers. Performers need to keep these motifs active in memory. Making connections among motifs is a highly valued skill, and audiences often applaud at a skillful weaving together of two or more motifs. A famous Chicago improv group, the ImprovOlympic, uses the "cocktail party" game to teach actors this skill. Eight actors are grouped into four pairs, and told they are couples at a cocktail party. Each couple is given a number. The scene begins with all four pairs engaged in simultaneous, parallel conversations. Every few seconds, the director calls out the number for one of the couples, and that couple begins to speak slightly louder so that the audience hears their conversation above the other three. When a new number is called out, this couple lowers their speech to a normal volume, and the new couple begins to speak louder. No matter how different the four topics are at the beginning, they always connect by the end of the game, often in unexpected ways. The director, Del Close, compared this game to the poles of a teepee: "At the bottom, the poles are far apart, but as they progress upward, they get closer together, until they finally connect at the top" (Halpern et al., 1994, p. 95).

The connections made during the cocktail party game should not seem unusual. We all recognize this as typical of good conversations. During a conversation, the ability to make these links is typical of good conversationalists; during a long-term relationship, making connections over time and over multiple encounters is associated with good friends. This is a fundamentally interactional skill that children must learn before they can participate effectively in social and conversational life. How do children's voices come together, join in unison, and separate again? What happens when two or more children, each with their own play voice, meet to play together? How do they negotiate the harmonizing of their voices? In this chapter, I draw on data from transcripts and field notes to identify broad patterns in children's improvisations. These analyses will set the stage for the theoretical discussion of chapter 8, in which I present a developmental model for these skills, drawing on Bakhtin's concepts of *voice* and *heteroglossia*. Younger children are not as accomplished at achieving a harmony of voices, and their voices frequently continue without successfully harmonizing. Many of the transcripts analyzed below were performed by the oldest children, the 5-year-olds.

A Typical Day

I began my taping on a Monday in January. I had decided to spend that week in the doll corner. I had already hidden the microphone and tape recorder early Monday morning. On Wednesday, my third day of taping, three girls were already playing when I turned on the tape recorder. They were taking care of baby dolls. In the first 17 lines of my transcript, Kathy is talking on the toy phone. She hangs up, and at line (18) announces that she is leaving:

Example 7.1. Kathy, Jennifer, and Rachel are playing in the doll corner.

(18)	Kathy	Alright, I'm a lawyer, I'll help you.	
(19)		Bye bye.	(Hangs up the phone.)
(20)		Gotta get my coat!	
(21)		Where's my coat?	
(22)		Put my coat on.	
(23)		I don't have any hood.	
(24)	Jennifer	Where are you going?	
(25)	Kathy	I'm going to somebody's house that=	
(26)		It's very dangerous.	

(27)		And do what happens?
(28)		There's a robber stealing I'm=
(29)		only lawyer.
(30)	Jennifer	What about your baby?
(31)		She's naked!
(32)	Rachel	(loud scream of laughter)
(33)	Kathy	My baby?
(34)		Well you guys,
(35)		You guys dress her,
(36)		and, and put her in,
(37)		this nice bed, cause that's my bed.
(38)	Jennifer	OK.
(39)	Rachel	Alright!
(40)		Kathy leaves the room.
(41)	Jennifer	Let's start dressing her!

This in-frame play departure was surprisingly common. Rather than simply leaving the play group, a child would often create a reason for their departure that made sense within the play frame. I noticed that when a child leaves in this fashion they are often going to the bathroom, soon to return to the play group. Kathy is back again by (51), when she walks in and announces "I'm home!" She then makes the sound of a phone ringing, and answers the phone, talking again about "catching the robber." While she's on the phone, she participates peripherally in Jennifer and Rachel's play with the baby dolls. At (115), Kathy tells Rachel that Yung-soo is on the phone, and wants to talk to her. Rachel takes the phone briefly for a conversation with Yung-soo, before returning to her doll.

At (145), Example 7.1 continues as the girls debate the next major play transformation, with three different new themes in play:

(145)	Kathy	Ring Ring!
(146)	Jennifer	It's time for my babies to go sleepy-bye!
(147)	Kathy	Hello?
(148)		Who are you?
(149)	Rachel	Time for dinner, everyone!
(150)	Kathy	You guys! (An exasperated tone.)
(151)		I'm on the=
(152)	Rachel	=Hang up that dumb phone.
(153)		Somebody's here.

Just after this, John jumps into the doll corner and scares them, and then runs out again. John and Matt return, with John speaking in a deep "bad guy" voice, saying "I need the ruby slippers," a pair of red plastic high-heeled shoes kept in the doll corner. The teachers always noticed whenever a group of boys went into the doll corner. By (185), Miss Benson has noticed a potential conflict brewing, and takes John and Matt back to the block area. After this, the girls move through several different play ideas:

(190)	Jennifer	John almost gonna kill us	
(191)	Kathy	Alright. Bye bye.	
(192)	Jennifer	They're gonna destroy us.	
(193)	Kathy	Now.	
(194)		Yung-soo called.	
(195)		and I, I, I said she could []	
(196)	Jennifer	OK, ring ring ring	(unenthusiastic.)
(197)	Kathy	You're gonna keep quiet.	
(198)		Allright.	
(199)	Jennifer	Who is it?	
(200)	Kathy	John!	(Scared tone)
(201)	Rachel	John!	(Also scared)
(202)	Jennifer	(3)It's dinner time!	(Gets a tablecloth, puts it on table.)
(203)	Rachel	Oh! Already?	
(204)	Kathy	I gotta cook dinner.	
(205)	Rachel	No. Now, don't cook too fast.	
(206)	Jennifer	Alright, I'll cook Rachel.	
(207)		Don't worry.	

Kathy seems to want to continue talking on the phone. She tries to weave in John's recent teasing, and Jennifer's continuation of the danger theme in (190), by announcing that John is on the phone. At (201), Rachel seems to be agreeing with Kathy's proposal; and then, Jennifer reactivates Rachel's dinner-time proposal from (149). It's almost as if Kathy and Jennifer are competing for Rachel's agreement. Jennifer chooses to re-introduce Rachel's dinner proposal, rather than accept Kathy's phone game. Rachel, in (203) and (205), seems like she doesn't want it to be dinner time yet. She may be wary that she will lose control of a theme that she introduced. Yet Jennifer's move works: Rachel has dropped the phone game. Kathy gives up the phone game, and Kathy and Jennifer compete over who gets to cook the dinner.

At (237), Yung-soo arrives. She is a frequent play partner with Kathy and Rachel, although not so much with Jennifer. Just after Yung-soo's arrival, Karl joins the play group. Their two entry attempts, both in the following segment, are quite different.

(237)	Yung-soo	OK, I'm here!	(She says as she enters the room.)
(238)	Rachel	Oh, hello, Yung-soo!	

(239) Kathy   You were calling us!
(240) Yung-soo   I forgot that []
(241) Kathy   Yung-soo, you were calling us!
(242)   You were calling Rachel and me.
(243)   You said []
(244) Yung-soo   []
(245) Kathy   You just made it, Yung-soo!
(246)   Of nine o'clock.
(247) Karl   Can I play with you?   (He enters the room.)
(248) Jennifer   OK?
(249) Rachel   Kathy, can he play with us?
(250) Kathy   OK.
(251) Karl   What could I be?
(252) Jennifer   You could be the (2) father
(253) Karl   I wanna be the kitty cat
(254)   Please?
(255) Kathy   Alright
(256) Rachel   OK
(257) Jennifer   I was thinking of that cat, OK?
(258) Rachel   Kitty cat!
(259)   Get back in your house!
(260)   Go! Go! Get back in your house!
(261) Kathy   Shoo Shoo! Get in there.
(262)   (Matt comes into the room.)
(263) Rachel   Stop it Matt!
(264)   (3) Get back in your house!
(265)   Shoo! Shoo!
(266)   (2) Shoo!
(267)   (4) Shoo!
(268) Jennifer   Maybe he wants some water.
(269) Rachel   (3) No.

Yung-soo's implicit bid for entry is accepted immediately; Kathy's acceptance is within-frame, referencing the earlier "phone" game, when Yung-soo was on the other end of the line. In contrast, Karl makes an explicit bid for entry, and the girls all have to agree to his entry, before assigning him the "kitty cat" role. They immediately place him in a subordinate status, by commanding him into his "house," or cage. When Matt tries to enter the room at (262), Rachel uses this same "kitty cat" frame to reject him: "Get back in your house!" Jennifer seems more willing to allow Matt to join the play. She counters Rachel by speaking within frame, and relatively implicitly, at (268), but Rachel rejects this proposal.

Soon the girls return to the dinner theme. Interestingly, it is now Kathy who re-introduces this theme, even though she was the last of the three to join this frame:

(284)	Kathy	I think dinner's almost ready!
(285)	Rachel	Dinner's ready!
(286)	Kathy	I cooked the dinner.
(287)	Rachel	Dinner's ready.
(288)	Kathy	No it's not. Not yet!
(289)		I have to put a bit of eggs
(290)		(Jennifer is tickling Karl)
(291)	Karl	(laughing)
(292)	Kathy	It's ready!
(293)		It's ready!
(294)		Everybody sit down, it's ready!
(295)	Jennifer	We [not] giving my poor babies!
(296)	Kathy	Jennifer, come on
(297)		(3) Jennifer
(298)		(3) I'll save you some [tea]
(299)	Jennifer	OK
(300)		But what about dinner for my baby?
(301)	Kathy	I got dinner!
(302)	Jennifer	Two babies!
(303)	Kathy	All right.
(304)		Sit down.

Just as they're sitting down, Muhammed and Matt enter at (311), growling like monsters. Yung-soo says, "We're not playing monster game! We're playing dinner!" They continue to play the dinner game through line (460). The rest of the dinner game involves many creative proposals: eating five desserts, serving stew, getting forks and knives. At (388), Karl, performing the kitty cat role, begins to lick "ice cream" from one of the bowls on the table. He is disciplined appropriately. At (396), Kathy announces that she has to lock the doors, to keep out turtles, then to keep out frogs.

Rachel reintroduces the bedtime theme at (460). Recall that this had been first proposed by Jennifer, at line (146). The other children accept the bedtime theme immediately. They argue about where they will each sleep. Jennifer and Rachel also decide that they have to put their babies to sleep. At (493), Yung-soo and Karl leave the doll corner. Jennifer and Kathy, performing in character, negotiate a plan to satisfy the goal of getting them back:

(498)	Kathy	Kitty cat run away, and Yung-soo!

(499)	Jennifer	You watch this.	
(500)		You watch my babies.	
(501)		You keep the house.	
(502)	Kathy	OK.	
(503)	Jennifer	Don't go away.	
(504)		Kitty cat!	(In distance, as she goes to get them.)
(505)		Kitty cat!	
(506)	Yung-soo	Momma, I'm back!	(She re-enters, alone.)
(507)	Kathy	I'm not momma.	
(508)		Know what?	
(509)		Jennifer's the mom.	
(510)	Yung-soo	What?	
(511)	Kathy	Jennifer's the mom.	
(512)	Yung-soo	Who are you?	
(513)	Kathy	I'm the um,	
(514)		Her um, the []	
(515)			(Jennifer and Karl return, Karl crawling.)
(516)	Jennifer	Get ready for bed!	
(517)	Yung-soo	What momma?	

Note how easily the children blend play character voices and their own voices, the play frame and the social structure of the classroom. At (498), Kathy doesn't say "Karl and Yung-soo left," she says "Kitty cat and Yung-soo." I believe that in this sort of role play, the children's real names serve as the names for their dramatic roles, as well. "Yung-soo" is the play Yung-soo. Also notice how easily Kathy and Jennifer weave into the play frame the goal of getting the two back into the doll corner. They decide that Kathy will stay and watch the babies and the house, while Jennifer goes to retrieve (rescue? find?) them. At (506), Yung-soo re-enters, speaking in a play voice, addressing Kathy as "Mommy." Kathy is relatively explicit in denying this implicit role assignment, but she provides a counter-proposal, that Jennifer is "Momma." This is clever, since Jennifer is out of the room at the time and can't object. Although Yung-soo addresses Jennifer as "Momma" upon her return, there is no uptake; this role assignment is never responded to by Jennifer, and is thus only shared by Kathy and Yung-soo.

Through (717), Kathy tries to get the children to "have a meeting" that she will direct. All of the children sit in a line, in a row of chairs. At (721), Jennifer and Karl leave this group, and they begin to draw on paper together. The meeting idea doesn't last very long, and Kathy proposes a new theme. At line (722), we see the first explicit metacommunication of the day:

| (722) | Kathy | You guys, pretend |

(723)		you guys, I'm the queen
(724)	Yung-soo	OK. And I'm a princess, she is a
(725)		sister of the princess.
(726)	Kathy	Pretend you were a queen, and, and, and
(727)		you were um, father, OK?
(728)	Yung-soo	Why?
(729)	Kathy	Cause, cause I want you to be big.
(730)		Alright?
(731)	Yung-soo	OK.
(732)	Rachel	I am big too!
(733)	Kathy	You are um, three, four.

At (772), Rachel introduces the idea that "somebody's coming!" Yung-soo extends this at (779) with a Christmas theme: "Oh no, he's coming down with the chimney!" But Kathy does not join in. Instead, she initiates a "medicine" theme. Rachel and Yung-soo pretend that they are sick, and Kathy feeds them medicine. After giving them medicine from (785) through (808), Kathy becomes concerned that her role has been misperceived; sometimes mothers give their children medicine, but Kathy does not want to be the mother. She makes an explicit statement: "Pretend I was a doctor now, OK?" Through clean-up time, Kathy applies "ice" to their heads, and then "weighs" them.

This play session shows how play frame relationships tend to mirror the social relations of the classroom. Kathy is older than Rachel and Yung-soo, and the transcripts demonstrate that she is the dominant player of the group. Jennifer is the same age as Kathy, and is an equally talented player. It's not surprising that Yung-soo would address Kathy as "Mommy"; it's a natural role, given her dominance over Yung-soo and Rachel. Although Kathy repeatedly rejects the Mother role, she still wants to be in a superior-status role, and assigns herself the role of doctor, with authority over the "patient" roles of the other girls. Note also that Kathy assigns Jennifer the role of mother, rather than choosing that role for Yung-soo or Rachel; such an assignment might challenge Kathy's dominance over these girls.

The transcript segments of Example 7.1 were taken from a relatively long play session, 59 minutes, with 965 utterances. For all of this time, Kathy and Rachel have been together, forming the core of the group. This is a remarkably stable play group, especially when contrasted with the shorter episodes described in Corsaro's ethnographic studies (1985). Although it's rare for a play group to continue for the entire hour, 20- and 30-minute sessions were very common.

The Polyphony of Play

I have taken the time to walk through an entire day's transcript to demonstrate how complex a play session can be. The operationalizations and statistics of the prior two chapters provide us with valuable data, but the full complexity of play cannot be observed in a two-turn exchange. There is a constant flux in the emergent, a slippage between the children's different perceptions of what is going on. It's almost as if several distinct play frames are active simultaneously, competing for prominence. Each child constantly introduces new ideas, new proposals for what should or could happen next. Many of these proposals are ignored. However, a proposal is sometimes accepted on the second or third repetition. Each repetition provides an opportunity to vary the proposal slightly. In Example 7.1, Kathy repeats her phone call theme, using a different variant each time, in an attempt to get Jennifer and Rachel interested. She finally gets Rachel to join this theme, by suggesting that the bad guy, John, is on the phone; but this is short-lived because Jennifer successfully introduces the dinnertime theme immediately after.

Children sometimes propose new play ideas almost in passing, which are ignored and seem to be forgotten. Yet several minutes later, either the same child, or one of the other children, might reintroduce the same idea. These reintroductions appear in a new context, because the play frame has moved on and transformed. There are several examples of this in Example 7.1. For example, Rachel first proposes the dinnertime theme (149). It remains dormant until reintroduced by Jennifer at (202). Rachel is somewhat hesitant at (203) and (205), perhaps because she senses that the dinnertime theme is leaving her control. Another example is the bedtime theme, first proposed by Jennifer at (146). This theme remains dormant until re-introduced by Rachel at (460).

To use a musical metaphor, these themes can be thought of as *motifs*, with repetition, variation, and embellishment. Jazz musicians refer to such themes as *riffs* or *figures*, which the other musicians may respond to immediately, but may also respond to further along in the performance. Because there are many motifs constantly active during play, the emerging play frame is *polyphonic*, with many voices participating. The dormant motifs form an ephemeral, potential play frame. The intersubjectively agreed upon, denotationally enacted frame is only the tip of the iceberg. Underneath the surface, there is a complex jumble of material that has been mentioned, but has not entered the frame because it has not been accepted by more than one child. These proposals are not yet intersubjective. But they are like seeds that the child plants, in the hopes that they may later grow.

This polyphonic aspect of children's play has parallels in improvisational theater. During an improv performance, the actors attempt to keep the many themes and ideas available preconsciously, so that they can be reintroduced at a dramatically correct moment. Actors have to store this information in the back of the mind, not relying on it too heavily, but keeping it available just below the level of consciousness so that they can pull it out when something in the scene triggers a connection (Halpern et al., 1994). The British director Keith Johnstone also emphasized the importance of these links: "The improviser has to be like a man walking backwards. He sees where he has been, but he pays no attention to the future. His story can take him anywhere, but he must still 'balance' it, and give it shape, by remembering incidents that have been shelved and reincorporating them" (1981, p. 116).

Children probably are not consciously aware of these inactive motifs to the extent that improv actors are. Yet, these motifs must be intersubjective to some degree, or the second mention of a motif could not be made by a different speaker. Even when there is no immediate visible uptake, the other children may be subconsciously registering the proposal, adding it to their own idiosyncratic version of the co-created play world. In groups of three or more children, a motif might be accepted by two of the children but not a third. This occurred in Example 7.1, when Kathy and Yung-soo agree that Jennifer is the Momma, even though Jennifer was out of the room and never picks up on the role assignment.

A motif is often carried by a single child until it becomes part of a play emergent. However, once a motif becomes intersubjective, it is carried by the entire group. The original participants may leave, and the motif may continue with new players. Motifs don't survive very long in isolation; they must stay intersubjective to stay an active part of the emergent. But, more than once, I observed motifs passing among children: For example, Child A begins a motif, Children B and C join, and then A and B leave while C, not the originator of the motif, continues awhile, alone, until D joins him. From D's perspective, C is the originator of the motif, but it actually has its roots in A's initiation.

I defined the group episode to begin when two children begin playing together. However, sometimes the roots of an episode's motifs extend back several minutes before the beginning of the episode, with a single child talking aloud, alone. On the day before Example 7.1 takes place, a Tuesday, my audiotape begins with Kathy alone in the doll corner, talking into the phone. Before any other children arrive, she has voiced many of the themes that she will later propose to the group.

In a larger sense, these motifs extend throughout the school year, because most of what gets played has been played at least once before. These girls have been playing dinnertime and bedtime in the doll corner all year. Each dyad and play group has a history that can be referenced. For example, one day in March, Muhammed said to Matt, "Let's do what we did yesterday!" He was referring to a game in which they dropped toy necklaces behind the toy stove, where I hid my tape recorder. The necklaces piled up on the tape recorder. Muhammed and Matt obviously thought that this might upset the teachers, because they conspiratorially looked through the doorways, but I was sitting 3 feet away and they didn't look at me. A play group collectively and individually has memory, refers to prior events, and makes comments about future events. Muhammed and Matt's game was created by them; no adult taught them the "dropping behind the sink" game. In another example of how friends share play histories, one day Jennifer mentioned a shared play location to Corinna: "We're moving to the plant, The plant we always play in." This was a strategy to get the two away from Kim, who Jennifer no longer wants to play with. But such an explicit discussion of play was unusual.

Many of the children had their own distinctive personal motifs, which they return to on different days and in different play groups. On February 3, John introduced the "robot" theme, which he played again the next day. This was a personal motif, because it was not picked up by anyone else, although John kept bringing it back into the play. It's particularly interesting that John brought this motif into a variety of different play contexts. Motifs can be blended with each other in novel, multiple ways. In the same episode, Jennifer uses the name Cera, which she has used many times with other play groups. This is one of her personal motifs.

When I first began to think of these musical metaphors, I recalled that the anthropologist Claude Levi-Strauss frequently used musical metaphors for culture. For example, much of the terminology and structure of *The Raw and the Cooked* (1969) draws on musical metaphors. Music was also Levi-Strauss's inspiration for the Theban myth chart, in which components of the myth are laid out in a form analogous to a musical score (1955). This made me think of using a new transcription method for conversation. Why couldn't I transcribe each child's voice as if it were a musical voice? I tried an experiment inspired by musical notation: transcribing each child's utterances in a row, horizontally, rather than the usual columnar method. All utterances by a specific child appeared in the same row. I also tried to identify groups and subgroups of children, which would correspond to sections of an orchestra. Sometimes sections play in unison, sometimes not. However, this method failed miserably, because the voices of play are collective and intersubjective. As in Example 7.1, each motif is shared by many children. It did not make sense to collect the utterances of a single child, because the motif, the voices, moved around from speaker to speaker. To be true to the musical metaphor, I would have had to transcribe each motif separately, across speakers. This would have been unwieldy, and not very rigorous either, because the transcription process would have been quite subjective. I am still intrigued by the possibilities for nonlinear transcription methodologies that might capture some of the parallelism, the polyphony, of play.

If only I could have followed every one of the 24 children during the 45-minute play session. Unfortunately, there are five rooms, connected in a circular fashion, and children frequently run around between the rooms. Even with the microphone placed immediately next to a play group, the children often enter and leave the aural space defined by my microphone; it's almost as if this space is a stage, with characters going off-stage and returning. When the children return, they are often playing the same activity as when they left, just like a musical motif returning into a performance.

Each play episode draws on personal, dyad, and group motifs. This is why play has been conceived to be variations on a script, or embellishments of a routine. But the musical metaphors of embellishment and of theme and variations don't do justice to the richness and complexity of improvisational interaction. For example, combining two themes to form a new episode could not be considered an embellishment of either one. A relatively trivial, but typical, example can be seen in line (200) of Example 7.1, when Kathy combines the "phone" theme with the "dangerous bad guys" theme, suggesting that the bad guy John is on the phone. I observed many cases of children blending two different motifs. In Example 7.2, Artie, Eddy, and Muhammed are building spaceships out of blocks in the block area. These structures are made from the largest blocks, and are big enough for the boys to sit on and "ride." They are building their ships, and loading them with food, in preparation for a trip to the moon. On other days, I had noticed both Muhammed and Eddy playing Teenage Mutant Ninja Turtles. Eddy, and later Muhammed, blend the spaceship theme and the ninja theme. Eddy is the first to propose this blend, mentioning the name of one of the TV show's turtle characters, Raphael, at line (105):

Example 7.2. Artie, Muhammed, and Eddy are building spaceships from blocks.

(94)	Artie	We're not going in space yet
(95)		the afternoon
(96)		now pretty soon it'll be nighttime
(97)		Don't go yet!
(98)		We're not in space
(99)	Muhammed	Who knocked my spaceship down?
(100)	Artie	Not time to go in space yet
(101)		We're just getting ready!
(102)		Remember what I said?
(103)	Muhammed	My seatbelt
(104)	Artie	We're not going in space yet
(105)	Eddy	A space Raphael
(106)	Muhammed	For the afternoon
(107)	Artie	Or we'll go in the nighttime
(108)	Muhammed	Or we could go in the afternoon
(109)		and get there at nighttime, right?
(110)	Artie	Right
(111)	Muhammed	That's why I got space food, right?

About 100 utterances later, Muhammed and Artie have "flown to the moon," by moving to the stairs. Eddy is no longer with them, when Muhammed re-introduces the ninja motif:

(225)	Artie	This is just the moon
(226)		We're on the moon!
(227)	Muhammed	This is my belt so I can fly around
(228)		I'm a ninja turtle
(229)		I'm a space ninja turtle
(230)		I'm a space Raphael

Often these motif blendings were centered around a single emotional theme, such as fear of a bad guy. Fein called this type of play organization an *affective template* (1985, 1987), and noted how the script model was particularly inadequate to this sort of play. I observed many instances of the three emotional themes that Corsaro identified, lost–found, danger–rescue, and death–rebirth (1985). The danger–rescue theme was the repeated motif on the Friday of my first week in the doll corner. Kathy is playing again with her usual friends, Yung-soo and Rachel, and Jennie as well. At line (346), Kathy announces in a scary voice: "Santa Claus is coming!" The other girls scream. The only protection is for them all to go to bed. Eventually Santa Claus arrives (483), and the children open presents for just a few utterances before Kathy warns them of the next threat (497): "It's a bunny! Easter rabbit!" All of the girls hide underneath blankets, as Kathy enacts the evil Easter bunny, chanting in a deep voice, "I am the Easter bunny!" At (600), Yung-soo asks, "Now what comes after Easter?" Kathy immediately replies, "Uh oh. Here comes the Halloween people!" All scream and hide once more.

The play emergents improvised by children are polyphonic, multileveled, and constantly changing. Much of what the children propose is never incorporated into any intersubjective play frame. But, when a new episode is successfully established, it tends to have thematic roots that can be identified retrospectively. One must keep Mead's warnings in mind: Just because we can identify these roots doesn't mean the emergence of a particular play theme was predetermined, or predicted, by these roots. The moment-to-moment invocation and embellishment of these multiple motifs is a collective improvisational process.

The Improvisationality of Play

In chapter 6, I analyzed the building blocks of improvisational performances, improvisational exchanges. The improvisational exchange is a two-turn conversational sequence. However, if children were skilled only at two-turn exchanges, their performances would still not look like adult improvisations. A series of unconnected two-turn exchanges doesn't make for a very interesting performance. Adult improvisers continue the same coherent drama for 5 minutes or 30 minutes, depending on the type of performance. Of course, we all know that good conversations, highly unstructured and improvised, can last for hours. The previous examples demonstrate that the children in my class-room engaged in connected, extended improvisations. There are many research questions that require that we examine these extended sequences. What are the effects of social context on these extended performances? Do the perform-ances become more elaborate or more coherent as the children get older?

In the remainder of this chapter, I present detailed analyses of several extended improvisations. In doing so, I am trying to move beyond a statistical focus on small units of analysis, by elaborating the rich, complex relationships between play frames, relationship histories, and individual personalities.

The Poetics of Play

In the improvisational exchanges of chapter 6, I coded each interactional turn on two metapragmatic dimensions. I assumed that a child used a single metapragmatic strategy through all of the utterances of the turn. Generally this was the case. However, in a few interesting cases, a child used different metapragmatic strategies in each utterance of the turn. Example 7.3 is a representative example:

Example 7.3. Jennifer and Corinna are playing with jungle animals in the block area.
(387) Corinna   Now, pretend it was raining, alright?
(388) Jennifer   OK.
(389) Corinna   And pretend the rhinos didn't like water.
(390)   Ooh, water, I hate it.
(391) Jennifer   And pretend the long necks loved water.
(392)   Pretend this one was poking a stone.
(393) Corinna   That one's mine!

Corinna's turn (389–390) contains a pair of utterances, each making the same proposal, but using different metapragmatic strategies. These two utter-ances demonstrate the sort of poetic parallelism that I discussed in chapter 2. (also see Sawyer, 1993). Corinna's first utterance is explicit and out of character. She uses the verb "pretend," and she refers to the toy rhinoceros in the third person. In her second utterance, she shifts in-character, and voices as the rhinoceros, stating the attitude that had been projected on it by the explicit statement of (389). These shifts in metapragmatic strategy, across successive utterances, seem to create an additional entailing force, strengthening the effect of the proposal. This additional interactional force is consistent with Silver-stein's (1984) claim that multiutterance poetic structures are commonly used in adult conversation.

Sometimes the strategy shift is from in-frame to out-of-frame. Here's an example from earlier the same day, while Jennifer was playing with Kathy at the sand table.

Example 7.4. Jennifer and Kathy are playing at the sand table. Jennifer has a duck she calls "Littlefoot."

(225)	Kathy	Pretend there was a earthquake right now.	
(226)		Dum, dum, dum	(Enacting the earthquake)
(227)	Jennifer	Littlefoot! Littlefoot!	
(228)		Are you with your mommy?	
(229)		Littlefoot, are you with your mommy?	
(230)		Pretend the Dad was calling them.	

In (225–226), Kathy shifts from explicitness to implicitness, from an out-of-frame directorial statement to an in-frame enactment. Jennifer responds by voicing as the Daddy toy, calling to his daughter Littlefoot. I think that at (230), Jennifer realized that her performance could be misinterpreted, that she did not specify her entailment clearly enough. For example, Kathy might think that Jennifer were speaking as herself, partially out-of-frame. Or Kathy might think that Jennifer is voicing as an older daughter, or as a superhero coming to the rescue. So Jennifer steps out of character to clarify, shifting to a strongly entailing, explicit strategy. This improvisational exchange combines four different metapragmatic strategies in an intriguing poetic structure:

out-of-frame	strongly entailing	(Kathy)
in-frame	weakly entailing	(Kathy)
in-frame	weakly entailing	(Jennifer)
out-of-frame	strongly entailing	(Jennifer)

Although I noticed these poetic combinations to be more frequent among the oldest children, they were occasionally used by younger children as well.

Example 7.5. Eddy, Matt, and Sam are playing bad guys and good guys in the block area. Although the teachers don't allow pretend guns, the boys often work them into the play when the teachers aren't looking.

(536)	Eddy	There's a gun for you, Sam.
(537)		There's a gun for you, Matt.
(538)		There's a gun for me!
(539)		Now we all have guns!
(540)		Ha ha ha ha!
(541)		Bernie! Oh a bad guy, let's all shoot.
(542)		Killed him.

The poetic structure of Eddy's turn has four components. In (536–538), he proposes that all three boys will have guns, using what I code as Level 3 explicitness. The continuative aspect of (539) indicates a shift to Level 2 explicitness: Eddy has moved to a present-tense statement of current fact. This shift toward implicitness is like Corinna's shift in Example 7.3. In (541), Eddy proposes that all three boys will use their guns to shoot Bernie, moving back to Level 3 to make a second proposal. Then in (542), Eddy shifts to past tense, Level 1 explicitness, to reinforce the entailment. Eddy's turn has the following poetic structure:

Entailment	Explicitness
All have guns	3
(repeat)	2
Shoot Bernie	3
(repeat)	1

These examples suggest a pattern: When a child proposes a new entailment for the first time, he or she shifts to a more explicit, more out-of-frame strategy. Once the entailment has been introduced explicitly, its entailing force can be strengthened by repeating the entailment using a more implicit, more in-frame strategy. Once Eddy has established the entailment that they all have guns, he shifts to a more explicit strategy to make the new proposal that they will shoot Bernie. Although implicitness reinforces the initial explicit proposal, moving too quickly to implicitness may not be effective. We see this in Example 7.4, when Jennifer has to shift from implicit to explicit to effectively project her entailment.

Extended Sequences

Many proposals to change the play frame are accepted, and then elaborated with a follow-on proposal, which I call an *extension*. If this follow-on proposal also receives a response, it becomes the first turn of another improvisational exchange. When play begins to flow smoothly, usually among play partners who are familiar with each other, improvisational exchanges chain together to form extended improvisational sequences. When children want to reject a proposal, they often use a *modification*, a rejection that simultaneously proposes an alternative to the proposal. The use of a modification helps the play performance to continue even in the presence of disagreement.

Example 7.6. Sam and Eddy are playing with jungle animals in the block area. Sam has a lion, Eddy has a giraffe, and there is an elephant nearby on the floor that neither has claimed.

(47) Sam   Come up and fight, Giraffe!
(48) Eddy   Oh, but don't knock me over,
(49)   [I have] put animals in
(50) Sam   I'll be your friend, said the lion.
(51) Eddy   OK.
(52)   Come on in here.
(53) Sam   OK.
(54)   So has the elephant!
(55)   He=was=wants to
(56)   sneak up on
(57) Eddy   Watch me, lion!
(58) Sam   What?
(59) Eddy   I can run [right] fast!
(60) Sam   So can I!
(61)   I won't eat you!
(62) Eddy   OK. Don't eat me!
(63)   Or I'll eat you!
(64) Sam   OK.
(65)   Come up, and=um=fight!
(66) Eddy   OK!

This sequence has a nice poetic structure, beginning and ending with Sam's proposal, "Come up and fight!" with Eddy finally agreeing, after some intervening negotiation. At no point do either of the boys explicitly mention play or pretend. The most explicit statement is the narrative voice of (50), "I'll be your friend, said the lion," but even this is in frame (coded as Level 3 frame). The example begins with Sam, voicing as the lion, challenging Eddy's giraffe to a fight. Eddy protests, and Sam modifies his original proposal, now suggesting that the lion and the giraffe can be friends. Eddy accepts this, and voicing as the giraffe, invites the lion inside his block structure: "Come on in here." At (54–56), Sam proposes a role for the elephant, sneaking up on them, but this theme is lost, because Eddy responds, speaking again as the giraffe, "Watch me lion!" and then, "I can run right fast!" This is an in-frame, Level 1 explicitness proposal. Sam responds in kind, and elaborates at (61), "I won't eat you." This extension is also in-frame and explicitness Level 1. Eddy's acceptance and extension, (62–63), is a threat, "Don't eat me or I'll eat you."

After this segment, Eddy and Sam continue playing. They build and expand cages for their animals. Then they decide they have to find and eat food. Bernie arrives at (192), and the three of them continue playing through the end of the play period, utterance (604), a total of more than 46 minutes.

Example 7.6 is in indirect performance style, with the children voicing as plastic figures. Some of the most interesting extended sequences occurred during indirect performance style, with the animals or toy people that were always available in the classroom.

Example 7.7. Muhammed and John are playing in the block area, with toy people figures and large blocks. John starts out enacting one of his toy people pushing a large block.

(290)	Muhammed	You can't push us
(291)		You're not [as strong]
(292)	John	Yes we are!
(293)		Look at him!
(294)		He's stronger than I am.
(295)		(makes explosion, fighting sounds.)
(296)		I don't know if I can push
		it myself. (He tries with his own hands, this time.)
(297)		Of course I can.
(298)	Muhammed	No you can't bad guy, see?
(299)		Ah hah
(300)	John	But you can push mine!
(301)		I'm telling on you
(302)	Muhammed	Why?
(303)	John	Because, you're
(304)		Your good guys are not being nice to my bad
(305)		They're supposed to not know them,
(306)		that these are bad guys
(307)	Muhammed	Well, they don't know they're bad guys.
(308)	John	Oh, OK, good.
(309)	Muhammed	The bad guys are just wearing a cost=
(310)		=a disguise, right?
(311)	John	Yeah.

This is another wonderful example of how easily the children shift between reality and fantasy, how often they combine different metapragmatic strategies in the same sequence. Muhammed starts out in character, using explicitness Level 2, projecting onto John's toy figure that he's not strong enough to push Muhammed's block. John's response is a modification, at the same explicitness level and also in character. Apparently, John can't make his toy figure push the block, so he tries it himself, stepping out of character at (296). Using his hands rather than his toy, he is successful at moving the block. But at (298), Muhammed responds to John's out-of-character block push with an in-character rejection, addressing John (or John's toy, the ambiguity is not unusual) as the bad guy. John is unhappy with Muhammed's rejection, and threatens to tell the teacher. (John often threatened "I'm telling," and the teachers tended not to take his complaints seriously.) Muhammed doesn't understand what he has done that John could complain about, and asks "Why?" at (302). Although the discussion about "telling" is clearly out of frame, John's explanation, (304–306), is in frame (coded as frame Level 3 and explicitness Level 3), and proposes an elaborate entailment: Muhammed's good guys think that John's bad guys are really good guys, and if they thought so, they would be nice to them. At (307), Muhammed agrees with this entailment, also with Level 3 frame, but with a shift to explicitness Level 2 (a continuative). At (309–310), Muhammed proposes an extension to John's entailment, suggesting that the bad guys are wearing a disguise that makes them appear to be good guys.

This blending of play and reality occurred in almost all of the play groups. The previous example shows these processes in a dyad, Muhammed and John, who are close friends and who play together frequently. Much of this confusion comes from the ambiguous indexical properties of pronouns like *I*, *you*, and *we*. These pronouns are often used in such a way that they can be interpreted to refer either to a play role or to the child's nonplay self. Example 7.8 contains a segment from a long play interaction in the block area:

Example 7.8. Muhammed, Corinna, and Artie are playing with jungle animals in the block area.

(532)	Corinna	Guess what?	
(533)		At the museum, someone is uh robbing us!	
(534)		And they wanta take us to jail!	
(535)	Muhammed	That very bad.	
(536)		How do you know a hippo, is robbing you?	
(537)	Artie	Uh, you saw them?	
(538)	Corinna	Yes, I saw him last night, he was robbing my owner.	
(539)		And I can't get him [drip of] my favorite food,	
(540)		mashed, mashed bugs.	
(541)	Artie	[] to get out of here.	
(542)		The [] took it out	
(543)		And I can get out, BOOM.	
(544)		I blasted open the door.	
(545)	Corinna	Artie, you killed, you, uh	
(546)		got killed, alright?	
(547)	Artie	And, we found him, OK?	
(548)		He wasn't dead, he just in [jail]	
(549)	Corinna	OK.	
(550)	Artie	[] where were you?	(Now they're voicing what they planned.)
(551)	Corinna	I'm in jail.	
(552)	Artie	OK!	
(553)		Boom	

(554)		And here's the bad guys coming in []	
(555)	Corinna	I wanna thank you	(Voicing as character)
(556)	Artie	Let's pretend when you turned around,	
(557)		the bad guys were [] in back of you, OK?	
(558)	Corinna	I love you for saving me!	
(559)	Artie	Let's pretend these guys were in back,	
(560)		all bad guys.	
(561)		Funny!	
(562)	Corinna	And they all tried to fight this guy, pretend that, alright?	
(563)	Artie	No, they all tried, to fight the good guy, OK?	
(564)	Corinna	No, pretend they all tried to fight me, because	
(565)		I am the bad guy.	
(566)	Artie	No you [] good guy.	
(567)	Corinna	[]	
(568)	Artie	Just pretend when you were	
(569)	Corinna	(cries)	(Voicing)
(570)		Boom, boom	
(571)		I kick you!	(The fight starts. Corinna's robot "kicks" Artie.)
(572)		Whoa.	
(573)	Artie	Uh oh.	
(574)	Corinna	Pretend you fixed my um, control	
(575)	Artie	Let's pretend you didn't know about he was behind,	
(576)		AHH!	(knocks over the dinosaurs)
(577)		Like this!	

Upon first reading, this segment seems almost incoherent. Several of the two-turn improvisational exchanges have a local coherence, but they don't necessarily add up to a globally coherent play episode. But these three children act as if they are sharing a play frame. They seem to know what's going on, and to not be confused about the play drama. Upon closer examination, it is possible to reconstruct the elaborate drama that these children are creating. At the beginning of this segment, (533), Corinna introduces a danger, or conflict, theme: "Someone is robbing us, and they wanta take us to jail." The "jail" theme stays active through (551), and after that, Artie introduces his "bad guy attack/fight" theme, which Corinna readily accepts.

At (535), in response to Corinna's proposal, "Someone is robbing us," Muhammed indirectly introduces the extension that it is the hippo who is robbing: "How do you know a hippo, is robbing you?" Artie extends this question at (537), "You saw them?" At (538), Corinna accepts both of these extended proposals. She answers, voicing as an animal, referencing her owner, and her favorite food, mashed bugs. At (541), Artie jumps ahead with the jail theme, enacting as if Corinna is already in jail (although note, she had only proposed "they wanta take us to jail.") This is explicitness Level 1, which is unusual for a new proposal, but it seems to work because it is closely related to Corinna's original proposal at (534). Artie proposes that he rescues Corinna by exploding the door to the jail. Corinna (545) extends this proposal, suggesting that Artie was killed in the explosion. Artie doesn't like the idea of his animal being killed, so he responds with a modification (547): We found him, but he wasn't dead, he was in jail. Corinna agrees, and then the two begin enacting the scene they have just constructed.

Note that even though they have been negotiating the play frame, most of the negotiation was in frame, and was relatively implicit. Artie and Corinna have not used any of the explicit metacommunication that we find described in most of the research on play. They have been using either a narratological voice, or else combining a narratological voice with their play character's voice, in a classically dialogic fashion. Utterances (541) through (548) are dialogic in this sense: Although they are speaking within the play frame, using pronouns that resolve to play frame characters, they combine this voice with a metapragmatic, narratological voice.

At (550), Artie speaks to Corinna's play character, "Where are you?" She answers as they have planned, "I'm in jail." Artie enacts the explosion that will free Corinna's character. But then, Artie introduces a new variant, the bad guys are coming in, not the good guys that would presumably rescue Corinna's character. At (555), Corinna hasn't picked up on this shift. She responds as if Artie's character is rescuing her, saying "I wanna thank you." Artie realizes that Corinna has not understood his implicit, within-frame entailment, so he shifts to a maximally explicit repeat of this proposal, saying "Let's pretend" (556). Corinna accepts this proposal, and extends it with another explicit proposal, at (562). Both Artie and Corinna continue with explicit metapragmatics until (569), when Corinna breaks out from the disagreement with an enacted series of events, a cry, an explosion, and then a kick to Artie's character. Artie elaborates this at (575) with a pair of parallel utterances, like the implicit shift previously described. He first repeats his proposal of (556), and then begins to enact the subsequent fight.

Much of children's play discourse is dialogic. Sometimes children speak in frame, but have non-play goals; other times, they are out of frame and explicit, but with in-frame goals. In chapter 6, I coded these two types of dialogic speech as frame Level 2 and frame Level 3, respectively. When a child proposes an extension, accepting the prior turn's proposal and elaborating with a proposal of their own, this turn is dialogic as well, because it combines two versions of the play frame, two potential interpretations of what is going on (Sheldon, 1992). The following example is a particularly telling case of the double-voicings of play, and the ways that the in-frame play discourse can reflect the social structure of the classroom. In example 7.9, Eddy began to play in the doll corner with Kathy's group of girls. I had never observed Eddy playing with this group before. Normally, Eddy played with Sam and Bernie. At (662), Muhammed and Sam enter the doll corner, and in the discussion about whether they should be allowed to join the play or not, Eddy and Kathy blend the play frame with their non-play goals.

Example 7.9. Kathy, Eddy, and Yung-soo are playing in the doll corner. At (662), Muhammed and Sam enter.

(663)	Kathy	Two strange boys!
(664)	Eddy	No these are good boys!
(665)		[] that guy.
(666)	Sam	I'm a good guy.
(667)	Muhammed	We're bad boys.
(668)	Yung-soo	You're bad.
(669)	Eddy	Uh uh!
(670)		They're good!
(671)		You're good too, Sam.
(672)	Sam	Yeah.
(673)	Kathy	Just Sam!
(674)	Yung-soo	I missed my slippers
(675)	Kathy	Just Sam's good. (She's rejecting Muhammed, more than Sam.)
(676)	Eddy	Yeah.
(677)	Muhammed	[I'm a] good turtle.
(678)		I'm a good guy.
(679)	Kathy	But you have to get out of here if you're,
(680)		if you're playing.
(681)	Muhammed	I'm not playing.
(682)	Eddy	Well you don't have to go [downstairs]
(683)	Kathy	No you have to get out of here.

Kathy responds first to the boys' entry, rejecting both of them as being "strange boys." This is the usual response among the girls in doll corner; when the boys enter, the girls usually treat it as an invasion. But this time, Eddy is playing with them, and these boys are his friends. The debate about whether they are allowed to play or not becomes an in-frame debate about whether they are good boys or bad boys. Sam seems to pick up on this, and claims that they are good boys, whereas Muhammed likes the idea of being bad boys. This could be because Sam is more interested in joining Eddy, his usual play partner, while Muhammed prefers to tease the girls. When Eddy insists that they are good boys, Kathy picks up on the discrepancy between Sam and Muhammed, and proposes a compromise: Only Sam is a good boy, and Muhammed, being a bad boy, will have to leave. When Eddy agrees at (676), Muhammed protests that he is a good guy. He seems to have realized that the in-frame play is really a debate about play entry. Kathy makes a very tricky proposal at (679), "You have to get out of here if you're playing." Because all of the children are playing, and because the purpose of the play entry attempt is to begin playing, this is a logical dilemma for Muhammed. He quickly responds (681) "I'm not playing," which is obviously false. By (690), all of the children have left the doll corner except for Muhammed and Sam; the play entry failed, and Eddy has chosen to continue with the girls.

Summary

The boundary between the play drama and the social world of the classroom is faint indeed. The children shift between these levels so readily, so smoothly, that it's almost as if they don't notice the difference at all. Unlike a theater performance, where the actors are always aware of the *fourth wall*, the boundary between the performed drama and the reality of the stage and audience, the children seem unconcerned with the boundary. All of these levels provide different metapragmatic strategies, which can be used with differential effectiveness, depending on the interactional context and on the interactional goals of the participants.

These examples show how children use metapragmatic strategies and improvisational exchanges to construct extended play improvisations. The previously mentioned examples seem fairly sophisticated, particularly when we analyze children's usage of different metapragmatic strategies, and how they select strategies to fit the conversational context and their interactional goals. Yet these transcripts are entirely typical; for each of the previous examples, there were 10 or 20 others that would have been just as interesting. These same phenomena are found in most preschool classrooms; the teachers told me that they did not find this classroom's play unusual.

8

Improvisation and Development

The view we take is that culture arises in the form of play, that it is played from the very beginning. ... It is through this playing that society expresses its interpretation of life and the world. By this we do not mean that play turns into culture, rather that in its earliest phases culture ... proceeds in the shape and mood of play. In the twin union of play and culture, play is primary.

—Johan Huizinga (1950, p. 46)

Although children's pretend play is sometimes repetitive and scripted, it is frequently improvisational. The preceding chapters explored how children collectively improvise play worlds. During the preschool years, pretend play is primarily collective, with each participating child creatively contributing to the construction of the drama. Because the play drama is collectively created, the meaning of each child's actions is determined and influenced by the subsequent flow of the interaction, and the change proposed by a child may be accepted, rejected, or elaborated by the other children.

The last four chapters presented a range of results with implications for the study of children's play and for the broader study of improvisational phenom-ena. At the broadest level, the results collectively demonstrate the face validity and practical utility of a performance metaphor for social play. Of course, this is not the first attempt to compare play to performance; I reviewed similar approaches in chapter 2. However, these approaches have not noted the uniquely improvisational nature of play performances. Improvisation is a unique type of performance, unlike scripted conventional theater in many respects. More so than scripted theater, in improvisational performance issues of crea-tivity, symbolic interaction, mediated action, intersubjectivity, and indexicality become salient. When play is viewed as a scripted performance, one is left with unsatisfactory structural models of social action, such as frame or script models. The performance metaphor must be elaborated: Children's play is *improvisational* performance.

This study of the improvisationality of play has four primary implications for play research. The first, perhaps most important, is a reevaluation of frame and script metaphors of play. Although suitable for some contexts, these metaphors seem inappropriate to the types of improvisation analyzed in this book. The second is an elaboration of the metacommunication concept by reference to the concepts of pragmatics and metapragmatics. This allowed us to consider dialogic speech, which is enacted in character, yet is still metacommunicative. The third set of issues involves the relationships between play metapragmatics and social context, with implications for research in play ecology and in peer relations. The fourth is the demonstrated importance of discourse sequence in the metapragmatic strategy used by a child. These findings suggest that children's negotiation of the play frame must be studied in interactional context, rather than focusing only on the skill level or developmental stage of a particular child.

Many of the findings of this study demonstrate the utility of a performance metaphor for play. First, recall that in chapter 4 I identified three different performance styles, based on the ways in which the children enacted their dramatic roles. The performance style had significant effects on the play. I found that the performance style, whether direct, indirect, or collective, was strongly correlated with the gender mix and the mean age of the play group. Second, recall that in chapter 6, the frame dimension of metapragmatic strategy was coded as one of four levels. These levels represent two features of a child's turn: the child being in character or out of character as well as the child's speech being in frame or out of frame. I presented evidence that these four strategies were used in different interactional contexts, and were used differently by children of different ages and between dyads of different friendship strengths. These findings emerge from the theoretical framework of play as framed performance.

The analyses presented in chapters 6 and 7 indicate that the metapragmatic level of interaction is constantly present, serving to construct and guide the emergence of the play drama. I have drawn on Silverstein's theory of metapragmatics (chapter 2) to elaborate on prior researchers' focus on explicit, out-of-frame metacommunication. This move from metacommunication to metapragmatics allows a more direct connection with studies of adult conversation. Prior studies of play assumed that metacommunication and enactment were mutually exclusive functions, associated with different utterances. That is, indexically entailing acts occur in exclusively metacommunicative utterances, and enacted utterances are fully determined by the indexical presuppositions of the play emergent. When a study separates explicit, out-of-frame metacommunication, and implicit, in-frame enactment, it is difficult to address these important theoretical questions: (a) How does the shifting blend of indexical presupposition and entailment result in an emergent, intersubjective interaction, and (b) how do children learn to combine the enacted and metapragmatic levels of interaction seamlessly in the same utterance, a skill that is second nature for adults? The analyses of the preceding chapters demonstrate that implicit and in-frame speech serves both enacting and negotiatory functions.

Another finding of this research is that social context has a significant influence on the metapragmatic practices of children. To explore the effects of social context, I focused on friendship, gender, age, and group size. The most striking finding was the influence of friendship on the success and the selection of a metapragmatic strategy, with both play entry sequences and improvisational exchanges. These findings suggest that metapragmatics would be difficult to study in a decontextualized experimental setting. Because the peer culture of the classroom is so intimately wrapped up with the metapragmatic layer of interaction, the researcher must incorporate a deep understanding of this local culture. It may be difficult to draw conclusions about metapragmatics without taking contextual variables into account.

The strongest finding to emerge from these analyses is that the metapragmatic strategy of any single play turn is dependent on its position in the ongoing play discourse. In the two-turn analyses of chapters 5 and 6, I demonstrated that the metapragmatic strategy of a turn was strongly correlated with the strategy of the preceding turn. For play entry sequences, the correlation of response strategy and entry attempt strategy was .56; for improvisational exchanges, the correlation was .69 for explicitness, and .77 for frame. For those exchanges in which the response strategy differed from the proposal strategy, the direction of the strategy shift and the goal of the responding child (to accept or reject the proposal) were strongly related. If the child was accepting the proposal, and the response was not the same strategy as the proposal, it was more implicit than the proposal. If the child was rejecting the proposal, and the response was not the same strategy, it was more explicit than the proposal. For entry sequences, this correlation was .92; for improvisational exchanges, the correlation was .76 for explicitness, and .66 for frame. These high correlations suggest that metapragmatics cannot be fully understood by focusing on the utterance level, because different interactional strategies are used in different discourse contexts. The metapragmatic strategies that a speaker uses in a specific turn are highly dependent on that turn's position in the ongoing flow of discourse.

Perhaps the most robust findings to emerge from this study are the importance of both explicit and implicit, both in-frame and out-of-frame metapragmatic strategies, and the value of models of play that emphasize its fluctuating, creative, contingent nature, rather than its static, imitative nature. The repeated importance of implicit and within-frame strategies in the previous analyses suggests that prior research may have neglected an important aspect of peer play interaction. Future studies should include analyses of both implicit and explicit metapragmatics, and should analyze how these strategies combine in different ways depending on the interactional and social context of the play.

Scripts and Improvisations

Script and frame models are useful ways of analyzing play that is relatively structured, when the children have either a shared relationship history or a peer culture that lets them know in advance what script they will be performing. I call these models structuralist because they focus on one or more of the static, structural characteristics of the play drama. They assume that the emerging play improvisation has a relatively static structure, which is understood in advance by the children. As with other forms of structuralism, they posit a "deep structure," for example, a script, and explain differences across play sessions as variations on this underlying structure.

There is a sense in which children's play is experimentation with social scripts, a way of learning through practice. When children play at putting the baby to bed, there are obvious parallels with their everyday home life. Domestic role play is perhaps the easiest type of play to analyze in this fashion. It's not surprising that much of the script- and frame-based research has focused on what I have referred to as direct performance style play. Most of the play in my classroom wasn't like this; it was instead creative fantasy play, in the performance styles that I called indirect and collective. The themes of this play were generally not taken from the everyday lives of these children. Instead, they seemed to be created out of their past media exposure. These play sessions combined themes from movies, TV, and children's books. There were rescues, fires, explosions, earthquakes, bad guys and good guys, spaceships, and families of animals.

On occasion, the children seemed to be enacting a single narrative from one of these sources. However, it was much more common for them to blend themes, characters, and events from many different narrative sources, to co-create a unique, improvised performance. Seeing these combinations of symbols from popular culture reminded me of Levi-Strauss's comparison of culture to *bricolage*, the French word for what a tinker does when he "knocks together" something. Levi-Strauss used this analogy to emphasize that culture is a combination of bits and pieces, forming a messy jumble. These preschool children were *bricoleurs* (French for "handymen" or "do-it-yourselfers"). They created minicultures in each new performance, by collecting bits and pieces from the adult culture.

Sometimes it's hard to make a distinction between a script, which is being enacted in a new variant, and a completely new improvisation. There is no sharp boundary, no easy way to characterize a given play session as being either "scripted" or "improvised." All social life is partially scripted and partially improvised, partially structured and partially performed. In the *bricolage* of social performance, there are always bits and pieces, some extended, some brief, which seem to be scriptlike.

For example, suppose the children at the sandtable are enacting a scene from *The Land Before Time*. Suppose the play is roughly identical to the movie except that a teenage mutant ninja turtle appears instead of one of the regular characters. The turtle's characteristics are woven into the drama to create a unique performance. Is this still the same script, but with a minor embellishment? Or is it a uniquely new improvisation? These distinctions are difficult to make. It's not very helpful to ask questions like, "How many different scripts have to be invoked before we say play is improvised? How extensive do the embellishments have to be?" Better to attempt to understand both the structured and the improvisational elements of children's play.

The script model proposes that children learn scripts through play. How can script play result in increasingly more intersubjective interaction? For most psychologists, a script is assumed to be a mental model. In this view, interaction is more successful, more coherent, and more intersubjective when the children's distinct mental models become more aligned. The reason that younger children's play has an improvisational, contingent character is because these children haven't learned the scripts well enough. It seems improvisational because they are failing to do the script right. Play is interesting because of how it contributes to the development of script competence.

The script model of development has one of the same weaknesses as the play theories of Piaget, Vygotsky, and Freud. All of them saw the randomness and chaos of social play, and argued that it occurred because children hadn't yet achieved the competence level of some later stage. These are negative views of play, of play as a lack of competence. These models miss the unique positive importance of play in development. The focus on play as improvisation suggests that its wandering, chaotic nature is what makes it so valuable for the children. Play is important because improvisation, fundamental to everyday social interaction, continues on in adult life. Adult conversations, although constrained in many ways by social and cultural factors, are also creative improvisations.

In this study of children's play, I have focused on notions of creativity and improvisation, of contextualization and social environment. I have introduced the metaphor of play as improvisation because I think it captures the contingent, creative aspects of play microgenesis more accurately than structural models. The improvisational metaphor led me to focus on interactional sequences, on indexical presupposition and entailment, and on the emergent, intersubjective nature of play interaction. The findings relating to the indexically entailing effects of interactional strategies provide us with a way to begin thinking about the improvisational aspects of interaction.

These issues are related to the so-called poststructural trend in the social sciences. Rather than a straightforward reproduction of the social structure through imitation, children seem to be active creators of their classroom culture. Other recent research (Corsaro, 1983, 1986, 1992; Corsaro & Rizzo, 1988; Hartup, 1979, 1981; Sawyer, 1993) suggested that children's play may not be a straightforward reproduction of socially appropriate scripts or routines; rather, children seem to creatively embellish these routines, extending them, and by doing so collectively creating a distinctive social world. Goncu (Goncu, 1987, 1993a, 1993b; Goncu & Kessel, 1984, 1988) suggested that the improvisational processes typical of social pretend play are critical in the development of intersubjectivity. Some researchers (Corsaro, 1986; Keenan & Schieffelin, 1976/1983) demonstrated structural and processual parallels between this type of fantasy play and adult conversational structures, suggesting that a creative competence is important in both forms of interaction.

Social life presents adults with a variety of interactional contexts, some more ritualized and structured, and others more improvisational. Yet all of these contexts display elements of both improvisationality and structure (Sawyer, 1996). The collective creation, maintenance, and alteration of culture depends on improvisational processes. Play is important because it is unscripted, because it allows the child to practice improvisation, and the blending of improvisation and structure.

Metapragmatics and Social Development

Many of the findings of this study relate to research in social development. This research includes studies of friendship, gender, and conversational development. Many studies have noted the importance of friendship during this age range (Challman, 1932; Corsaro, 1985; Gottman, 1983; Green, 1933; Howes, 1987a, 1992; Marshall & McCandless, 1957; Parten, 1932). However, these studies have not analyzed metacommunication or metapragmatics. In the most sociolinguistic of these studies, Corsaro (1979a, 1985) suggested that friendship was primarily a tool to be manipulated explicitly to achieve two play goals: play access and the protection of play space. Yet he did not explore how friendship could have these implicit, unstated effects on play.

I found significant relationships between friendship and metapragmatic strategy, for both play entry sequences and for improvisational exchanges. Friends are more implicit and more in-frame, with both proposals and responses. In addition, friends are better at using metapragmatic strategies appropriate to the interactional context. For example, when responding to a play entry attempt by a friend, children were more likely to use the strategy shifts appropriate to their goal, shifting to explicitness to reject, or shifting to implicitness to accept.

The identification of relationships between friendship and metapragmatics suggests how peer relations could contribute to social development. Chapter 1 discussed how peer relations play a unique and important role in the social development of the child, yet prior research has rarely explored the interactional mechanisms that mediate this influence. Although friendship is only one aspect of peer relations, the identification of relationships between friendship and metapragmatic strategy suggests how the improvisational processes of play interaction may mediate the developmental effects of peer relations during the preschool years. Further research should extend this analysis to incorporate other aspects of peer culture, including the breadth of social contacts, the popularity of children, and the interactional histories of each child through the school year.

Some recent research into the sociolinguistics of gender development has suggested that women's talk is more indirect, more polite than male speech (see chapter 4). Sachs (1987), defining indirectness in syntactic terms, as a question, and directness as a statement, found that preschool girls were more indirect than boys. It's unclear how such a definition of indirection would translate into our metapragmatic dimensions. Yet it seems reasonable to hypothesize that implicitness and being in frame are more indirect than explicitness and being out-of-frame. If we make this assumption, the results presented here contain conflicting evidence. Girls were more implicit in their play entry attempts, but boys were more implicit when proposing changes to the play frame. These results suggest that the relationships between indirectness and gender require further elaboration and analysis. Specifically, the notion of indirectness must be elaborated theoretically to incorporate these multiple metapragmatic dimensions. These results confirm Goodwin and Goodwin's (1987) hypothesis that the use of different interactional strategies depends on the context of use, and that future work on the indirectness of conversation must incorporate analyses of conversational context.

My strongest gender-related finding was the influence of performance style. Studies of role playing have concentrated on the content of the roles, rather than the performance style. Role type categories include, for example, domestic, occupational, and fantasy roles (Marshall, 1961; McLoyd, Warren, & Thomas, 1984b; Sanders & Harper, 1976; Singer, 1973). Most of these studies found that boys engage in more fantasy play than girls. By focusing on performance style, rather than role content, I found a somewhat different relationship between gender and performance style. Boys performed collectively, while girls performed directly. The relationship between gender and indirect style was not significant. These results suggest that future studies of role play should analyze both the role content and the performance style.

In addition to these specific findings, studies of social development that incorporate a focus on language should keep in mind the more general findings summarized previously. For example, future studies should include analyses of both implicit and explicit metapragmatics, and should analyze how these strategies combine in different ways depending on the interactional and social context of the play.

These are the immediate implications for the near-term study of children's play. In the remainder of this chapter, I use the improvisational metaphor to discuss how play might contribute to social development. After presenting this developmental trajectory, I close the chapter with a discussion of the broader implications for psychology and other studies of situated interaction, and some suggestions for future work in children's social play.

A Model of Improvisational Socialization

The complex play improvisations in my preschool classroom seemed to repli-cate, in microcosm, the complex relations between the social world and ways of talking found among adults. Sociolinguists have studied many of these relations. Such relationships include the use of different pronouns of address to indicate social relationship (Brown & Gilman, 1960; Errington, 1985), and the use of different styles of talking, often called *registers*, to strategically manipulate social relations (Gumperz, 1982). Although the organization of my classroom isn't as complete and complex as the macrosocial structure, the *processes* of interaction characteristic of adult language use are salient in a classroom of over 20 children. For example, a group's improvisation is sometimes influenced by the improvisations of nearby groups, much like topics can bounce from group to group at a cocktail party. The large number of children in the classroom results in several distinct play groups; the classroom environment has multiple conversational voices active at all times.

Many theories of the relations between language and social context address similar phenomena, including those of Bakhtin, Blumer, Mead, Wertsch, and Vygotsky. Bakhtin's writings on literary theory (Bakhtin, 1981, 1986) have only recently been explored by developmentalists (Wertsch, 1991; Wortham, 1994). Bakhtin's concepts of *heteroglossia*, *voice*, and *speech genre* are useful in presenting a developmental model for how interactional skills may be learned. Bakhtin argued that the social individual participates in a complex, multifaceted linguis-tic world, with many different ways of speaking, or *voices*, which are each indexical of a recognizable social role and status. In such a complex heteroglos-sic social environment, one with many ways of talking available to speakers, each interaction provides the individual with a wide range of strategies for socially locating themselves relative to their interlocutors. Bakhtin's writings focus on how members of the society creatively manipulate these voices for particular interactional effects. These creative processes are remarkably similar to many of the improvisational processes I have identified in children's play discourse.

Children often speak with distinctive speech styles when enacting a play role. These styles can be characterized at several linguistic levels, including prosodic (pitch, tone, rhythmic contour), lexical (distinctive word choices), and pragmatic (stereotypic use of idiomatic speech). For example, a helpless baby may be enacted with a high-pitched, plaintive tone; an evil monster with a deep, slowly enunciated tone (recall the examples of chapters 6 and 7). Several of Bakhtin's concepts are useful in understanding how children employ different ways of talking to enact play roles. Bakhtin took a linguistic, rhetorical approach to concepts of *style* and *genre* in literature, and his important essay, "Discourse in the Novel" (1981) is directed toward the then current (1934) debate over the novel's prose style. Bakhtin argued that the novel was a unique development in literature because it could not be characterized by any single style, or defined as a traditional genre. Rather, the novel was best viewed as a forum in which the author could experiment with combinations of different genres and styles. He located each style in an individual character, and referred to that character's manner of speaking and relating to others as a *voice*. In the novel, these voices blend and merge in a single text: "The novel as a whole is a phenomenon multiform in style and variform in speech and voice. In it the investigator is confronted with several heterogeneous stylistic unities, often located on different linguistic levels and subject to different stylistic controls" (p. 261). Bakhtin termed this distinguishing characteristic of the novel *heteroglossia*, defining the novel by the presence of multiple voices: "The novel can be defined as a diversity of social speech types and a diversity of individual voices, artistically organized" (p. 262).

Bakhtin developed a concept related to voice, *speech genre*, in an essay written in 1952–1953, "The Problem of Speech Genres" (Bakhtin, 1986). This concept is also relevant to children's play because different types of play have many of the characteristics of a speech genre. In the context of peer sociodramatic play, one might differentiate *genre* and voice as follows. The term *genre* can be used for a type of play activity, for example, playing with dinosaurs in the sandtable, or rescuing a good guy from an attack by a bad guy. The term *voice* then can be interpreted as a way of speaking within the genred activity, usually, but not necessarily, associated with specific roles of that genre. Thus, each play genre may contain several distinct voices, each typically associated with a distinct role in the interaction.

The extent to which Bakhtin's theory is applicable to children's play would be discovered through empirical observation and analysis. To what extent do children voice in interaction? To what extent are these voices dialogized? Does the heteroglossic nature of the classroom affect individual interactions? Children's play may be a context for learning the voices and interactional genres that predominate in the culture. But more fundamentally, it may be that what children learn is how the different voices that compose a culture can interact, struggle, and be resolved, in a fundamentally heteroglossic social environment:

They learn how to "do heteroglossia." When play becomes social, the child's tentative ability to voice is forced to encounter other children's distinct, idiosyncratic, novice abilities to voice. Even if attempting to voice in the same genre, each child may have learned different variants of the genre from other sources; thus, peer play is a locus for the intersubjective negotiation and co-construction of voice. The heteroglossic social encounter is the interactional space within which children confront a social world, and within which individual behavior and play worlds are continually created, through processes of improvisational interaction.

Improvisational Play and Development

The model of improvisation presented in chapter 2 provides us with the theoretical tools needed to analyze how negotiation occurs in the heteroglossic environment of children's play. The heteroglossia of play is similar to the polyphonic voices of a musical performance, as suggested in chapter 7. Both concepts suggest that one can view each child's voice as an ongoing, parallel contribution to a *polyphonic composition*, an improvised collective performance. This perspective allows a study of several aspects of conversation that have not been amenable to past sociolinguistic approaches. First, a view of conversation as polyphonic allows one to examine the pretend play encounter as a fundamentally heteroglossic speech environment, where many voices are present simultaneously. The polyphonic metaphor introduced in chapter 7 emphasizes that a voice is not always carried by a single child. Several of the examples in chapter 7 show how a theme can rotate among several children (also see Sawyer, 1993). Second, the polyphonic metaphor provides a basis for explaining the dynamic, constantly fluctuating nature of the temporary play reality; in the presence of multiple distinct voices, a constantly shifting situational definition would be expected. Third, our analyses have demonstrated that much of the negotiation of voice and genre is not phrased explicitly by the children. Instead, it occurs implicitly, often while enacting the pretend activity.

In social play, children improvise an emergent temporary interactional reality that in turn constrains their actions. To what extent do adults engage in the same type of improvisational interaction? What is the relationship between specific adult interactions and the macrosocial order? I'll attempt to answer these questions by elaborating a developmental link between children's group play and adult interaction.

I suggest that there is a continuous developmental trajectory in communicative competence through the ages of peak pretend play, roughly from age 2 to age 6. Although such a developmental continuity has been proposed by many researchers, most theorists have not connected this trajectory with peer play development. Rather, perhaps because of the recent influence of Vygotsky

(1978, 1934/1986) and his concept of the *zone of proximal development*, the focus in psychology has tended to be on parent–child interaction. However, Vygotsky also considered peer play to be such a zone (1978).

Piaget first presented the concept of *egocentric speech*, a developmental stage in which the child talks out loud, but is incapable of integrating his speech with that of others around him. The image of two children sitting next to each other, speaking continuously, while seeming not to attend to each other's speech, gave rise to the terms *parallel play* and *collective monologue*. As I noted in chapter 1, many studies have questioned Piaget's solitary-to-social continuum. Recent theorists inspired by Vygotsky have argued that social interaction precedes egocentrism, and that the child's early thought and language develops through an internalization of social interaction. Regardless of the relative percentage of social play, there is substantial evidence that interactive pretend play becomes progressively more complex between 3 and 6 years (Corsaro, 1979b; Howes, 1980; Iwanaga, 1973; Rubin et al., 1978; Sanders & Harper, 1976; Smilansky, 1968).

Bakhtin's concepts can be used to characterize these social skills, to characterize *how* children's play increases in complexity. Although there are significant individual differences, most children at the age of 3 are just beginning to acquire the competence to integrate their play with that of other children. By the age of 6, almost all children have developed a facile ability for social play. Given that this change does not happen in a discontinuous fashion, what are the developmental parameters that must change during ages 3 to 6? The previous discussion of Bakhtin's notions of voice and heteroglossia suggest a possibility. Using Bakhtin's terminology, one could say that a child of 3 is unable to *dialogize*, and unable to participate in the heteroglossic environment of the classroom. The child's speech might be called *monoglossic*. Although the child is far from egocentric—by this age, interacting extensively with caregivers and siblings—the child cannot blend voices in a single utterance.

The first developmental step toward heteroglossic ability would be an increasing competence at dialogic speech with a single interactant. These dyadic encounters allow the child to learn to incorporate the addressee's voice into his own voice, taking the first steps toward a truly dialogic competence. As many psychologists have noted, this initial dialogic competence tends to develop in interaction with the caregiver, Vygotsky's classic zone of proximal development (Fiese, 1990; Miller & Garvey, 1984; Sachs, 1980; Sneider, 1985). Thus, children entering preschool have already moved beyond the early state of monoglossia, and are capable of rudimentary dialogic interaction.

The second developmental phase is dialogic interaction with peers. There is evidence that peer interactions are important and possibly contribute to social development independently of relations with the caregiver (Fein & Fryer, 1995; Guralnick, 1981; Hartup, 1979, 1983; Lewis & Rosenblum, 1975). In one study, Dunn (1986) found that mothers almost never engaged in pretend play with children; instead, mothers "usually act as spectators to children's fantasies.

They make pretend suggestions and offer comments, but rarely enter the game as full partners. In play between child and sibling, however, both child and sibling collaborate as partners in the shared pretend" (p. 159).

Peer interaction seems to require a more advanced dialogic ability than interaction with an adult. In the preschool classroom, the 3-year-old repeatedly has to interact with others his own age, with no clear status relationship. The child must learn additional skills at dialogic interaction before becoming facile with peers. This ability is distinguished from dialogic interactions with the caregiver primarily by the *interactional techniques* employed: The metapragmatic strategies necessary to achieve the child's interactional goals must be more sophisticated, because other children cannot be expected to be as concerned as the parents would be with a given child's goals. Although the parents create a zone of proximal development by clarifying the interactional parameters for the child, in play with peers, the children must do additional work to achieve intersubjectivity (Goncu, 1993a, 1993b).

The third and final phase is that of *full heteroglossia*. The heteroglossic environment of group play differs from caregiver interaction in several ways. First, play with peers is more egalitarian. Second, a heteroglossic environment like preschool is not found in the home. There are two levels of heteroglossia in the classroom: the voices present in a single interactional episode or play group, and the collective voices of each distinct play group's emergent. Other children's voices, either from within the group or from a nearby group, can influence the direction of the play. For example, children often move from one group to another, taking a group voice with them. Even without changes in group composition, I frequently observed an interesting phenomenon: Voices jumped between groups that were sitting close enough together to overhear each other, even when they were not (visibly) playing together. A portion of one group's emergent play frame moves to a nearby group, becoming integrated with this nearby group's own emergent.

This developmental trajectory is compatible with research on the development of the child's theory of mind (Astington, Harris, & Olson, 1988) and the development of role-taking skills (Selman, 1971, 1976). This research demonstrates that the child is just beginning to develop the ability to represent mental states of interlocutors at age 3. To generate a dialogic utterance, one that incorporates the voices of the addressee as well as the speaker, the child must be cognitively capable of representing the perspective, or voice, of the addressee. Selman's (1976) Levels 0 through 3 of *social perspective taking* are parallel to the previously mentioned progression, although his parallel levels occur at much later ages: Level 0 is egocentric; Level 1 is subjective, differentiating the subjective perspectives of self and other (dialogic with caregiver); Level 2 is "reciprocal dyadic," viewing the self as a subject reciprocally (dialogic with peers); Level 3 is "third-person dyadic," constructing reality from interpsychic subjectivity (full heteroglossia); Level 4 is the societal, adult perspective (post-preschool).

Interacting skillfully in a complex heteroglossic environment requires a well-developed ability to use interactionally appropriate metapragmatic strategies. In Mrs. Winston's preschool classroom, both explicit and implicit techniques were required for successful social interaction. Since my data show that the older children of the classroom were more explicit, the eventual shift to being exclusively implicit must come after preschool. At the same time, my data show that the older children were more in-frame. But most interesting are the findings that show that different strategies are effective in different interactional and social contexts. Rather than simply becoming more explicit, or more implicit, during the preschool years, children seem to be learning how to use different strategies effectively in different contexts.

The final stage of preschool development is the ability to negotiate skillfully, using sophisticated techniques of implicit metapragmatics, within multiple levels of heteroglossia. As I noted in chapter 2, implicit and in-frame skills are required for adult conversational competence. Some prior research has shown that children stop engaging in improvisational fantasy play around age 6 (Auwarter, 1986), about a year or two after preschool. Perhaps children stop this type of play because it has served its developmental purpose. By this age, children are recognized as socially competent individuals. They have mastered the interactional skills practiced in fantasy play, and are able to use them during everyday conversation. These skills also allow children to participate in more complex social relationships, developing relatively permanent friendships and entering primary school.

Implications for Developmental Research

In the preceding chapters, I have demonstrated that metapragmatic strategies are an important aspect of pretend play between ages 3 and 5. Many interactional and social skills develop rapidly during these same years. These skills include pretend play, theories of mind, the ability to represent and construct narratives, social cognitive abilities, and intersubjective skills. Because metapragmatics is a constant and important feature of improvised interaction, the use of metapragmatics in play may be related to the development of these abilities.

For example, many of the skills required to represent and construct narratives are the same skills required to engage in social pretend play. In play, children frequently combine their play character's voice with a narrator's voice. This form of dialogism is an important characteristic of narrative, as well. The ability to construct and present a narrative requires a basic ability at role taking, and an understanding of the perspective of the listener, both abilities that are important in pretend play. In the advanced play improvisations presented in chapter 7, children accept their partner's proposals and elaborate on them with their own novel proposals. To do this effectively, children must be able to understand their partner's proposal, and to understand their partner's perspective on the play frame. Narratives often make use of quoted speech, a form of *reportive metapragmatics* (Lucy, 1993; Silverstein, 1993). Many of the examples of dialogism that Bakhtin provides are quoted speech. The metapragmatic strategies used in advanced play may contribute to the reportive metapragmatics required for narrative.

Like narrative skill, social cognition requires role-taking abilities. In pretend play, children need to take the perspective of the other, to construct dialogic utterances that integrate multiple perspectives, and to effectively propose indexical entailments. These skills are important to social cognition. These skills are also important to the development of intersubjectivity in play (Goncu, 1993a, 1993b). These parallels suggest that the practice of collectively constructing an intersubjective play emergent may be related to the development of social cognition.

When we think of play as improvisational, it helps us understand why play is fun for children—why it is a context where *flow* is experienced (Csikszentmihalyi, 1979, 1990). It takes skill to manage the balance between structure and innovation, between maintaining coherence with the changing emergent and creating a novel entailment. Improvisational performers, both in jazz and improvisational theater, say that their greatest satisfaction comes from this interplay with coperformers (Berliner, 1994; Halpern, Close, & Johnson, 1994; Sawyer, 1992). I have suggested that improvisational skills develop continuously through preschool. If so, the child's level of skill is constantly matched by the challenges of the interactional situation, resulting in the balance of individual skill and situational challenge that leads to a flow state. This perspective may explain why group pretend play fades away around age 6: By this age, children have mastered the interactional skills that were practiced during pretend play. The skills of the child advance beyond the challenges of pretend play. Having mastered these skills, children can begin to engage in non-play social interactions within an increasingly complex peer culture.

An important implication for psychology is the need to incorporate the social group level of analysis, and the need to focus on situated action as a unit of analysis. My studies were done at the event level of analysis, using either the group episode or the interactional routine. Of course, a focus on the individual child as the unit of analysis is equally essential to developmental research. Yet, it seems that much of what happens in the preschool classroom cannot be explained fully through an analysis of individual traits or interactional dispositions. Many of the findings presented here would have been difficult, in some cases impossible, to identify without focusing on collective action. For example, the sequential effects of one turn on the next, and the influence of social context on these effects, are not possible to detect and study by operationalizing measures of any single child. Future studies of play metapragmatics should analyze children in social and interactional contexts.

Implications for the Study of Situated Action

Many of the studies in this book have focused on the ways that sociocultural context affects play, and the ways that children simultaneously contribute to the creation and reproduction of their microsocial reality. In taking this approach, I have drawn on many of the insights of sociocultural psychology. The study of children's social play provides a unique window onto sociocultural processes. In social play, the metapragmatic strategies that are skillfully blended in adult interaction are differentiated and differentially manipulated. Children learn metapragmatics by collectively creating and inhabiting temporary play realities.

Developmental psychology's increasing incorporation of sociocultural approaches is a manifestation of a broader trend in the social sciences: the relations between the individual, society, and culture. In recent decades, a variety of social theorists have attempted to explore these relationships through a focus on linguistic interaction between individuals. In focusing on interaction, these theorists recall the symbolic interactionists, and I refer to this trend as interactionism. Interactionist theorists have explored how the macrosocial structure influences and constrains individuals during interactions with others, and how individuals contribute to the construction of the social order through interactions with others. This approach has been an attempt to integrate and reconcile two opposing epistemological positions within the social sciences that, following Bourdieu (e.g., Bourdieu, 1990), I refer to as subjectivist (including phenomenology, rational action theory, much of interpretive sociology and anthropology, and some clinical and cultural psychology) and objectivist (Saussurean semiology and the various structuralisms in language and anthropology, scientific psychology, and most social theory, including Marxism and critical theory).

Subjectivism posits that human psychology is primary, and that human nature determines macrosocial structure. A canonical representative of this position is Adam Smith, who claimed in a famous passage that the social structure of capitalism arises from "a certain propensity in human nature...the propensity to truck, barter and exchange one thing for another" (Smith, 1976, p. 17). This is an implicit assumption of most psychology as well. In contrast, objectivism posits that macrosocial structure is primary, and that human nature is relative and socioculturally determined. A canonical representative of this position is Karl Marx, writing in an equally famous passage: "This sum of productive forces, capital funds and social forms of intercourse, which every individual and generation finds in existence as something given, is the real basis of what the philosophers have conceived as 'substance' and 'essence of man' " (Marx, 1978, p. 165). Marx went so far as to claim that the fields of philosophy and psychology would become obsolete, subsumed by economics. The Frankfurt school extended these notions by arguing that knowledge itself, including social science knowledge, is socially constructed.

Interactionism has appeared in different manifestations in each social science discipline. In Europe, often broadly labeled "poststructural" or "postmodern," interactionist theories include Bourdieu's (1977) notion of *habitus*, Derrida's (1978) focus on the play of the sign in interaction, Foucault's (1972) concept of discursive practices, and Habermas's (1987) theory of communicative action. In the United States, interactionism originated with the American pragmatists, particularly G. H. Mead (who also influenced many European interactionists including Habermas, 1987, and Berger & Luckmann, 1966), and has continued in its microsociological descendants, symbolic interactionism, ethnomethodology, conversation analysis, and social constructivism. To generalize, the continental tradition, while emphasizing the role of interaction, has not attributed a great deal of creative potential to the individuals participating in the interaction; in contrast, the American tradition has tended to focus more on the creative, constituting roles played by social actors. Yet both traditions have given a central role to symbolic processes of microinteraction.

Contemporary European social theorists have taken different positions on the relationship between microinteraction and macrosocial structure; what seems to unify many of these theorists is that all of them give symbolic interaction a prominent role in their theory. Habermas (1987) drew on speech act theory and Mead's pragmatism to develop his theory of communicative action, as a way of connecting action theory with structural analysis to resolve a variety of issues resulting from the earlier Frankfurt School writings. Foucault's focus on *discursive practices* (1972, 1978) suggested that the analyst must focus closely on specific linguistic interactions (whether spoken or via texts) to understand how macrosocial forces regiment and control individuals.[1] Bourdieu (1977) frequently used the term *improvisation* in explaining the notion of *habitus*, describing the practices through which individuals manipulate and interpret social structures to advantage in specific interactions.[2]

Although U.S. interactionists (including symbolic interactionists, ethnomethodologists, and social constructionists) argue that individuals coconstruct their social reality through interaction, on the face of it there is a

---

[1]Although the term *discourse* is often used indiscriminately to refer to all instances of what Foucault called in his later works "power–knowledge relations" (e.g., 1979, pp. 24–29), he was careful to reserve the term *discourse* for interactions involving language; although he included direct verbal interactions, his own methodology focused on written texts, which are also referred to as *discursive*.

[2] Bourdieu defined *habitus* in terms that might apply to a jazz quartet: "Objectively 'regulated' and 'regular' without being in any way the product of obedience to rules, they can be collectively orchestrated without being the product of the organizing action of a conductor" (1977, p. 72).

great deal of stability in social life. Individuals occupy particular locations in a social order which change infrequently: occupation, family role, friendship networks. Thus, a direct empirical evaluation of interactionism is difficult. Studies have tended to be either historical (e.g., the Foucauldian tradition) or theoretical. Apparently more so than in social life, in many improvisational genres, the participants are constantly creating and recreating a temporary social reality, and then enacting that reality. This temporary reality includes social role assignments, role relationships, and complex processes of negotiating this microsocial order. In improvisational performance, we see in stark relief the primary moments of the interactionist dialectic. The tension in performance between script and improvisation is a manifestation of a broader tension, between structure and individual agency.

A study of improvisation allows the empirical evaluation of interactionist theories. Because everyday life is relatively stable, with opportunities for impro-visationality confined to informal social interactions, the study of improvisational performance genres may be a more effective way of analyzing interactional creativity. While the social context of adult life is broad and difficult to analyze, the immediate context of an improvisational performance is the ephemeral, emergent dramatic frame, a clearly defined and bounded context. Children's pretend play is an improvisational genre that allows the evaluation and development of interactionist theory. Study in preschool has several methodological benefits. First, rather than study the entirety of U.S. society, a preschool classroom provides a more limited social context, allowing a more thorough and rigorous specification of the sociocultural context oper-ating on individual interactions. The preschool classroom represents a clearly defined, bounded social environment (Corsaro, 1985, 1986; Hartup, 1981). Second, the bounded nature of the classroom allows the researcher to record the entirety of interaction using audio or videotape. It is much easier to acquire audiotapes of naturalistic interaction between children than it is to acquire similar data on adult linguistic interaction. Adults rarely ignore the presence of the researcher and the microphone to the extent that my subjects did; a parallel study with adults would require surreptitious taping, a project with ethical difficulties.[3]

Sociology and psychology have traditionally studied play from opposite ends of the interactionist spectrum. Traditional macrosociology, an objectivist disci-pline, suggests that children's play is a context for the reproduction of the social order. Sociologists call this period *socialization*, implying a passive internalization of social structures and practices (see Cook-Gumperz & Corsaro, 1986, for a history of the use of this term). The implication is that children imitate

---

[3] Note that ethnomethodology, an interactionist subdiscipline that has focused on adult interaction, has avoided these issues by focusing almost exclusively on semipublic interactions, including the courtroom, the classroom, and the doctor–patient encounter.

interactional patterns that they have observed among adults. This perspective does not attribute a great deal of creativity to children at play. In contrast, psychology is based on subjectivist assumptions, and uses the term *development* rather than socialization, reflecting the assumption that this process is internally driven. Beginning with Piaget's staged structuralist models, psychological theory argued that children's play demonstrates the individual child's developing cognitive competence to engage in social activity. In the traditional structuralist formulation, these individual-centered developmental processes are universal, and there is no need to study the influence or specificity of individual societies or contexts.

This book is part of a recent trend toward examining these interactionist questions, by examining the influence of social structure on individual development, and the child's own creative role in that development. Rather than a straightforward reproduction of the social structure through imitation, children seem to be active creators of their own classroom culture that builds on the adult culture. Researchers like Corsaro (1983, 1986, 1992; Corsaro & Rizzo, 1988) and Rogoff (1990) have emphasized the improvisational creativity of children, suggesting that children's play is not a straightforward reproduction of social structure. Instead, children appropriate these structures and use them to create new, improvised interactions. These recent studies are critical of the view that socialization is a passive internalization of macrosocial structures. Viewing children's play as improvisational suggests how it may play a developmental role in teaching children how to manage the balance between social structure and individual creative action. As an example of an empirical interactionist study, this research may contribute to these broader social theoretic issues.

Suggestions for Future Work

Because much of this book has focused on phenomena that have been neglected by prior research, it has an exploratory quality. For many reasons, I chose to focus closely on a single classroom. Although many of my observations and analyses benefited from the ethnographic method, a drawback is that the results cannot necessarily be generalized. For example, in this study, the play groups were self-selected. Thus, groups were not randomly sampled, and accordingly one should be cautious in interpreting the statistical results. However, these results are valuable in part because the groups were self-selected, because that is the way selection really happens in preschool. The introduction of random sampling would at the same time be an imposition of researcher-imposed structure, making the study less naturalistic and potentially affecting the children's play behavior. These are the difficult compromises that have to be made when selecting a method (Rogoff, 1982).

Keeping these concerns in mind, future studies of play metapragmatics could include more classrooms and could use a more structured quasiexperimental design to control for factors such as age, gender, and friendship. However, any move in this direction would run the risk of losing some of the depth that one gets from an ethnographic approach. The researcher should try to observe children in an environment that is already an accepted part of their everyday world.

There are many other analyses that could have been conducted on this type of play data. The theoretical framework, and the results presented, suggest several follow-up analyses:

1. *Analysis of longer sequences of play* to evaluate to what extent interactional routines of three or more turns in length influence individual turns. What are the relationships between these broader interactional patterns and the interactional strategies of specific turns? Do multiutterance patterns have indexically entailing effects, beyond those of the immediately prior utterance?

2. *Analysis of the overall trajectory of a group episode.* Does the blend of interactional strategies change throughout the course of a group episode? Do children become progressively more implicit, more in-frame, as play progresses? If the play frame shifts radically, will children then become more explicit? The studies of pair-part routines and of longer sequences presented in this book are suggestive, and could be explored with statistical and sequential analysis.

3. *Analysis of more complex interactional sequences.* This book has focused on two relatively simple interactional sequences, play entry sequences and improvisational exchanges. A sequential analysis of the extended sequences could be conducted, to identify sequences of three or more turns. Children may also combine strategies in a single turn, and these within-turn sequences could be analyzed.

4. *The content of play:* the type of play theme, the role types enacted (domestic, occupational, fantasy), and the relationships between types of play, play location, and play objects. Does the play theme or activity have an effect on the interactional strategies used? Do some themes result in more coherent interaction?

5. *Comparison of metapragmatics across performance styles.* Are different strategies predominant in different styles? Are there different blends of the 16 types of interactional strategy across styles? Does play in some styles contain a higher percentage of improvisational exchanges? These analyses would help us understand how different types of play contribute to the development of interactional skill.

6. *Comparative study of other social and cultural groups.* Because this was an ethnographic study of a single classroom, one should be cautioned against extending the results to other preschools. In particular, the results may be hard to generalize to children of other social classes or cultures. Similar studies could

be conducted among children of different social classes, or in other cultures, to explore how these macrocontexts influence the metapragmatic level of inter-action.

7. *Experimental and quasiexperimental designs.* Although I have chosen to conduct contextualized, observational research, many of the effects identified here could be explored using quasiexperimental designs. For example, friends could be randomly selected from preschools, and videotaped playing for a controlled period of time, in a controlled setting. Several of the relationships identified in chapter 6 could be evaluated with such a design, providing verification and increasing the validity of the previously mentioned findings.

8. *Older children.* Because many of the developmental trends identified seem to continue beyond preschool, a kindergarten (ages 5–6) study is sug-gested. For example, chapter 4 showed that the percentage of indirect style play increases from 3 to 5. Does the percentage of this type of play continue to increase after age 5? Also, the findings of chapter 5 suggested that at age 5, children were still learning to be implicit at play entry; the relative use of implicit strategies, although increasing with age, was still only 75% for 5-year-olds. A comparative study of kindergarten pretend play would allow a more complete analysis of the development of these skills.

I have argued that children's play provides a unique window onto the interactional processes through which children create intersubjective worlds and peer relations. I have used the metaphor of play as improvisation to analyze how children's play contributes to the development of social and conversational skills. Both Piaget and Vygotsky considered group play to be rule-governed. This structuralist perspective lives on in frame and script theories of play. The results presented here extend these perspectives by demonstrating that pretend play is both rule-governed and improvised, and that both aspects are critical in its analysis. Children's social pretend play is a quintessentially improvisational encounter. Children collectively create a shared situational definition through play. Rather than refer to this as a play frame, I have borrowed a term from Mead, the emergent, to better represent the constantly changing and fluctuat-ing nature of the play drama. Children create the emergent through creative acts that are indexically entailing, even while they maintain coherence with the emergent. The improvisational metaphor suggests that although children may learn scripts through play, they also creatively reproduce and embellish these scripts. When we think of pretend play as improvisation, we can understand why it is so important to social and conversational development: Play provides children with an opportunity to manage the tension between social structure and individual creativity.

References

Al-Shatti, A., & Johnson, J. (1984, April). *Free play behaviors of middle class Kuwaitis and American children*. Paper presented at the annual meeting of the American Educational Research Association, New Orleans, LA.

Andersen, E. S. (1986). The acquisition of register variation by Anglo-American children. In B. Schieffelin & E. Ochs (Eds.), *Language socialization across cultures* (pp. 153–161). New York: Cambridge University Press.

Andersen, E. S. (1990). *Speaking with style: The sociolinguistic skills of children*. London: Routledge.

Ariel, S., & Sever, I. (1980). Play in the desert and play in the town: On play activities of Bedouin Arab children. In H. B. Schwartzman (Ed.), *Play and culture* (pp. 164–175). New York: Leisure Press.

Astington, J. W., Harris, P. L., & Olson, D. R. (Eds.). (1988). *Developing theories of mind*. New York: Cambridge University Press.

Austin, J. L. (1962). *How to do things with words*. Oxford: Clarendon Press.

Auwarter, M. (1986). Development of communicative skills: The construction of fictional reality in children's play. In J. Cook-Gumperz, W. A. Corsaro, & J. Streeck (Eds.), *Children's worlds and children's language* (pp. 205–230). New York: Mouton de Gruyter.

Bakeman, R., & Brownlee, J. R. (1980). The strategic use of parallel play: A sequential analysis. *Child Development, 51*, 873–878.

Baker-Sennett, J., & Matusov, E. (in press). School "performance": Improvisational processes in development and education. In R. K. Sawyer (Ed.), *Creativity in performance*. Norwood, NJ: Ablex.

Baker-Sennett, J., Matusov, E., & Rogoff, B. (1992). Sociocultural processes of creative planning in children's playcrafting. In P. Light & G. Butterworth (Eds.), *Context and cognition: Ways of learning and knowing* (pp. 93–114). Hillsdale, NJ: Lawrence Erlbaum Associates.

185

Bakhtin, M. M. (1981). Discourse in the novel. In M. M. Bakhtin, *The dialogic imagination* (pp. 259–422). Austin, TX: University of Texas Press.

Bakhtin, M. M. (1986). The problem of speech genres. In M. M. Bakhtin, *Speech genres and other late essays* (pp. 60–102). Austin, TX: University of Texas Press.

Bar-Hillel, Y. (1954). Indexical expressions. *Mind, 63,* 359–379.

Barker, R. G., & Wright, H. F. (1955). *Midwest and its children.* New York: Harper & Row.

Bates, E. (1975). Peer relations and the acquisition of language. In M. Lewis & L. A. Rosenblum (Eds.), *Friendship and peer relations* (pp. 259–292). New York: Wiley.

Bates, E. (1976). *Language and context: The acquisition of pragmatics.* New York: Academic Press.

Bates, E., Benigni, L., Bretherton, I., Camaioni, L., & Volterra, V. (1977). From gesture to the first word: On cognitive and social prerequisites. In M. Lewis & L. A. Rosenblum (Eds.), *Interaction, conversation, and the development of language* (pp. 247–307). New York: Wiley.

Bateson, G. (1971). The message "This is play." In R. E. Herron & B. Sutton-Smith (Eds.), *Child's play* (pp. 261–266). Malabar, FL: Robert E. Krieger Publishing Company. (Original work published 1956)

Bateson, G. (1972). A theory of play and fantasy. In G. Bateson (Ed.), *Steps to an ecology of mind* (pp. 177–193). New York: Chandler. (Original work published 1955)

Bauman, R., & Briggs, C. L. (1990). Poetics and performance as critical perspectives on language and social life. *Annual Review of Anthropology, 19,* 59–88.

Bearison, D. J. (1994). *Interpersonal collaboration and children's cognitive development.* Project Summary, Peer Interaction Laboratory, CUNY Graduate Center, New York.

Bearison, D. J. (1995, May). *Interpersonal collaboration: Games and negotiations.* Brown Bag Seminar Series, CUNY Graduate Center, New York.

Berger, P. L., & Luckmann, T. (1966). *The social construction of reality: A treatise in the sociology of knowledge.* Garden City, NY: Doubleday.

Berliner, P. (1994). *Thinking in jazz: The infinite art of improvisation.* Chicago: University of Chicago Press.

Black, B., & Hazen, N. L. (1990). Social status and patterns of communication in acquainted and unacquainted preschool children. *Developmental Psychology, 26,* 379–387.

Bloch, M. N. (1989). Young boys' and girls' play at home and in the community: A cultural-ecological framework. In M. N. Bloch & A. D. Pellegrini (Eds.), *The ecological context of children's play* (pp. 120–154). Norwood, NJ: Ablex.

Blumer, H. (1969). *Symbolic interactionism: Perspective and method.* Englewood Cliffs, NJ: Prentice-Hall.

Boggs, S. T. (1990). The role of routines in the evolution of children's peer talk. In B. Dorval (Ed.), *Conversational organization and its development* (pp. 101–130). Norwood, NJ: Ablex.

Bourdieu, P. (1977). *Outline of a theory of practice.* New York: Press Syndicate of the University of Cambridge.

Bourdieu, P. (1990). *The logic of practice.* Stanford, CA: Stanford University Press.

Bower, E., Ilgaz-Carden, A., & Noori, K. (1982). Measurement of play structures: Cross-cultural considerations. *Journal of Cross-Cultural Psychology, 13,* 315–329.

Bretherton, I. (1984). Representing the social world in symbolic play: Reality and fantasy. In I. Bretherton (Ed.), *Symbolic play: The development of social understanding* (pp. 1–41). Orlando, FL: Academic Press.

Bretherton, I. (1986). Representing the social world in symbolic play: Reality and fantasy. In A. W. Gottfried & C. C. Brown (Eds.), *Play interactions: The contribution of play materials and parental involvement to children's development* (pp. 119–148). Lexington, MA: Lexington Books.

Bretherton, I. (1989). Pretense: The form and function of make-believe play. *Developmental Review, 9,* 383–401.

Briggs, C. (1986). *Learning how to ask: A sociolinguistic appraisal of the role of the interview in social science research*. New York: Cambridge University Press.

Bronfenbrenner, U. (1979). *The ecology of human development*. Cambridge, MA: Harvard University Press.

Brown, P., & Levinson, S. (1978). Universals in language usage: Politeness phenomena. In E. N. Goody (Ed.), *Questions and politeness: Strategies in social interaction* (pp. 56–289). New York: Cambridge University Press.

Brown, R., & Gilman, A. (1960). The pronouns of power and solidarity. In T. A. Sebeok (Ed.), *Style in language* (pp. 253–276). Cambridge, MA: MIT Press.

Brownell, C. A. (1990). Peer social skills in toddlers: Competencies and constraints illustrated by same-age and mixed-age interaction. *Child Development, 61*, 838–848.

Bruner, J. (1975). The ontogenesis of speech acts. *Journal of Child Language, 2*, 1–19.

Bruner, J. (1981). The pragmatics of acquisition. In W. Deutsch (Ed.), *The child's construction of language* (pp. 39–55). New York: Academic Press.

Bruner, J. (1983). *Child's talk: Learning to use language*. New York: Norton.

Bruner, J. (1990). *Acts of meaning*. Cambridge, MA: Harvard University Press.

Burke, K. (1968). "Dramatism." Under entry: "Interaction." In David L. Sills (Ed.), *International encyclopedia of the social sciences*, (Vol. 7, pp. 445–452). New York: Macmillan and The Free Press.

Burke, K. (1969). *A grammar of motives*. Berkeley: University of California Press.

Butterworth, G. (1992). Context and cognition in models of cognitive growth. In P. Light & G. Butterworth (Eds.), *Context and cognition: Ways of learning and knowing* (pp. 1–13). Hillsdale, NJ: Lawrence Erlbaum Associates.

Camaioni, L. (1986). From early interaction patterns to language acquisition: Which continuity? In J. Cook-Gumperz, W. A. Corsaro, & J. Streeck (Eds.), *Children's worlds and children's language* (pp. 69–82). New York: Mouton de Gruyter.

Cazden, C. B. (1988). *Classroom discourse: The language of teaching and learning*. Portsmouth, NH: Heinemann.

Challman, R. C. (1932). Factors influencing friendships among preschool children. *Child Development, 3*, 146–158.

Cicourel, A. V. (1974). *Cognitive sociology: Language and meaning in social interaction*. New York: The Free Press.

Clark, H., & Haviland, S. E. (1977). Comprehension and the given-new contract. In R. Freedle (Ed.), *Discourse production and comprehension* (pp. 1–40). Hillsdale, NJ: Lawrence Erlbaum Associates.

Coleman, J. (1990). *The compass: The improvisational theatre that revolutionized American comedy*. Chicago: University of Chicago Press.

Connolly, J. A., & Doyle, A. B. (1984). Relation of social fantasy play to social competence in preschoolers. *Developmental Psychology, 20*, 797–806.

Cook-Gumperz, J. (1986). Caught in a web of words: Some considerations on language socialization and language acquisition. In J. Cook-Gumperz, W. A. Corsaro, & J. Streeck (Eds.), *Children's worlds and children's language* (pp. 37–64). New York: Mouton de Gruyter.

Cook-Gumperz, J., & Corsaro, W. A. (1977). Social-ecological constraints on children's communicative strategies. *Sociology, 2*, 411–434.

Cook-Gumperz, J., & Corsaro, W. A. (1986). Introduction. In J. Cook-Gumperz, W. A. Corsaro, & J. Streeck (Eds.), *Children's worlds and children's language* (pp. 1–11). New York: Mouton de Gruyter.

Corsaro, W. A. (1979a). "We're friends, right?": Children's use of access rituals in a nursery school. *Language in Society, 8*, 315–336.

Corsaro, W. A. (1979b). Young children's conception of status and role. *Sociology of Education, 52,* 46–59.

Corsaro, W. A. (1981). Friendship in the nursery school: Social organization in a peer environment. In S. R. Asher & J. M. Gottman (Eds.), *The development of children's friendships* (pp. 207–242). New York: Cambridge University Press.

Corsaro, W. A. (1983). Script recognition, articulation, and expansion in children's role play. *Discourse Processes, 6,* 1–19.

Corsaro, W. A. (1985). *Friendship and peer culture in the early years.* Norwood, NJ: Ablex.

Corsaro, W. A. (1986). Discourse processes within peer culture: From a constructivist to an interpretive approach to childhood socialization. *Sociological Studies of Child Development, 1,* 81–101.

Corsaro, W. A. (1992). Interpretive reproduction in children's peer cultures. *Social Psychological Quarterly, 55,* 160–177.

Corsaro, W. A. (1993). Interpretive reproduction in children's role play. *Childhood, 1,* 64–74.

Corsaro, W. A., & Rizzo, T. A. (1988). *Discussione* and friendship: Socialization processes in the peer culture of Italian nursery school children. *American Sociological Review, 53,* 879–894.

Csikszentmihalyi, M. (1979). The concept of flow. In B. Sutton-Smith (Ed.), *Play and learning* (pp. 257–274). New York: Gardner Press.

Csikszentmihalyi, M. (1988). Society, culture, and person: A systems view of creativity. In R. J. Sternberg (Ed.), *The nature of creativity* (pp. 325–339). New York: Cambridge University Press.

Csikszentmihalyi, M. (1990). *Flow: The psychology of optimal experience.* New York: Harper & Collins.

Csikszentmihalyi, M., & Sawyer, R. K. (1995). Creative insight: The social dimension of a solitary moment. In R. J. Sternberg & J. E. Davidson (Eds.), *The nature of insight* (pp. 329–363). Cambridge, MA: MIT Press.

Damon, W. (1977). *The social world of the child.* San Francisco: Jossey-Bass.

Derrida, J. (1978). Structure, sign, and play in the discourse of the human sciences. In *Writing and difference* (pp. 278–294). Chicago: University of Chicago Press.

Dewey, J. (1934). *Art as experience.* New York: Perigree Books.

Dewey, J. (1925). *The later works, 1925–1953: Volume 1.* Carbondale, IL: Southern Illinois University Press.

Dodge, K. A., & Schlundt, D. C. (1983). Social competence and children's sociometric status: The role of peer group entry strategies. *Merrill-Palmer Quarterly, 29,* 309–336.

Doyle, A. B. (1982). Friends, acquaintances, and strangers: The influence of familiarity and ethnolinguistic background on social interaction. In K. H. Rubin & H. S. Ross (Eds.), *Peer relationships and social skills in childhood* (pp. 229–252). New York: Springer-Verlag.

Doyle, A. B., & Connolly, J. (1989). Negotiation and enactment in social pretend play: Relations to social acceptance and social cognition. *Early Childhood Research Quarterly, 4,* 289–302.

Doyle, A. B., Connolly, J., & Rivest, L. P. (1980). The effect of playmate familiarity on the social interactions of young children. *Child Development, 51,* 217–223.

Doyle, A. B., Doehring, P., Tessier, O., & de Lorimier, S. (1992). Transitions in children's play: A sequential analysis of states preceding and following social pretense. *Developmental Psychology, 28,* 137–144.

Dunn, J. (1986). Pretend play in the family. In A. W. Gottfried & C. C. Brown (Eds.), *Play interactions: The contribution of play materials and parental involvement to children's development* (pp. 149–162). Lexington, MA: Lexington Books.

Dunn, J., & Dale, N. (1984). I a Daddy: 2-year-olds' collaboration in joint pretend with sibling and mother. In I. Bretherton (Ed.), *Symbolic play: The development of social understanding* (pp. 131–158). New York: Academic Press.

El'konin, D. B. (1969). Some results of the study of the psychological development of preschool-age children. In M. Cole & I. Maltzman (Eds.), *A handbook of contemporary Soviet psychology* (pp. 163–208). New York: Basic Books.

Emmerich, W. (1977). Evaluating alternative models of development: An illustrative study of preschool personal-social behaviors. *Child Development, 48,* 1401–1410.

Errington, J. J. (1985). On the nature of the sociolinguistic sign: Describing the Javanese speech levels. In E. Mertz & R. J. Parmentier (Eds.), *Semiotic Mediation: Sociocultural and Psychological Perspectives* (pp. 287–310). Orlando, FL: Academic Press.

Ervin-Tripp, S. (1972). On sociolinguistic rules: Alternation and co-occurrence. In J. J. Gumperz & D. Hymes (Eds.), *Directions in sociolinguistics: The ethnography of communication* (pp. 213–250). New York: Basil Blackwell.

Ervin-Tripp, S. (1979). Children's verbal turn-taking. In E. Ochs & B. B. Schieffelin (Eds.), *Developmental pragmatics* (pp. 391–414). New York: Academic Press.

Fein, G. G. (1981). Pretend play in childhood: An integrative review. *Child Development, 52,* 1095–1118.

Fein, G. G. (1985). The affective psychology of play. In C. C. Brown & A. W. Gottfried (Eds.), *Play interactions: The role of toys and parental involvement in children's development* (pp. 19–28). Skillman, NJ: Johnson & Johnson Baby Products Company.

Fein, G. G. (1987). Pretend play: Creativity and consciousness. In D. Gorlitz & J. F. Wohlwill (Eds.), *Curiosity, imagination, and play: On the development of spontaneous cognitive and motivational processes* (pp. 281–304). Hillsdale, NJ: Lawrence Erlbaum Associates.

Fein, G. G., & Fryer, M. G. (1995). Maternal contributions to early symbolic play competence. *Developmental Review, 15,* 367–381.

Fein, G. G., Moorin, E. R., & Enslein, J. (1982). Pretense and peer behavior: An intersectoral analysis. *Human Development, 25,* 392–406.

Feitelson, D. (1977). Cross-cultural studies of representational play. In B. Tizard & D. Harvey (Eds.), *Biology of play* (pp. 6–14). Philadelphia: J. B. Lippincott.

Feitelson, D., Weintraub, S., & Michaeli, O. (1972). Social interactions in heterogeneous pre-schools in Israel. *Child Development, 43,* 1249–1259.

Field, T. (1981). Early peer relations. In P. S. Strain (Ed.), *The utilization of classroom peers as behavior change agents* (pp. 1–30). New York: Plenum Press.

Fiese, B. H. (1990). Playful relationships: A contextual analysis of mother-toddler interaction and symbolic play. *Child Development, 61,* 1648–1656.

Forbes, D., & Yablick, G. (1984). The organization of dramatic content in children's fantasy play. In F. Kessel & A. Goncu (Eds.), *Analyzing children's play dialogues* (pp. 23–36). San Francisco: Jossey-Bass.

Foucault, M. (1972). *The archeology of knowledge and the discourse on language.* New York: Pantheon Books.

Foucault, M. (1978). *The history of sexuality, Volume 1: An introduction.* New York: Vintage Books.

Franklin, M. (1983). Play as the creation of imaginary situations: The role of language. In S. Wapner & B. Kaplan (Eds.), *Towards a holistic developmental psychology* (pp. 197–220). Hillsdale, NJ: Lawrence Erlbaum Associates.

Freedle, R., & Lewis, M. (1977). Prelinguistic conversations. In M. Lewis & L. A. Rosenblum (Eds.), *Interaction, conversation, and the development of language* (pp. 157–185). New York: Wiley.

Freud, S. (1966). *Introductory lectures on psycho-analysis.* New York: Norton.

Friedrich, P. (1971). Structural implications of Russian pronominal usage. In W. Bright (Ed.), *Proceedings of the UCLA sociolinguistics conference, 1964* (pp. 214–259). Los Angeles: Center for Research in Languages and Linguistics.

Gadamer, H. (1975). *Truth and method.* New York: The Seabury Press.

Galda, L. (1984). Narrative competence: Play, storytelling, and story comprehension. In A. Pellegrini & T. Yaukey (Eds.), *The development of oral and written language in social contexts* (pp. 105–117). Norwood, NJ: Ablex.

Garvey, C. (1974). Some properties of social play. *Merrill-Palmer Quarterly, 20,* 163–180.

Garvey, C. (1982). Communication and the development of social role play. In D. Forbes & M. T. Greenberg (Eds.), *Children's planning strategies* (pp. 81–101). San Francisco: Jossey-Bass.

Garvey, C. (1984). *Children's talk.* Cambridge, MA: Harvard University Press.

Garvey, C., & Berndt, R. (1977). *The organization of pretend play.* Corte Madera, CA: Select Press.

Garvey, C., & Hogan, R. (1973). Social speech and social interaction: Egocentrism revisited. *Child Development, 44,* 562–568.

Garvey, C., & Kramer, T. L. (1989). The language of social pretend play. *Developmental Review, 9,* 364–382.

Gaskins, S., & Goncu, A. (1988). Children's play as representation and imagination: The case of Piaget and Vygotsky. *The Quarterly Newsletter of the Laboratory of Comparative Human Cognition, 10,* 104–107.

Gaskins, S., & Goncu, A. (1992). Cultural variation in play: A challenge to Piaget and Vygotsky. *The Quarterly Newsletter of the Laboratory of Comparative Human Cognition, 14,* 31–35.

Gaskins, S., Miller, P. J., & Corsaro, W. A. (1992). Theoretical and methodological perspectives in the interpretive study of children. In W. A. Corsaro & P. J. Miller (Eds.), *Interpretive approaches to childhood socialization* (pp. 5–23). San Francisco: Jossey-Bass.

Giffin, H. L. N. (1982). The metacommunicative process in collective make-believe play (Doctoral dissertation, University of Colorado, 1982). *Dissertation Abstracts International, 43,* 972A.

Giffin, H. L. N. (1984). The coordination of meaning in the creation of a shared make-believe reality. In I. Bretherton (Ed.), *Symbolic play: The development of social understanding* (pp. 73–100). Orlando, FL: Academic Press.

Gilligan, C. (1982). *In a different voice: Psychological theory and women's development.* Cambridge, MA: Harvard University Press.

Goffman, E. (1959). *The presentation of self in everyday life.* New York: Anchor Books.

Goffman, E. (1961). *Encounters.* Indianapolis: Bobbs-Merrill.

Goffman, E. (1963). *Behavior in public places.* New York: The Free Press.

Goffman, E. (1967). *Interaction ritual: Essays on face-to-face behavior.* New York: Pantheon Books.

Goffman, E. (1971). *Relations in public.* New York: Basic Books.

Goffman, E. (1974). *Frame Analysis: An essay on the organization of experience.* New York: Harper & Row.

Goncu, A. (1987). Toward an interactional model of developmental changes in social pretend play. In L. Katz (Ed.), *Current topics in early childhood education* (pp. 108–125). Norwood, NJ: Ablex.

Goncu, A. (1993b). Development of intersubjectivity in social pretend play. *Human Development, 36,* 185–198.

Goncu, A. (1993a). Development of intersubjectivity in the dyadic play of preschoolers. *Early Childhood Research Quarterly, 8,* 99–116.

Goncu, A. (in press). Harout and I: A short story for the becoming teacher. In W. Ayers (Ed.), *Becoming teachers.* New York: Columbia University Teacher's College Press.

Goncu, A., & Kessel, F. S. (1984). Children's play: A contextual-functional perspective. In F. S. Kessel & A. Goncu (Eds.), *Analyzing children's play dialogues* (pp. 5–22). San Francisco: Jossey-Bass.

Goncu, A., & Kessel, F. S. (1988). Preschooler's collaborative construction in planning and maintaining imaginative play. *International Journal of Behavioral Development, 11,* 327–344.

Goodwin, M. H., & Goodwin, C. (1987). Children's arguing. In S. U. Philips, S. Steele, & C. Tanz (Eds.), *Language, gender, and sex in comparative perspective* (pp. 200–248). New York: Cambridge University Press.

Gottman, J. M. (1983). How children become friends. *Monographs of the Society for Research in Child Development, 48* (2, Serial No. 201).

Gottman, J. M., & Parkhurst, J. (1980). A developmental theory of friendship and acquaintanceship processes. In W. A. Collins (Ed.), *Minnesota Symposia on Child Psychology* (pp. 197–253). Hillsdale, NJ: Lawrence Erlbaum Associates.

Green, E. H. (1933). Friendships and quarrels among preschool children. *Child Development, 4,* 237–252.

Griffin, P., & Mehan, H. (1981). Sense and ritual in classroom discourse. In F. Coulmas (Ed.), *Conversational routine: Explorations in standardized communication situations and pre-patterned speech* (pp. 187–213). The Hague, Netherlands: Mouton.

Gumperz, J. J. (1972). Introduction. In J. J. Gumperz & D. Hymes (Eds.), *Directions in sociolinguistics: The ethnography of communication* (pp. 1–25). New York: Basil Blackwell.

Gumperz, J. J. (1977). Sociocultural knowledge in conversational inference. In M. Saville-Troike (Ed.), *Linguistics and anthropology* (pp. 191–212). Washington, DC: Georgetown University Press.

Gumperz, J. J. (1982). *Discourse strategies.* New York: Cambridge University Press.

Guralnick, M. J. (1981). Peer influences on the development of communicative competence. In P. S. Strain (Ed.), *The utilization of classroom peers as behavior change agents* (pp. 31–68). New York: Plenum Press.

Habermas, J. (1987). *Theory of communicative action.* Boston: Beacon Press.

Haight, W. L., & Miller, P. J. (1993). *Pretending at home: Early development in a sociocultural context.* Albany, NY: SUNY Press.

Halliday, M. A. K. (1984). Language as code and language as behavior: A systemic-functional interpretation of the nature and ontogenesis of dialogue. In R. P. Fawcett, M. A. K. Halliday, S. M. Lamb, & A. Makkai (Eds.), *The semiotics of culture and language, Vol 1: Language as a social semiotic* (pp. 3–35). London: Frances Pinter.

Halliday, M. A. K., McIntosh, A., & Strevens, P. (1964). *The linguistic sciences and language teaching.* London: Longman.

Halpern, C., Close, D., & Johnson, K. (1994). *Truth in comedy: The manual of improvisation.* Colorado Springs, CO: Meriwether Publishing.

Harre, R., & Gillett, G. (1994). *The discursive mind.* Thousand Oaks, CA: Sage.

Hartup, W. W. (1979). Peer relations and the growth of social competence. In M. W. Kent & J. E. Rolf (Eds.), *Primary prevention of psychopathology, Vol. 3: Social competence in children* (pp. 150–170). Hanover, NH: University Press of New England.

Hartup, W. W. (1981). Peer relations and family relations: Two social worlds. In M. Rutter (Ed.), *Scientific foundations of developmental psychiatry* (pp. 280–292). Baltimore: University Park Press.

Hartup, W. W. (1983). Peer relations. In P. Mussen (Ed.), *Handbook of child psychology: Vol. 4* (pp. 103–196). New York: Wiley.

Hays, R. B. (1989). The day-to-day functioning of close versus casual friendships. *Journal of Social and Personal Relationships, 6,* 21–37.

Hazen, N. L., & Black, B. (1989). Preschool peer communication skills: The role of social status and interaction context. *Child Development, 60,* 867–876.

Hickmann, M. (1985). Metapragmatics in child language. In E. Mertz & R. J. Parmentier (Eds.), *Semiotic mediation: Sociocultural and psychological perspectives* (pp. 177–201). Orlando, FL: Academic Press.

Hirschfeld, L. A. (1994). The child's representation of human groups. *The Psychology of Learning and Motivation, 31,* 133–185.

Howes, C. (1979). *Toddler social competence in family and center day care.* Unpublished doctoral dissertation, Boston University, Boston, MA.

Howes, C. (1980). Peer play scale as an index of complexity of peer interaction. *Developmental Psychology, 16,* 371–372.

Howes, C. (1981, April). *Patterns of friendship.* Paper presented at the biennial meeting of the Society for Research in Child Development, Boston, MA.

Howes, C. (1983). Patterns of friendship. *Child Development, 54,* 1041–1053.

Howes, C. (1987a). Peer interaction of young children. *Monographs of the Society for Research in Child Development, 53*(1, Serial No. 217).

Howes, C. (1987b). Social competence with peers in young children: Developmental sequences. *Developmental Review, 7,* 252–272.

Howes, C. (1992). *The collaborative construction of pretend: Social pretend play functions.* Albany, NY: State University of New York Press.

Huizinga, J. (1955). *Homo ludens: A study of the play element in culture.* Boston: Beacon Press. (Original work published 1944)

Hymes, D. (1972). Models of the interaction of language and social life. In J. J. Gumperz & D. Hymes (Eds.), *Directions in sociolinguistics: The ethnography of communication* (pp. 35–71). New York: Basil Blackwell.

Hymes, D. (1974). Ways of speaking. In R. Bauman & J. Sherzer (Eds.), *Explorations in the ethnography of speaking* (pp. 433–451). New York: Cambridge University Press.

Iwanaga, M. (1973). Development of interpersonal play structure in three, four, and five year-old children. *Journal of Research and Development in Education, 6,* 71–82.

Jakobson, R. (1960). Closing statement: Linguistics and poetics. In T. A. Sebeok (Ed.), *Style and language* (pp. 350–377). Cambridge, MA: MIT Press.

Jakobson, R. (1971). Shifters, verbal categories, and the Russian verb. In *Selected writings of Roman Jakobson. Volume 2: Word and language* (pp. 130–147). The Hague, Netherlands: Mouton.

Jakobson, R. (1985). Metalanguage as a linguistic problem. In S. Rudy (Ed.), *Roman Jakobson: Selected writings* (pp. 113–121) New York: Mouton. (Original work published 1956)

Jennings, K. D. (1975). People versus object orientation, social behavior, and intellectual abilities in preschool children. *Developmental Psychology, 11,* 511–519.

John-Steiner, V. (1993). Creative lives, creative tensions. *Creativity Research Journal, 5,* 99–108.

John-Steiner, V., & Tatter, P. (1983). An interactionist model of language development. In B. Bain (Ed.), *The sociogenesis of language and human conduct* (pp. 79–97). New York: Plenum Press.

Johnstone, K. (1981). *Impro: Improvisation and the theatre.* New York: Routledge.

Kane, S. R., & Furth, H. G. (1993). Children constructing social reality: A frame analysis of social pretend play. *Human Development, 36,* 199–214.

Keenan, E. L. (1971). Two kinds of presupposition in natural language. In C. J. Fillmore & D. T. Langendoen (Eds.), *Studies in linguistic semantics* (pp. 45–54). New York: Holt.

Keenan, E. O., & Schieffelin, B. B. (1983). Topic as a discourse notion: A study of topic in the conversations of children and adults. In E. Ochs & B. B. Schieffelin (Eds.), *Acquiring conversational competence* (pp. 66–113). London: Routledge & Kegan Paul. (Original work published 1976)

Konner, M. (1975). Relations among infants and juveniles in comparative perspective. In M. Lewis & L. A. Rosenblum (Eds.), *Friendship and peer relations* (pp. 99–129). New York: Wiley.

Krampen, M. (1981). The developmental semiotics of Jean Piaget. *Semiotica, 34,* 193–218.

Labov, W., & Fanshel, D. (1977). *Therapeutic discourse: Psychotherapy as conversation.* New York: Academic Press.

Lakoff, R. (1975). *Language and women's place*. New York: Harper & Row.

Lawrence, J. A., & Valsiner, J. (1993). Conceptual roots of internalization: From transmission to transformation. *Human Development, 36*, 150–167.

Lever, J. (1978). Sex differences in the complexity of children's play and games. *American Sociological Review, 43*, 471–483.

Levi-Strauss, C. (1955). The structural study of myth. *Journal of American Folklore, 68*, 428–444.

Levi-Strauss, C. (1969). *The raw and the cooked: Introduction to a science of mythology: 1.* (J. Weightman & D. Weightman, Trans.). New York: Harper & Row.

LeVine, R. A., & LeVine, B. B. (1963). Nyansongo: A Gusii community in Kenya. In B. B. Whiting (Ed.), *Six cultures: Studies of child rearing* (pp. 15–202). New York: Wiley.

Levinson, S. C. (1983). *Pragmatics*. New York: Cambridge University Press.

Lewin, K. (1935). *A dynamic theory of personality*. New York: McGraw-Hill.

Lewis, M., & Rosenblum, L. A. (1975). Introduction. In M. Lewis & L. A. Rosenblum (Eds.), *Friendship and peer relations* (pp. 1–9). New York: Wiley.

Lucy, J. A. (1988). The role of language in the development of representation: A comparison of the views of Piaget and Vygotsky. *The Quarterly Newsletter of the Laboratory of Comparative Human Cognition, 10*, 99–103.

Lucy, J. A. (Ed.). (1993). *Reflexive language*. New York: Cambridge University Press.

Magee, M. A. (1989). Social play as performance. *Play and Culture, 2*, 193–196.

Magnusson, D., & Endler, N. S. (Eds.). (1977). *Personality at the crossroads: Current issues in interactional psychology*. Hillsdale, NJ: Lawrence Erlbaum Associates.

Mandler, J. H. (1979). Categorical and schematic organization in memory. In C. K. Puff (Ed.), *Memory organization and structure* (pp. 259–299). New York: Academic Press.

Marshall, H. R. (1961). Relations between home experiences and children's use of language in play interaction with peers. *Psychological Monographs, 75*(5, Whole No. 509).

Marshall, H. R., & McCandless, B. R. (1957). A study in prediction of social behavior of preschool children. *Child Development, 28*, 149–159.

Marx, K. (1978). The German ideology. In R. C. Tucker (Ed.), *The Marx-Engels reader* (pp. 146–200). New York: Norton & Company.

Masur, E. F. (1978). Preschool boys' speech modifications: The effect of listeners' linguistic levels and conversational responsiveness. *Child Development, 49*, 924–927.

Matthews, W. S. (1977). Modes of transformation in the initiation of fantasy play. *Developmental Psychology, 13*, 212–216.

McLoyd, V. C. (1982). Social class differences in sociodramatic play: A critical review. *Developmental Review, 2*, 1–30.

McLoyd, V. C. (1983). Class, culture, and pretend play: A reply to Sutton-Smith and Smith. *Developmental Review, 3*, 11–17.

McLoyd, V. C. (1986). Social class and pretend play. In A. W. Gottfried & C. C. Brown (Eds.), *Play interactions: The contribution of play materials and parental involvement to children's development* (pp. 175–196). Lexington, MA: Lexington Books.

McLoyd, V. C., Thomas, E. A. C., & Warren, D. (1984a). The short-term dynamics of social organization in preschool triads. *Child Development, 55*, 1051–1070.

McLoyd, V. C., Warren, D., & Thomas, E. A. C. (1984b). Anticipatory and fantastic role enactment in preschool triads. *Developmental Psychology, 20*, 807–814.

McTear, M. (1985). *Children's conversation*. London: Basil Blackwell.

Mead, G. H. (1932). *The philosophy of the present*. Chicago: University of Chicago Press.

Mead, G. H. (1934). *Mind, self, and society*. Chicago: University of Chicago Press.

Mehan, H. (1979). *Learning lessons*. Cambridge, MA: Harvard.

194 REFERENCES

Miller, P., & Garvey, C. (1984). Mother–baby role play: Its origin in social support. In I. Bretherton (Ed.), *Symbolic play: The development of social understanding* (pp. 101–130). New York: Academic Press.

Moore, N. V., Evertson, C. M., & Brophy, J. E. (1974). Solitary play: Some functional reconsiderations. *Developmental Psychology, 10,* 830–834.

Mueller, E. (1972). The maintenance of verbal exchanges between young children. *Child Development, 43,* 930–938.

Nelson, K., & Gruendel, J. M. (1979). At morning it's lunchtime: A scriptal view of children's dialogues. *Discourse Processes, 2,* 73–94.

Nelson, K., & Seidman, S. (1984). Playing with scripts. In I. Bretherton (Ed.), *Symbolic play: The development of social understanding* (pp. 45–71). Orlando, FL: Academic Press.

Nezlek, J. B. (1993). The stability of social interaction. *Journal of Personality and Social Psychology, 65,* 930–941.

Ochs, E. (1979). Transcription as theory. In E. Ochs & B. B. Schieffelin (Eds.), *Developmental pragmatics* (pp. 43–72). New York: Academic Press.

Ochs, E. (1983). Planned and unplanned discourse. In E. Ochs & B. B. Schieffelin (Eds.), *Acquiring conversational competence* (pp. 129–157). Boston: Routledge & Kegan Paul. (Reprinted from T. Given, ed., 1979, *Discourse and syntax*).

Ochs, E., & Shieffelin, B. B. (Eds.). (1979). *Developmental pragmatics.* New York: Academic Press.

Packer, M. (1995, March). *The logic of interpretive inquiry.* Society for Research in Child Development, Indianapolis, IN.

Paley, V. G. (1984). *Boys & girls: Superheroes in the doll corner.* Chicago: University of Chicago Press.

Paley, V. G. (1988). *Bad guys don't have birthdays.* Chicago: University of Chicago Press.

Paley, V. G. (1992). *You can't say you can't play.* Cambridge, MA: Harvard University Press.

Parsons, T. (1937). *The structure of social action.* New York: The Free Press.

Parten, M. B. (1932). Social participation among pre-school children. *Journal of Abnormal and Social Psychology, 27,* 243–269.

Parten, M. B. (1971). Social play among pre-school children. In R. E. Herron & B. Sutton-Smith (Eds.), *Child's play* (pp. 83–95). Malabar, FL: Robert E. Krieger Publishing Company. (Reprint from *Journal of Abnormal and Social Psychology*, 1933, 28, 136–147).

Parten, M. B., & Newhall, S. M. (1943). Social behavior of preschool children. In E. A. Barker (Ed.), *Child behavior and development.* New York: McGraw-Hill.

Peirce, C. S. (1931). *Collected papers of Charles Sanders Peirce, Vol. 2.* Cambridge, MA: Harvard.

Peters, A. M., & Boggs, S. T. (1986). Interactional routines as cultural influences upon language acquisition. In B. B. Schieffelin & E. Ochs (Eds.), *Language socialization across cultures* (pp. 80–96). New York: Cambridge University Press.

Philips, S. U. (1972). Participant structures and communicative competence: Warm Springs children in community and classroom. In C. B. Cazden, V. P. John, & D. Hymes (Eds.), *Functions of language in the classroom* (pp. 370–394). New York: Teacher's College Press.

Phillips, E. L., Shenker, S., & Revitz, P. (1951). The assimilation of the new child into the group. *Psychiatry, 14,* 319–325.

Phinney, J., & Rotherham, M. (1981). *The influence of friendship on type and outcome of social overtures in a preschool setting.* Paper presented at the biennial meeting of the Society for Research in Child Development, Boston, MA.

Piaget, J. (1955). *The language and thought of the child* (Marjorie Gabain, Trans.). Cleveland: The World Publishing Company. (Original work published 1923)

Piaget, J. (1960). *The moral judgment of the child.* Glencoe, IL: The Free Press.

Piaget, J. (1962). *Play, dreams, and imitation in childhood* (C. Gattegno & F. M. Hodgson, Trans.). New York: Norton and Company. (Original work published 1946)

Potter, J., & Edwards, D. (1992). *Discursive psychology.* Thousand Oaks, CA: Sage.

Putallaz, M., & Gottman, J. M. (1981). An interactional model of children's entry into peer groups. *Child Development, 52*, 986–994.

Putallaz, M., & Wasserman, A. (1990). Children's entry behavior. In S. R. Asher & J. D. Coie (Eds.), *Peer rejection in childhood* (pp. 60–89). New York: Cambridge University Press.

Rabinow, P., & Sullivan, W. M. (1979). *Interpretive social science: A reader.* Berkeley: University of California Press.

Rawlins, W. K. (1991). On enacting friendship and interrogating discourse. In K. Tracy (Ed.), *Understanding face-to-face interaction: Issues linking goals and discourse* (pp. 101–115). Hillsdale, NJ: Lawrence Erlbaum Associates.

Reuter, J., & Yunik, G. (1973). Social interaction in nursery schools. *Developmental Psychology, 9,* 319–325.

Rogoff, B. (1982). Integrating context and cognitive development. In M. E. Lamb & A. L. Brown (Eds.), *Advances in developmental psychology* (pp. 125–170). Hillsdale, NJ: Lawrence Erlbaum Associates.

Rogoff, B. (1990). *Apprenticeship in thinking: Cognitive development in social context.* New York: Oxford University Press.

Rogoff, B. (in press). Observing sociocultural activity on three planes: Participatory appropriation, guided participation, apprenticeship. In A. Alvarez, P. del Rio, & J. V. Wertsch (Eds.), *Sociocultural studies of mind.* New York: Cambridge University Press.

Rogoff, B., Baker-Sennett, J., & Matusov, E. (1994). Considering the concept of planning. In M. Haith, J. Benson, R. Roberts, & B. Pennington (Eds.), *The development of future-oriented processes* (353–373). Chicago: University of Chicago Press.

Rubin, K. H. (1976). Relation between social participation and role-taking skill in preschool children. *Psychological Reports, 39,* 823–826.

Rubin, K. H., Watson, K. S., & Jambor, T. W. (1978). Free-play behaviors in preschool and kindergarten children. *Child Development, 49,* 534–536.

Rubin, K. H., Fein, G. G., & Vandenberg, B. (1983). Play. In P. H. Mussen (Ed.), *Handbook of child psychology: Vol. 4. Socialization, personality, and social development* (pp. 693–774). New York: Wiley.

Rubin, K. H., & Maioni, T. L. (1975). Play preference and its relationship to egocentrism, popularity and classification skills in preschoolers. *Merrill-Palmer Quarterly, 21,* 171–179.

Rubin, K. H., Maioni, T. L., & Hornung, M. (1976). Free play behaviors in middle- and lower-class preschoolers: Parten and Piaget revisited. *Child Development, 47,* 414–419.

Ruesch, J., & Bateson, G. (1951). *Communication: The social matrix of psychiatry.* New York: Norton.

Sachs, J. (1980). The role of adult–child play in language development. In K. Rubin (Ed.), *Children's play* (pp. 33–48). San Francisco: Jossey Bass.

Sachs, J. (1987). Preschool boys' and girls' language use in pretend play. In S. U. Philips, S. Steele, & C. Tanz (Eds.), *Language, gender, and sex in comparative perspective* (pp. 178–188). New York: Cambridge University Press.

Sachs, J., & Devin, J. (1975). Young children's use of age-appropriate speech styles in social interaction and role-playing. *Journal of Child Language, 3,* 81–98.

Sachs, J., Goldman, J., & Chaille, C. (1984). Planning in pretend play: Using language to coordinate narrative development. In A. Pellegrini & T. Yaukey (Eds.), *The development of oral and written language in social contexts* (pp. 119–128). Norwood, NJ: Ablex.

Sacks, H., Schegloff, E., & Jefferson, G. (1974). A simplest systematics for the organization of turn-taking in conversation. *Language, 50,* 696–735.

Sanders, K. M., & Harper, L. V. (1976). Free-play fantasy behavior in preschool children: Relations among gender, age, season, and location. *Child Development, 47,* 1182–1185.

de Saussure, F. (1966). *Course in general linguistics* (Wade Baskin, Trans.). New York: McGraw-Hill. (Original work published 1915)

Sawyer, R. K. (1992). Improvisational creativity: An analysis of jazz performance. *Creativity Research Journal, 5*, 253–263.

Sawyer, R. K. (1993). The pragmatics of play: Interactional strategies during children's pretend play. *Pragmatics, 3*, 259–282.

Sawyer, R. K. (1995a). Creativity as mediated action: A comparison of improvisational performance and product creativity. *Mind, Culture, and Activity, 2*, 172–191.

Sawyer, R. K. (1995b). A developmental model of heteroglossic improvisation in children's fantasy play. *Sociological Studies of Children, 7*, 127–153.

Sawyer, R. K. (1996). The semiotics of improvisation: The pragmatics of musical and verbal performance. *Semiotica, 108*, 269–306.

Scarlett, W. G., & Wolf, D. (1979). When it's only make-believe: The construction of a boundary between fantasy and reality in storytelling. In E. Winner & H. Gardner (Eds.), *Fact, fiction, and fantasy in childhood* (pp. 29–40). San Francisco: Jossey-Bass.

Schank, R. C. (1982). *Dynamic memory: A theory of reminding and learning in computers and people.* New York: Cambridge University Press.

Schank, R. C., & Abelson, R. P. (1977). Scripts, plans, and knowledge. In P. N. Johnson-Laird & P. C. Wason (Eds.), *Thinking: Readings in cognitive science* (pp. 421–432). New York: Cambridge University Press.

Schegloff, E. A. (1968). Sequencing in conversational openings. *American Anthropologist, 70*, 1075–1095.

Schegloff, E. A. (1990). On the organization of sequences as a source of "coherence" in talk-in-interaction. In B. Dorval (Ed.), *Conversational organization and its development* (pp. 51–77). Norwood, NJ: Ablex Publishing Corp.

Schegloff, E., Jefferson, G., & Sacks, H. (1977). The preference for self-correction in the organization of repair in conversation. *Language, 53*, 361–382.

Schegloff, E., & Sacks, H. (1973). Opening up closings. *Semiotica, 8*, 289–327.

Schenkein, J. (Ed.). (1978). *Studies in the organization of conversational interaction.* New York: Academic Press.

Schiffrin, D. (1977). Opening encounters. *American Sociological Review, 42*, 679–691.

Schiller, F. (1967). *On the aesthetic education of man.* New York: Oxford University Press.

Schutz, A. (1967). *The phenomenology of the social world* (George Walsh & Frederick Lehnert, Trans.). Evanston, IL: Northwestern University Press. (Original work published 1932)

Schwartzman, H. (1978). *Transformations: The anthropology of children's play.* New York: Plenum Press.

Schwarz, J. C. (1972). Effects of peer familiarity on the behavior of preschoolers in a novel situation. *Journal of Personality and Social Psychology, 24*, 276–284.

Searle, J. R. (1969). *Speech acts.* New York: Cambridge University Press.

Selman, R. L. (1971). Taking another's perspective: Role-taking development in early childhood. *Child Development, 42*, 1721–1734.

Selman, R. L. (1976). Toward a structural analysis of developing interpersonal relations concepts: Research with normal and disturbed preadolescent boys. *Minnesota Symposia on Child Psychology, 10*, 156–200.

Shantz, C. U. (1983). Social cognition. In J. Flavell & E. Markman (Eds.), *Handbook of child psychology: Vol. 3. Cognitive development* (pp. 496–560). New York: Wiley.

Shatz, M., & Gelman, R. (1973). The development of communication skills: Modifications in the speech of young children as a function of listener. *Monographs of the Society for Research in Child Development, 38* (5, Serial No. 152).

Sheldon, A. (1992). Conflict talk: Sociolinguistic challenges to self-assertion and how young girls meet them. *Merrill-Palmer Quarterly, 38,* 95–117.

Shweder, R. A. (1990). Cultural psychology—What is it? In J. W. Stigler, R. A. Shweder, & G. Herdt (Eds.), *Cultural psychology: Essays on comparative human development* (pp. 1–43). New York: Cambridge University Press.

Silverstein, M. (1976). Shifters, linguistic categories, and cultural description. In K. Basso & H. Selby (Eds.), *Meaning in anthropology* (pp. 11–55). Albuquerque, NM: University of New Mexico Press.

Silverstein, M. (1979). Language structure and linguistic ideology. In P. R. Clyne (Ed.), *The elements: A parasession on linguistic units and levels* (pp. 193–247). Chicago: Chicago Linguistic Society.

Silverstein, M. (1984). On the pragmatic "poetry" of prose: Parallelism, repetition, and cohesive structure in the time course of dyadic conversation. In D. Schiffrin (Ed.), *Meaning, form, and use in context: Linguistic applications* (pp. 181–198). Washington, DC: Georgetown University Press.

Silverstein, M. (1985). The functional stratification of language and ontogenesis. In J. Wertsch (Ed.), *Culture, communication, and cognition: Vygotskian perspectives* (pp. 205–235). Cambridge, UK: Cambridge University Press.

Silverstein, M. (1991). A funny thing happened on the way to the form: A functionalist critique of functionalist developmentalism. *First Language, 11,* 143–179.

Silverstein, M. (1993). Metapragmatic discourse and metapragmatic function. In J. A. Lucy (Ed.), *Reflexive language* (pp. 33–58). Cambridge, UK: Cambridge University Press.

Simon, T., & Smith, P. K. (1985). Play and problem solving: A paradigm questioned. *Merrill-Palmer Quarterly, 31,* 265–277.

Sinclair, J. M., & Coulthard, R. M. (1975). *Towards an analysis of discourse: The English used by teachers and pupils.* London: Oxford University Press.

Singer, D. G., & Singer, J. L. (1990). *The house of make-believe: Play and the developing imagination.* Cambridge, MA: Harvard.

Singer, J. L. (1973). *The child's world of make-believe: Experimental studies of imaginative play.* New York: Academic Press.

Singer, J. L. (1979). Affect and imagination in play and fantasy. In C. Izard (Ed.), *Child personality and psychopathology.* New York: Wiley-Interscience.

Slaughter, D. T., & Dombrowski, J. (1989). Cultural continuities and discontinuities: Impact on social and pretend play. In M. N. Bloch & A. D. Pellegrini (Eds.), *The ecological context of children's play* (pp. 282–310). Norwood, NJ: Ablex.

Slobin, D. I. (1973). Cognitive prerequisites for the development of grammar. In C. A. Ferguson & D. I. Slobin (Eds.), *Studies of child language development* (pp. 175–208). New York: Holt, Rinehart, & Winston.

Slobin, D. I. (1978). Suggested universals in the ontogenesis of grammar. In V. Honsa & M. J. Hardman-de-Bautista (Eds.), *Papers on linguistics and child language: Ruth Hirsch Weir memorial volume* (pp. 249–264). The Hague, Netherlands: Mouton.

Smilansky, S. (1968). *The effects of sociodramatic play on disadvantaged preschool children.* New York: Wiley.

Smith, A. (1976). *An inquiry into the nature and causes of the wealth of nations.* Chicago: University of Chicago Press.

Smith, P. K. (1977). Social and fantasy play in young children. In B. Tizard & D. Harvey (Eds.), *Biology of play* (pp. 123–145). Philadelphia, PA: J. B. Lippincott.

Smith, P. K. (1978). A longitudinal study of social participation in preschool children: Solitary and parallel play reexamined. *Developmental Psychology, 14,* 517–536.

Sneider, L. (1985). *Mothers and toddlers: Partners in early pretend*. Paper presented at the biennial meeting of the Society for Research in Child Development, Toronto, Ontario.

Spolin, V. (1963). *Improvisation for the theater*. Evanston, IL: Northwestern University Press.

Sutton-Smith, B. (1979). Epilogue: Play as performance. In B. Sutton-Smith (Ed.), *Play and learning* (pp. 295–322). New York: Gardner Press.

Sutton-Smith, B. (1983). Commentary on social class differences in sociodramatic play in historical context: A reply to McLoyd. *Developmental Review, 3*, 1–5.

Trabasso, T., Stein, N. L., Rodkin, P. C., Munger, M. P., & Baughn, C. R. (1992). Knowledge of goals and plans in the on-line narration of events. *Cognitive Development, 7*, 133–170.

Udwin, O., & Shmukler, D. (1981). The influence of sociocultural, economic and home background factors on children's ability to engage in imaginative play. *Developmental Psychology, 17*, 66–72.

Vygotsky, L. S. (1978). *Mind in society* (Alex Kozulin, Trans.). Cambridge, MA: Harvard University Press.

Vygotsky, L. S. (1986). *Thought and language* (E. Hanfmann & G. Vakar, Trans.). Cambridge, MA: MIT Press. (Original work published 1934)

Watzlawick, P., Beavin, J. H., & Jackson, D. D. (1967). *Pragmatics of human communication: A study of interactional patterns, pathologies, and paradoxes*. New York: Norton.

Wertsch, J. V. (Ed.). (1985a). *Culture, communication, and cognition: Vygotskian perspectives*. New York: Cambridge University Press.

Wertsch, J. V. (1985b). The semiotic mediation of mental life: L. S. Vygotsky and M. M. Bakhtin. In E. Mertz & R. J. Parmentier (Eds.), *Semiotic mediation: Sociocultural and psychological perspectives* (pp. 49–71). Orlando, FL: Academic Press.

Wertsch, J. V. (1985c). *Vygotsky and the social formation of mind*. Cambridge: Harvard University Press.

Wertsch, J. V. (1991). *Voices of the mind*. Cambridge, MA: Harvard.

Whiting, B. B. (1980). Culture and social behavior: A model for the development of social behavior. *Ethos, 8*, 95–116.

Whiting, B. B., & Whiting, J. W. M. (1975). *Children of six cultures*. Cambridge, MA: Harvard University Press.

Wortham, S. (1994). *Acting out participant examples in the classroom*. Philadelphia, PA: John Benjamins.

Yawkey, T., & Alverez-Dominques, J. (1984). *Comparisons of free play behaviors of Hispanic and Anglo middle-class SES five-year-olds*. Paper presented at the annual meeting of the American Educational Research Association, New Orleans, LA.

Youniss, J. (1975). *Another perspective on social cognition*. Minneapolis, MN: University of Minnesota Press.

Zarbatany, L., Brunschot, M. V., Meadows, K., & Pepper, S. (in press). Effects of friendship and gender on peer group entry. *Child Development*.

Zinchenko, V. P. (1985). Vygotsky's ideas about units for the analysis of mind. In J. V. Wertsch (Ed.), *Culture, communication, and cognition: Vygotskian perspectives* (pp. 94–118). Cambridge, MA: Cambridge University Press.

Author Index

A

Abelson, R. P., 2
Al-Shatti, A., 6
Alverez-Dominques, J., 6
Andersen, E. S., 25
Ariel, S., 6
Astington, J. W., xix, 4, 176
Austin, J. L., 17
Auwarter, M., 35, 36, 44, 124, 127, 177

B

Bakeman, R., 14
Baker-Sennett, J., 2, 9, 33
Bakhtin, M. M., 34, 42, 172, 173
Bar-Hillel, Y., 39
Barker, R. G., 5
Bates, E., xxii, 16, 18
Bateson, G., xxiii, 1, 34, 35, 37
Baughn, C. R., 4
Bauman, R., 49
Bearison, D. J., 9
Benigni, L., 16, 18
Berger, P. L., 180
Berliner, P., 178
Berndt, R., 24, 35
Black, B., 5, 20, 119

Bloch, M. N., 5, 6, 15
Blumer, H., 30
Boggs, S. T., 2, 17, 22, 23, 45
Bourdieu, P., 3, 179, 180
Bower, E., 6
Bretherton, I., 2, 3, 10, 16, 18, 24, 34, 43
Briggs, C. L., 33, 49
Bronfenbrenner, U., 4, 77
Brophy, J. E., 14
Brown, P., 42, 88
Brown, R., 26, 172
Brownell, C. A., 87
Brownlee, J. R., 14
Bruner, J., xxii, 16, 17, 18, 33, 38, 45
Burke, K., 2
Butterworth, G., 33

C

Camaioni, L., 16, 18, 22, 45
Cazden, C. B., 18
Chaille, C., 125
Challman, R. C., 90, 170
Cicourel, A. V., 3
Clark, H., 21
Close, D., 141, 143, 150, 178
Coleman, J., xviii
Connolly, J. A., 5, 36, 49, 90, 126, 129

199

Subject Index

A

Age of play group, 87–88
Audio data
    estimating obtrusiveness of, 57–59
    recording procedures, 66–67
    sampling locations, 60–66
    transcription of, 73–76

C

Classroom map, 60
Conversation analysis, 21–23
Conversational turns, 82

D

Developmental pragmatics, 15–27
Dialogism, 41–45, 86, 162–164
Discourse analysis, 20–21

E

Egocentric speech, 8–10, 175
Emergent, the, 31, 46, 48–49

E

Event, as unit of analysis, 33–34, 76–78,
    178–179
Explicitness of metapragmatic strategy, 128–131

F

Field notes, 54, 66, 74–75
Flow, 178
Frame, 1–4, 127–128
Friendship, *see also* Improvisational exchange
    and friendship, Play entry sequence
    and friendship
    friendship index, defined, 89–91

G

Gender, *see also* Performance style and gender
    composition, Play entry sequence
    and gender, Improvisational ex-
    change and gender
    gender composition of play group, 88–89
Generalized other, 86
Group episode, defined, 81–82
Group size, 89

H

Heteroglossia, 42–45, 172–177

203

DATE DUE

5/1/04			